Pedagogy, Politics and Philosophy of Peace

Bloomsbury Critical Education Series

Series Editor: Peter Mayo

This series is fundamentally concerned with the relationship between education and power in society and is therefore committed to publishing volumes containing insights into ways of confronting inequalities and social exclusions in different learning settings and society at large. The series will comprise books wherein authors contend forthrightly with the inextricability of power/knowledge relations.

Also available from Bloomsbury

On Critical Pedagogy, Henry A. Giroux
Peace Education, edited by Monisha Bajaj and Maria Hantzopoulos

Pedagogy, Politics and Philosophy of Peace

Interrogating Peace and Peacemaking

Edited by Carmel Borg and Michael Grech

Bloomsbury Academic
An imprint of Bloomsbury Publishing Plc

B L O O M S B U R Y
LONDON · OXFORD · NEW YORK · NEW DELHI · SYDNEY

Bloomsbury Academic

An imprint of Bloomsbury Publishing Plc

50 Bedford Square	1385 Broadway
London	New York
WC1B 3DP	NY 10018
UK	USA

www.bloomsbury.com

BLOOMSBURY and the Diana logo are trademarks of Bloomsbury Publishing Plc

First published 2017

British Library Cataloguing-in-Publication Data
A catalogue record for this book is available from the British Library.

ISBN: HB: 978-1-4742-8279-6
ePDF: 978-1-4742-8280-2
ePub: 978-1-4742-8281-9

Library of Congress Cataloging-in-Publication Data
A catalog record for this book is available from the Library of Congress.

Typeset by Deanta Global Publishing Services, Chennai, India
Printed and bound in Great Britain

To Frei Betto (Carlos Alberto Libânio Christo) –
for preaching the good news of peace

Contents

Notes on Contributors   ix

Foreword *Peter Mayo*   xv

Introduction *Carmel Borg and Michael Grech*   1

Part 1   The Contents of Peace

1   Where does True Peace Dwell? *Marianna Papastephanou*   7

2   A Gramscian Analysis of Passive Revolution and its Contribution to the Study of Peace *Joseph Gravina*   32

3   Breathing Peace, Relating with the Other and the Maternal *Simone Galea*   47

4   The Limits of Exogenous Initiatives in Peacemaking, Focusing on Iraq after the US Invasion *Arsalan Alshinawi*   62

5   Critical Peace in the Digital Era of Austerity and Crisis *Nicos Trimikliniotis and Dimitris Trimithiotis*   81

Part 2   Challenges to Peace Education

6   Dreaming of Peace in a Culture of War *Antonia Darder*   97

7   The Myth of the Inevitability of War *Clive Zammit*   110

8   Liberal Peace and Media Debates around the Cases of *Jyllands-Posten* and *Charlie Hebdo* *Carmen Sammut*   127

Part 3   Pedagogy of Peace

9   Some Reflections on Critical Peace Education *Michalinos Zembylas and Zvi Bekerman*   147

10   School Textbooks and Entanglements of the 'Colonial Present' in Israel and Palestine *André Elias Mazawi*   161

11   The Long Shadow Thrown over the Actions of Men
     Michael Zammit   181

12   Schooling for Democracy: Music and Critical Pedagogy
     in Egypt *Linda Herrera*   200

Epilogue *Carmel Borg and Michael Grech*   217

Index   243

Notes on Contributors

Arsalan Alshinawi studied pharmacy and diplomacy at the University of Malta, and international relations and international political economy at the Universities of Amsterdam and Nijmegen. He is senior lecturer at the Department of International Relations (Faculty of Arts) of the University of Malta. Dr Alshinawi was also a lecturer at the Faculty of Oriental Studies and at the School of International Relations in St. Petersburg State University, Russia. He is currently a visiting lecturer at the Faculty of Economics, Management and Accountancy of the University of Malta, Malta, and the American University of Iraq in Sulaimani. The author of several publications and a member of the foreign editorial board of the Annual of Asian and African Studies Journal of St. Petersburg State University, he is fluent in Maltese, Arabic, Kurdish and Persian languages. His research interest is in the field of political economy of development, notably in the Muslim – Arab world, and the impact of Western dominance in IR theory. Dr Alshinawi has also served at the Ministry of Foreign Affairs in Valletta and in Maltese diplomatic missions in Tunisia and Libya.

Zvi Bekerman teaches anthropology of education at the School of Education and the Melton Center, the Hebrew University of Jerusalem, Israel. His research interests are in the study of cultural, ethnic and national identity, including identity processes and negotiation during intercultural encounters as these are reflected in inter/multicultural, peace and citizenship education and in formal and informal learning contexts. He has widely published on these issues in a variety of academic journals. Among his recent books are *The Promise of Integrated and Multicultural Bilingual Education: Inclusive Palestinian-Arab and Jewish Schools in Israel* (2016), and *Teaching Contested Narratives: Identity, Memory And Reconciliation In Peace Education And Beyond* (with Michalinos Zembilas 2012).

Carmel Borg is former head of department and dean of the Faculty of Education, University of Malta, Malta. He lectures in curriculum studies, critical pedagogy, parental involvement in education, and community and adult education. He has authored and co-authored, presented, often as keynote speaker, and published extensively in several languages around the foregoing issues. As a public intellectual and community activist, professor Borg promotes education as a liberating experience and challenges technologies of oppression within education systems. He has a long-standing involvement in curriculum development at all levels of the education process, locally and internationally. Professor Borg is the editor of the *Malta Review of Education Research* (MRER) and associate editor of several other peer-reviewed, international journals. He is also editor of the *Education Research Monograph Series* (ERMS).

Antonia Darder is a distinguished international Freirian scholar. She holds the Leavey Presidential Endowed Chair of Ethics and Moral Leadership at Loyola Marymount University, Los Angeles, USA, and is Professor Emerita of Education Policy, Organization and Leadership at the University of Illinois at Urbana-Champaign, USA. Her scholarship focuses on issues of racism, political economy, social justice and education. Her work critically engages the contributions of Paulo Freire to our understanding of inequalities in schools and society. Darder's critical theory of biculturalism links questions of culture, power and pedagogy to social justice concerns in education. In her scholarship on ethics and moral issues, she articulates a critical theory of leadership for social justice and community empowerment. Her work also engages issues of culture and its relationship to recent developments in neuroscience. She is the author of numerous books and articles in the field, including *Culture and Power in the Classroom* (20th Anniversary edition), *Reinventing Paulo Freire: A Pedagogy of Love, A Dissident Voice: Essays on Culture, Pedagogy, and Power* and *Freire and Education*. She is also co-author of *After Race: Racism After Multiculturalism* and co-editor of *The Critical Pedagogy Reader, Latinos and Education: A Critical Reader,* and the *International Critical Pedagogy Reader*.

Simone Galea is associate professor in the Department of Education Studies, Faculty of Education, University of Malta, Malta. Her teaching and research are mainly in philosophy of education, feminist philosophy and theory, narrative research and research methodology. Her publications explore the notions of femininity and the maternal and their relation to educational thought and practice, and the ethical and political relations of doing research with others. Her recent publications include The *Teacher, Literature and the Mediterranean* (2014, co-edited with Adrian Grima); *My Teaching, My Philosophy: Kenneth Wain and the Lifelong Engagement with Education* (2014, co-edited with John Baldacchino and Duncan Mercieca). Her chapter 'Engendering Knowledge: Education, the

Maternal and Doing Research with Women' has been published in Victoria Perselli's (ed.) *Education, Theory and Pedagogies of Change in a Global Landscape* in 2016. She also writes poetry and children's stories.

Joseph Gravina holds a PhD in comparative political economy and education. He currently teaches systems of knowledge at the Junior College of the University of Malta, Malta. Dr Gravina is a Gramsci specialist. His earliest study on Gramsci focused on 'The educational relevance of Antonio Gramsci's political writings'. In 2003 he published 'Values in Systems of Knowledge'. He has also published works on politics, human rights and positivism, most notably, 'So close and yet so far: The Malta Labour Party's cultural politics during the 1970s and 1980s', in *Revisiting Labour History* (2012), edited by John Chircop; 'Democracy? What democracy?' in Michael Grech's *Jottings ... and reflections* (2015); and, in Maltese, '*L-Isfond soċjali, politiku u ekonomiku ta' hidmet Lorenzo Milani – Riflessjoni Gramxjana*', a Gramscian reflection on the social, political and economic background to Don Milani as a public figure, in *Lorenzo Milani: Bejn ilbierah u llum* (2010), edited by Carmel Borg.

Michael Grech is currently reading for a PhD in philosophy at the University of Birmingham, UK. His interests in philosophy include metaphysics and philosophy of language. Apart from philosophy, Grech is also interested in politics, cultural issues, religion, immigration and the relationship between these. On these issues, he has authored and edited a number of publications and produced and hosted a number of radio programmes. Grech teaches philosophy at a post-secondary institution and with a local NGO.

Linda Herrera is professor in the department of Education Policy, Organization and Leadership at the University of Illinois at Urbana-Champaign, USA, and director of the Global Studies in Education program. She works on the politics of education and youth policy and movements in the Middle and North Africa. Her two most recent books are *Revolution in the Age of Social Media: The Egyptian Popular Insurrection and the Internet* (2014) and *Wired Citizenship: Youth Learning and Activism in the Middle East* (2014). She is currently curating an online video project and website inspired by the Arab Uprisings called 'Democracy Dialogue' (www.democracydialog.com).

André Elias Mazawi is professor in the Department of Educational Studies at the University of British Columbia, Canada. A political sociologist of education, he is interested in the roles of the state, geopolitics and popular culture on the construction of imaginaries of schooling and higher education and their effects on the articulation of governance regimes and policyscapes. He has published widely on these issues, with particular reference to Mediterranean and Middle East societies. He is also an affiliate professor with the Euro-Mediterranean Centre of Educational Research at the University of Malta, Malta, and serves on the Advisory Editorial Board of *Postcolonial Directions in Education.*

Marianna Papastephanou is currently teaching philosophy of education in the Department of Education at the University of Cyprus. She has studied and taught at the University of Cardiff, UK. She has also studied and researched in Berlin, Germany. Her research interests include political philosophy, the 'modern vs. postmodern' divide, utopia, the Frankfurt School and epistemological, linguistic and ethical issues in education. She has written numerous articles and participated in various conferences on the above topics. She is the editor of *K-O Apel. From a Transcendental-Semiotic Point of View* (Manchester: Manchester University Press, 1997); *Philosophical Perspectives on Compulsory Education* (Dordrecht: Springer, 2014), and she is the author of *Educated Fear and Educated Hope: Utopia, Dystopia and the Plasticity of Humanity* (Rotterdam: Sense Publishers, 2009) and *Eccentric Cosmopolitanism and a Globalized World* (Boulder: Paradigm, 2012).

Carmen Sammut is pro-rector and head of the Department of International Relations at the University of Malta. She is a senior lecturer in media, culture and international relations; political communication; media and forced migration; and Journalism. Her research and publications revolve around these themes. She obtained her PhD as a Commonwealth Scholar from the Media and Communications Department at Goldsmiths College, University of London, UK, and a Master's, PGCE and BA from the University of Malta, Malta. She originally started her career in journalism and for many years sat on the Media Ethics Commission of the Institute of Journalists, where she chaired a commission that aimed to update the Code of Ethics. She is still engaged with the media as a news analyst. In recent years, she has served as chair of the Majjistral Nature and History Park; she advised the Ministry for Foreign Affairs on the European Commission-League of Arab States Liaison Office (ECLASLO); she currently moderates meetings of the Council of Maltese Living Abroad and is a member of the board that reviews applications for Overseas Development Aid (ODA). At an international level, she is governor for Malta in the board of the Asia-Europe Foundation (ASEF).

Nicos Trimikliniotis is an associate professor at the School of Social Sciences, University of Nicosia, Cyprus. He heads the Cyprus team of experts for the Fundamental Rights Agency of the European Union. He is also a practising barrister. He has researched on integration, citizenship, education, migration, racism, free movement of workers, EU law, discrimination and Labour Law. He is the National Expert for Cyprus for the European Labour Law Network. He is part of the international team working on world deviance, which has produced *Gauging and Engaging Deviance 1600-2000*, Tulika press (2014). His works include *Mobile Commons, Migrant Digitalities and the Right to the City*, 2015; *Beyond a Divided Cyprus: A State and Society in Transformation*, 2012; and *The Nation-State Dialectic and the State of Exception*, 2010.

Dimitris Trimithiotis holds a PhD in sociology from Aix-Marseille University, France. He is currently adjunct lecturer at the University of Cyprus, Department of Social and Political Sciences. He is also research associate at the Mediterranean Laboratory of Sociology, France. In 2008, he was awarded a research fellowship from the French Ministry of Higher Education and Research for his thesis on the process of production of the political dimension of the European Union. Since then, he has participated in several research projects and published articles and monographs in the field of sociology of media, journalism and political communication.

Clive Zammit is currently a senior lecturer in the recently set up Department of Cognitive Science within the Faculty of Media and Knowledge Sciences at the University of Malta. He is the course director of the MSc in Cognitive Science run by the same department and also collaborates in EU FP7 research projects related to Online Privacy and Surveillance. After graduating in philosophy and economics from the College of Charleston, USA, and the University of Malta, Malta, Clive Zammit read for a PhD in philosophy at the University of Essex, UK, where he wrote on the possibilities of an Ethics of Witnessing. Over the past twenty years, he has lectured in philosophy in various academic and non-academic institutions. His main research interests and recent publications focus on Heidegger's use of the Middle Voice and the relations between Ethics and Temporality. He is also interested in the relations between philosophy and practice-based research, mainly in the digital arts.

Michael Zammit is associate professor in the Department of Philosophy of The University of Malta. A pioneer in introducing the study of Sanskrit and the

Advaita Vedanta philosophy in the Maltese academic context, he also lectures in various fields in Western philosophy, including ethics, logic, philosophy of language, Plato, Seneca, Plotinus and Marsilio Ficino. Apart from writing academic papers and poetry, Professor Zammit has prepared a number of translations, including the translation of the *Bhagavad Gītā* from the original Sanskrit to Maltese. He is a member of the scientific board of the Elémire Zolla International Research Society (A.I.R.E.Z., Italy), contributing to the scientific and editorial projects promoted by the society. Some of Prof. Zammit's several adaptations for the theatre are currently being used as texts by the Drama Unit Theatre Programme.

Michalinos Zembylas is associate professor of educational theory and curriculum studies at the Open University of Cyprus. He is also visiting professor and research fellow at the Institute for Reconciliation and Social Justice, University of the Free State, South Africa. He has written extensively on emotion and affect in relation to social justice pedagogies, intercultural and peace education, human rights education and citizenship education. His recent books include *Teaching Contested Narratives: Identity, Memory and Reconciliation in Peace Education and Beyond* (with Zvi Bekerman), and *Integrated Education in Conflicted Societies* (with C. McGlynn and Z. Bekerman). His latest book is titled *Emotion and Traumatic Conflict: Re-claiming Healing in Education.*

Foreword[1]

This new book series is being introduced against an international background that comprises situations that are disturbing as well as interesting. There are concerns regarding the distribution of wealth and its concentration in the hands of a few to the detriment of the many, 'the multitudes', as referred to by Michael Hart and Toni Negri.[2] The series is launched at a time when the 'social contract' is continuously being shredded as several people are removed from the index of human concerns. Many are led to live in a precarious state. Contract work has become the norm, a situation that renders one's life less secure. There is also criticism targeted at the very nature of production and consumption themselves with their effects on people and their relationship to other social beings and the rest of the planet.

These are also difficult times because the initial enthusiasm for the popular quest for democracy in various parts of the world has been tempered by eventual realism based on the fact that strategically entrenched forces are not removed simply by overthrowing a dictator. Far from ushering in a 'spring', the uprisings in certain countries have left political vacuums – fertile terrain for religiously motivated terrorism that presents a real global security threat. This threat, though having to be controlled in many ways, not least tackling the relevant social issues at their root, presents many with a *carte blanche* to trample on hard-earned democratic freedoms and rights. The situation is said to further spread the 'culture of militarization' that engulfs youth, about which much has been written in Critical Education. Terrorist attacks or aborted coups allow scope for analyses on these grounds, including analyses that draw out the implications for education.

The security issue, part of the 'global war on terror', is availed of by those who seek curtailment of human beings' right to asylum seeking and who render impoverished migrants as scapegoats for the host country's economic ills. The issue of migration would be an important contemporary theme in the large domain of Critical Education.

We are also living in challenging times in which an attempt is made for politics to be rescued from the exclusive clutches of politicians and bankers.

A more grass-roots kind of politics has been constantly played out in globalized public arenas such as the squares and streets of Athens, Madrid, Istanbul (Gezi Park), Cairo, Tunis and New York City. A groundswell of dissent, indignation and tenacity was manifest and projected throughout all corners of the globe, albeit, as just indicated, not always leading to developments hoped for by those involved. Yet, hope springs eternal. Some of these manifestations have provided pockets for alternative social action to the mainstream, including educational action. Authors writing on Critical Education have found, in these pockets, seeds for a truly and genuinely democratic pedagogy that will hopefully be explored and developed, theoretically and empirically, in this series.

It is in these contexts, and partly as a response to the challenges they pose, that this new series on Critical Education has been developed. Education, though not to be attributed powers it does not have (it cannot change things on its own), surely has a role to play in this scenario – from exposing and redressing class politics to confronting the cultures of militarization, consumerism, individualism and ethnic supremacy. The call among critical educators is for a pedagogy of social Solidarität that emphasizes the collective and communal in addition to the ecologically sustainable.

Critical educators have for years been exploring, advocating and organizing ways of seeing, learning and living that constitute alternatives to the mainstream. They have been striving to make their contribution to changing the situation for the better, governed by a vision or visions of systems that are socially more just. The ranks of the oppressed are swelling. Hopefully, it is the concerns of these people that are foremost in the minds and hearts of those committed to a social-justice-oriented Critical Education. I would be the first to admit that even a professed commitment to a Critical Education can degenerate into another form of radical chic or another form of academic sterility. We need to be ever so vigilant towards not only others but also ourselves, coming to terms with our own contradictions, therefore seeking, in Paulo Freire's words, to become less incoherent.

This series offers a platform for genuinely socially committed critical educators to express their ideas in a systematic manner. It seeks to offer signposts for an alternative approach to education and cultural work, constantly bearing in mind the United Nations Sustainable Development Goals that, albeit difficult to realize, serve as important points of reference when critiquing current policies in different sectors, including education. The series' focus on Critical Education, comprising the movement known as critical pedagogy, is intended to contribute to maintaining the steady flow of ideas that can inspire and allow for an education that eschews the 'taken for granted'.

This first volume raises the issue of peace within the context of social justice, indicating that the former cannot exist without the latter. This is no sanitized version of peace but, to the contrary, one rooted in radical forms of social justice and pedagogy. It brings together a number of writers from different parts of the world, some living in zones of conflict. It does so in the spirit of internationalism that guides this series.

Peter Mayo
Series Editor
University of Malta,
Msida, Malta

Notes

1 This Series Preface draws on these two works: Mayo, P. (2012a). *Politics of Indignation. Imperialism, Postcolonial Disruptions and Social Change.* Winchester and Washington: Zero Books/John Hunt publishers; Mayo, P. (2012b). 'Critical Pedagogy in Hard Financial Times', *Lifelong Learning in Europe (LLinE)*, (2): 23–7. I am indebted to my friend Michael Grech for his comments on an earlier draft. The usual disclaimers apply.

2 See Hart and Negri (2001). *Empire.* Massachusetts: Harvard University Press.

Introduction

Carmel Borg and Michael Grech

In an age where official and sponsored violence is becoming normalized and conceived of as a legitimate tool of peacekeeping, a number of academics and activists represented in this timely volume are interrogating the intensification of the militarization of civil life and of international relations, and problematizing the very concept of peace. Coming from different areas of study, the authors discuss peace from their particular perspective; the nature of peace, myths related to peace, the logistics of peace and peacemaking, as well as the relation of peace and pedagogy in the broadest meaning of the term, constitute the main themes of the book. One thread that binds the chapters together is the distinction between genuine peace, based on revisualized (inter/intra) social relations and transformational struggles, and false peace or pacification. Another thread that weaves through the twelve contributions that constitute this book is the importance given to critical reflection in relation to peace-oriented actions. Editorially, we would like the reader to conceive of the book as a set of chapters that collectively contribute to a coherent vision and pedagogy of authentic peace.

This book emerged from our understanding that power operates in concrete and historical realities of individuals and groups situated in asymmetrical social and political locations. Such a view prompts us to ask ethically and politically loaded questions like: Who is benefiting from peace arrangements? Is peace always desirable? Is stability a sign of peace? Can peace be imposed? Whose peace is being legitimized? How can we best educate for peace? In the course of answering such questions, the contributors to this volume emphatically reject dysfunctional peace processes and stability without justice. Such peace processes contrast heavily with peace initiatives that are informed by cognitive, social, economic and ecological justice.

Pedagogically, we, the editors, regard a commitment to genuine peace as entailing the ongoing search for the right cognitive and emotional frameworks, a process where critical peace education plays an important role in the process of forming critical citizenships that speak to the fragility and precariousness of millions of lives; marginalized people whose humanity is routinely threatened through exploitation and dispossession. Critical peace education is possibilitarian. It offers dialogical opportunities for consciousness building around social justice, equity, democracy, critical literacy, fundamental human rights, international solidarity, indigenous and minority rights, workers' rights, to mention a few generic themes, which may lead to concrete actions that contribute to realities where the disenfranchised (in more than one sense) emerge from their status, as squatters on their own land, to become protagonists in transforming structural changes that currently oppress and dehumanize so many people. Critical peace education as a lifelong and lifewide interaction with the human built and natural environments is possibilitarian and, therefore, it is a pedagogy of hope. In fact, it is based on the belief that oppression, colonization and cultural invasion can be resisted and subverted through cognitive mobilization and collective actions. We see this book as an integral part of our resolve to contribute to this gaol; to transform the world and make it other than it is: a world that currently negates fairness, inclusion, quality of life, safety and dignity in the name of industrial 'peace' and economic stability and growth.

While some of the chapters are country-specific, most of the lessons learnt from this book can speak to people in different geographies and situations. The chapters are open invitations to readers from across the world to engage, doubt, challenge and problematize hegemonic messages about peace and about what needs to be done to re/establish peace. The book is also conceived of as an antidote to the growing cynicism and fatalism that dominate the pedagogical encounters that both of us, editors of this book, are engaged in: cynicism and fatalism that block possibilities for transformative thinking and action.

As it unfolds, the book establishes signposts for a socially just and critical curriculum. Inspired by classical texts, Marianna Papastephanou sets as a presupposition of future efforts toward peace an ontology of peace that sees the wilderness of our world as created rather than natural. Reclaiming genuine peace requires unveiling the world, retrieving the non-thematized issues, rethinking the existent and imagining radical ways out of the wilderness. Clive Zammit also draws inspiration form classical texts and argues that Eirene, goddess of peace, and its heritage have been largely lost through scepticism and cynicism. Zammit's contribution to the peace curriculum takes the form of a heightened awareness of linguistic structures that support and empower the destructive discourse and the mindset of war.

Michalinos Zembylas and Zvi Bekerman challenge some of the taken-for-granted premises on which peace education, over the past thirty years, has been founded, like the premises about the goodness of peace, the fideistic approach to peace and the idea that peace is the opposite of war. Zembylas and Bekerman critique psychologized assumptions about peace and advocate a peace education curriculum that reinstates the materiality of things and practices, and engages in critical cultural analysis, reontologizes research and practice, and reinventing educators as critical experts of design.

Michael Zammit invites us to consider a non-dualist approach to peace education: a curriculum that promotes the universal, non-egocentric and praxial dimensions of peace. The non-dual approach is essentially philosophical and aims to promote the whole of one's being rather than privileging the intellect.

In the context of a book that advocates genuine peace, Linda Herrera calls for the reclaiming of humanistic curricula and pedagogies as a response to what she refers to as the intensification of political and economic injustices and the invigoration of nativism, sectarianism and religious fundamentalism. Adopting a life-history approach, Herrera, through the narrative of a musical maestro, underscores the urgency for pedagogies, educational spaces and learning communities that promote the principles of respect, pluralism, rational critical inquiry, justice and excellence.

André Mazawi's work provides a reflection on the potential of textbooks as instruments of hegemony. While accounting for agency, textbooks constitute powerful tools for the reproduction of dominant discourses and views of the world. Against such a realization, Mazawi examines and reports on the struggle over content and curricula in a region marked by geopolitical and intracommunal, social and political conflicts.

Using Jyllands-Posten and Charlie Hebdo as case studies, Carmen Sammut offers an important analysis of how media, like textbooks, constitute sites of struggle. True to the pedagogy of hope, Sammut advocates for social responsibility theories of communication as viable media intermediaries for more dialogue and peaceful encounters with the 'other'.

The importance of border-crossing as a powerful pedagogical tool in a curriculum for peace is foregrounded by Simone Galea, who problematizes the essentially patriarchal paradigms of peace. Galea pushes for a pedagogical third space where people meet and share 'breath' in an attempt to open up possibilities for rethinking relations with the different 'other'.

Joseph Gravina's chapter reveals how popular 'revolutions', based on critical consciousness and community-oriented action, rather than 'revolutions from above' (read political and economic settlements grafted by local and transnational elites), could provide concrete possibilities for genuine peace. While the former promotes agency and engagement, the latter, in Gravina's words, often lead to adaptation and, appeasement and as a result, precarious peace. Gravina emphasizes the 'pedagogical' role of passive revolutions as selective agents of change that does not lead to genuine peace.

Similarly, Arsalan Alshinawi illustrates how attempts to impose 'peace' arrangements that are completely insensitive to the historical realities and present tensions of geographic, cultural, economic and political spaces are bound to inflame tensions rather than contribute to lasting peace. Alshinawi makes a case for endogenous solutions to oppressive and violent social relations.

Nicos Trimikliniotis and Dimitris Trimithiotis propose that more than quick-fix solutions, we should think anew peace building and peacekeeping, in ways that actually transform current thinking and practices of peace-seeking in the world, which, in the authors' view, are predominantly Euro- and Western-centric in nature. They promote a critical-sociological approach to peace building, based on a sense of place and contextualized policies and frameworks for peace.

This book, in Antonia Darder's words, dares to dream of peace in a culture of war. It is revolutionary because it resists cynicism and fatalism. In understanding the search for peace as a critical moral imperative, this volume unveils some of the most glaring elements of the hidden curriculum of violence while contributing to the possibility of a peacefully just world.

Part One

The Contents of Peace

1

Where does True Peace Dwell?

Marianna Papastephanou

Introduction

In Cornelius Tacitus's[1] *Agricola*, the Scottish (Caledonian) leader Calgacus addresses the people with a speech urging them to war against the Roman Empire to secure their freedom. The first paragraph of the harangue ended with the famous dictum: 'Auferre trucidare rapere falsis nominibus imperium, atque ubi solitudinem faciunt, pacem appellant' (§30): 'Theft, slaughter and rape, the liars call Empire; they create a wilderness and call it peace'.[2]

Ever since, 'they create a wilderness and call it peace' has been an emblematic phrase of much political criticism that takes place both in public fora and in specialized departments. This chapter maps some of the multiple political operations of the 'metaphoricity'[3] of wilderness and tentatively explores how this metaphoricity may heighten our awareness of the world of today, a world where peace is absent and various excuses and alibis for this absence play a pacifying and soporific role. Contemporary reality will be sketched as a constructed wilderness, unsuitable and unlikely *qua* peace's dwelling place. The figurative substratum of this critique will be formed through brief references to Aristophanes' comedy *Peace*.[4] Finally, the chapter questions the naturalization and normalization of the homelessness of peace that may be extrapolated from some postmodern discourses. Such postmodern discourses make room for viewing the lack of abode as ontologically more appropriate for peace since the very search for a home for peace, that is, for a stable, conflict-free and orderly world, ostensibly reflects a by now obsolete metaphysics of presence. Such discourses acknowledge that a nuanced notion of conflict and the inescapability and significance of some conflicts for life have been neglected in a modern utopianism obsessed with order. But, by also failing to discern between detrimental conflict and desirable controversy, these postmodern discourses ironically run the risk of metaphysically, though unwittingly, naturalizing and normalizing the human-made wilderness that blocks true peace.

Wilderness

In Calgacus' dictum, *solitudo*, wilderness, often translated as 'solitude', 'desolation' or 'desert', is not natural but constructed, since 'they create' it, that is, it is human-made. The subject creating it is in plural; an aggressive, imperialist 'they' committing atrocities and cloaking them with the euphemism 'peace'. But, beyond the dictum, in many cases, the 'they' having the upper hand cannot be clearly distinguished from a subjected, docile and impotent 'we'. In such cases, even if the creation of wilderness burdens a specific agential collective subject, the perpetuation of wilderness burdens a passive recipient. The latter tolerates and often condones, instead of combating, wilderness – a wilderness that becomes eternal pacification much against hopes for perpetual peace. For instance, it is well known that Harold Pinter made precisely this point regarding the passivity and unquestioning manner with which his compatriots in the UK accepted their country's involvement in warfare in the 1990s.

Combating the constructed wilderness requires awareness of, and faith in, the possibility of the conceptual doubleness of peace – a doubleness that comprises a true and ideal peace as well as a pseudo-peaceful state (of affairs). Discerning a wilderness that is only nominally peace inserts a critical distance between a façade of peaceful coexistence and a true or genuine irenic life. To adapt here Carmel Borg and Michael Grech's views concerning peace, critique should distinguish 'between authentic peace and pacification, that is, between just peace and a pseudo-peace arrangement that violently reproduces the social and economic status quo on a global scale' (Borg and Grech, 2014, p. 1).

The distinction between true peace and pseudo-peace is compatible with (and throws light upon) another distinction, that of negative and positive peace. Whereas positive peace involves notions such as justice and equality (Bartolucci and Gallo, 2008, p. 8), negative peace is 'simply the absence of direct violence or war' (ibid., p. 7). It is a state of affairs where 'no active and organized military violence is taking place'. The negative sense is 'the most common understanding of peace, not only in the context of international politics', but also 'in the context of the peace and war debate' (ibid.). *Pax romana* is an example of negative peace[5] sliding into a façade of harmony, a state of affairs where the absence of violence through legal arrangements, military forces and social repression secures a pseudo-peace. The critical distance that Calgacus inserted between the created wilderness and the name 'peace' indicates the necessary critical contrast between a facile negative peace and a positive one of genuine transcendence of the constructed wilderness.

Yet, criticality[6] also invites us to think about whether wilderness is inherently connected to peace or to war: whereas in the dictum, wilderness is created, in much modern philosophy (and less explicitly in postmodern philosophy) the wilderness obstructing peace has been thought as natural. Considered in these terms, war has been seen as inherent to the *condition humaine*. Thomas Hobbes, for instance, whose overriding concern (Marshall, 1980, p. 194) had been a kind of peace, had naturalized war as a pre-contractual state of affairs – a 'state of nature where, without law and order, life is nasty, brutish and short' (p. 199). As a natural state of war against all, an anarchy of equals naturally inclined to fight and always in danger of mutual extinction, wilderness represented for many moderns the dystopian, though original, human condition that reflected their anthropological self-understanding *qua* egoistic and belligerent beings. Such beings can avoid and mitigate their natural condition and inclinations (the natural wilderness) only through a pact. In Hobbes' case, this pact secures a peace that we may regard only as negative: to obtain and maintain it 'men's opinions must be well governed' (ibid., p. 196). To this end, 'the Sovereign has the duty and the power not only to decide what "doctrines and opinions are averse, and what conducing to peace"', but also to ensure 'what men are to be trusted' 'in speaking to the multitudes of people' and 'who shall examine the doctrines of all books before they be published' (ibid.). Thus, the 'natural' wilderness described by the English philosopher is abandoned in exchange of freedom for safety and for a securitized sense of peace. But, in an early and interesting twist of the assumption that peace, even in servitude, is safer than war, the Scottish leader Calgacus seems to treat this assumption as expedient scaremongering and begins his speech to the multitude precisely by stating that, given the prospect of subjection, 'in war and battle, in which the brave find glory, even the coward will find safety' (Tacitus, §30). Calgacus makes a counter-intuitive connection of striving for freedom with safety. In doing so, he reverses the intuitive impression that pseudo-peace at least guarantees security and prosperity.

Though John Locke's version of the pact differed from that of Hobbes, it shared some of the Hobbesian naturalization and anthropological accommodation of strife at the pre-contractual level. And it slid into the constructed wilderness that Calgacus chastised by practically attenuating or disregarding claims to justice and equality of women, the poor and the 'uncivilized' (Gregoriou and Papastephanou, 2013). As a contractual state of a hierarchy of appeased, 'safe' and tamed egoists, wilderness (this time in Calgacus' sense of a state that passes for peace) represented the limit to utopia of modern imagination, the only attainable best possible world – for a naturally tarnished human being is unable of the perfection pertaining to the true and genuine peace in tension with the constructed wilderness.

Especially from modernity onwards, with few exceptions such as J. J. Rousseau, war rather than peace was viewed as the true and natural human condition, one that could only be mitigated contractually. A state of war against all, a Hobbesian state of nature that supposedly frames the human condition, has been a strong spatial metaphor, raising 'natural' obstacles to peace or naturalizing the sociopolitical failures to construct a permanent residence for peace. In a wilderness conceived as natural, or, when constructed, as framed by natural parameters, true peace cannot find a home. The peace that suits such spatiality can only be 'pseudo' or, at best, a brittle balance or a dim semblance.

The social contract tradition from Hobbes and Locke down to much current liberalism legitimizes itself *via* the intro-state wilderness that it presupposes as symbolic yet natural and aspires to surpass. Immanuel Kant's (1992) perpetual peace and vision of international right/cosmopolitan law extends the social contract to inter-state relations to lead the world beyond its wilderness and turn it into peace's stable, everlasting and proper home. Kant is rather ambivalent about the naturalness of the wilderness of the pre-cosmopolitan state of affairs: at times it seems more constructed than natural, but, at times, Kant attributes it to anthropological parameters such as the 'unsocial sociability of men', the 'foul stain of our species' and the 'radical' *qua* rooted cruelty inherent in humanity (Papastephanou, 2013).[7]

But natural wilderness was at times also conceived as an idyllic and happy state, a golden age long surpassed, 'an age before strife and suffering' (Zammit, 2014, p. 81). Often, this wilderness utopianized and romanticized the 'primitive' spatialities that Westerners encountered outside their ever-receding borders and construed as pre-contractual. But more often, it offered the means for what can be called 'inverted utopianization': the utopia of 'primitive' simplicity was wholly grafted on foreign lands though not affirmatively as in most utopianizing tactics, but, rather, negatively and dismissively. The remote space offered no ground for a nostalgic longing for a return to humanity's original home. Rather, its Golden

Age utopianization opened it up as a primitive space, a hitherto empty though fertile land for Western inscription (Gregoriou and Papastephanou, 2013). A case in point is the logic of *terra nullius* (empty, uncultivated land) in Locke. Locke saw the colony of Virginia as in a 'state of nature', which 'state of nature' justified the colonial enterprise and exploitation. In fact, 'Locke's image of the state of nature was constructed from a range of colonial sources on Indigenous peoples, depicting a condition without settled private property and legislative authority' (Buchan, 2005, p. 5). Virtue, for Locke, is, then, associated with the kind of productive labour that replenishes earth and justifies peoples' earning of titles to lands and goods (Glausser, 1990, p. 210). Conversely, people inhabiting land 'that they either cannot or will not develop' may be treated as 'aggressors against those who can and would develop that land' (p. 208). Wayne Glausser (1990) gives a detailed account of how such assumptions framed Locke's endorsement of slave trade and participation in the institutions of slavery (p. 200), and his exceptions to people's right to defend their country when it is threatened by conquest. Such an exception is the following: 'If a native population should "resist conquest of their waste land, they become aggressors in war", and the developers may justly kill them and enslave captives' (Glausser, 1990, p. 208). 'Eager to make his mark on the *tabula rasa* of American waste land' (p. 209), Locke considered wasteland a 'wilderness' awaiting 'the virtuous energy of European developers, who may find themselves killing, enslaving and philosophizing in the interests of development' (p. 215).

Through such operations, *inter alia*, philosophy often reflected, abetted, crystallised or sleepwalked its society's way to various injustices. In a context of powerful empires (often misrecognized as nation-states) that continued to form the setting of Western states of exception throughout (post-)modernity, injustices were bequeathed to later generations as impossible and intractable legacies. For instance, such a case of Western states of exception was the reality effected by the fact that a colonial metropolis would issue the Atlantic Charter[8] by which the principle of peoples' self-determination was affirmed, only to come some years later to exempt some colonies from the exercise of that principle in order to keep them under its control for geopolitical purposes. Creating exceptions to self-determination rendered the Western state in control of the colony exceptional, a case where the relativization of principles is supposedly appropriate. The colonial spaces that suffered such an exception (denial of their freedom) were burdened with the impossible situation that this very exception created, and are still struggling with the concomitant political 'legacy'.

Such injustices tended to occur mostly elsewhere, and were inflicted by the philosophers' mother countries upon other spatialities; on supposed 'wildernesses' in 'need' of the Western man's taming and civilizing industriousness. Many cases in point can be drawn from colonial imperialism. But, (post-)modern times also provide relevant examples. Such could be the case of Iraq. The West considered the Iraq of the Saddam era (not of the past; how could it given Iraq's rich history?) a havoc, a threat, a rogue state, a not-quite-contractual society (thus in this way, pre-political) that required the Western smoothing of its (Iraq's) affairs, an intervening process that would undo Iraqi wilderness by turning Iraq into a 'democratic' (in the Western model) state.

To sum up, the colonial context of *terra nullius* has provided yet another sense of wilderness, that of the foreign, uncultivated natural spatiality whose supposed non-utilization by its inhabitants legitimized in the Western mind[9] the Western intervention and conquest.

Against such 'natural' wildernesses, Western colonialism counterposed a *pax romana* of exploitation and slavery destined to be extremely profitable for the West as it secured for it peaceful (in the sense of unobstructed) *dominium* and free (in the sense of got-for-nothing) labour. In some cases, the only eternal peace thus attained was of the dead, as many people died on both sides of the civilizing mission. Nevertheless, such occurrences made the West rich, though the thus-secured wealth, like all unqualified wealth, is 'pseudo', not only because it generates illusions of peace but also because it is as such volatile and constantly threatened by the true (constructed) wilderness that the (unevenly enjoyed) wealth itself constitutes and perpetuates.

Beginning with the metaphoricity of world-as-wilderness that frames philosophy concerning peace, this chapter has so far unpacked some tensions between natural and constructed meanings of wilderness to associate them with true and pseudo-peace. We may now subtly connect the above with an ancient, comical account of war as effected, human-made rather than natural, and of peace as positive rather than negative. In Aristophanes' *Peace*, the dwelling place of a deified though exiled peace is sought beyond the then-current state of affairs.

Peace, the comedy

Three Aristophanic anti-war comedies, *Acharnians* (425 BC), *Peace* (421 BC) *Lysistrata* (411 BC) deal with the wilderness of war as created and are woven around the efforts of peacemakers to restore peace's dwelling among the societies at war. In the *Acharnians*, the Ur-peacemaker is Dikaeopolis, whose name (*dikaia polis*, evoking a city of justice) establishes an early conception of positive peace, not just as absence of war but as presence of justice. In *Lysistrata* (whose name evokes the dissolution of the army), the peacemaker is a woman who aspires to undo the constructed wilderness through appeal to natural inclinations towards a peaceful and pleasurable life.

In *Peace*, the homonymous divinity can be found nowhere; no space or home is a point of reference where she could be sought. Here we have an early connection of the constructed state of war with the spatiality hosting peace, the search for it and the de-naturalized causes of war. The peacemaker, Trygaeus, undertakes a peace initiative, namely, to transcend the city by flying to the skies to search for the eclipsed goddess. He does not search for a negative peace but for a positive peace that strikes a utopian note. The goddess of peace is not just the opposite of war, its mere absence, but a divine presence that precludes the eventuality of desert, desolation and wasteland: 'This lovable deity has the odour of sweet fruits, of festivals, of the Dionysia, of the harmony of flutes, of the tragic poets, of the verses of Sophocles, of the phrases of Euripides', 'of ivy, of straining-bags for wine, of bleating ewes', 'of the upturned wine-jar, and of a whole heap of other good things'. When Trygaeus prays to Peace, he asks her to 'cause the Greeks once more to taste the pleasant beverage of friendship and temper all hearts with the gentle feeling of forgiveness'. The state that peace creates attracts the eye: 'Then look how the reconciled towns chat pleasantly together, how they laugh.'

But peace was nowhere and war was prepared. Flying away to search for peace, hovering above the imminent wilderness, Trygaeus harkened to the words of the gods who accused his co-citizens of expelling peace from their land. As for the gods themselves, their relative rather than absolute ontological distance from humanity constituted a living presence of divine 'otherness' in people's everydayness. But, because war scenes caused divine aversion, that presence was yet another war victim, as the gods themselves had gone away.

TRYGAEUS
And why have the gods moved away?

HERMES
Because of their wrath against the Greeks. They have located War in the house they occupied themselves and have given him full power to do with you exactly as he

pleases; then they went as high up as ever they could, so as to see no more of your fights and to hear no more of your prayers.

Gods' averted eyes at the sight of war, a theme common to Homer[10] and to Aristophanes, the change of abode of the divine Other and peace's lack of abode psychoanalytically complicate the social imaginary of people who are about to commit the hubris of an aggressive war. Peace's lack of abode is not something that people 'naturally' tend towards or accept. It troubles their subconscious and this is obvious from the fact that they imagine their gods as displeased with them and their wars. This discomfort, this *Unbehagen* (a German psychoanalytic term for things about which people feel a vague sense of unease), attested in the comedy, complicates facile assumptions that peace's lack of abode in times of war was reflected as 'natural' or taken for granted in the social imaginary of those involved in the warfare.

TRYGAEUS
What reason have they for treating us so?

The answer questions the assumption of the inevitability of war and stresses that the state of war is human-made, as humans have been offered opportunities of peace that they have not taken up:

HERMES
Because they have afforded you an opportunity for peace more than once, but you have always preferred war. If the Laconians got the very slightest advantage, they would exclaim, 'By the Twin Brethren! The Athenians shall smart for this.' If, on the contrary, the latter triumphed and the Laconians came with peace proposals, you would say, 'By Demeter, they want to deceive us. No, by Zeus, we will not hear a word; they will always be coming as long as we hold Pylos.'<Quote>

Mutual distrust thus emerges as the cause, at least the apparent one, of war. But this would be too simplistic and psychologist an explanation. Despite the importance of its de-naturalization of the causes of war, this explanation singles out just one possible cause.

The wide spectrum of causes of war delimits and 'queers' the solutions. To queer something is to complicate it, to explore its limits, to question its foundations and to examine its assumptions. Full awareness of the complex and true (instead of superficial) causes of war helps us perform such queering of the proposed solutions to the problem of war since some solutions reflect precisely the flat and facile accounts of what counts as the cause of war. The following is a case in point: obviously thinking that the ideal solution to the problem of wars might be the non-lethal ending of a war with the victory of one's forces (and the concomitant *pax romana* effects), and thus presupposing that the cause of war may be just the aggressive 'other' that has to be neutralized, a laboratory in Ohio in 1994 produced the so-called 'gay bomb'.[11] One wonders, even if the American Air Force manages to utilize such a 'gay-bomb' to spray the battlefield with pheromones and make enemy soldiers become sexually irresistible to each other, would that stop the breaking out of wars, their lethal outcomes and their *pax romana* realities? Beyond behaviourist measures, what are the true causes of the absence of true peace? Would a thoughtful theorization of such causes not expose behaviourist solutions as the ridiculous nostrums that they are (to say the least)? Even more, would it not expose the underlying homophobic instrumentalization of eroticism and its subjection to expedience in 'efforts' such as those of the Air Force?

The causes of war

A more sophisticated (compared to mutual distrust), though still psychologistic and reductive, explanation of war might be obtuseness, lack of foresight and of knowledge of a war's stakes. For instance, if the wilderness effected in Iraq after the Western invasion were less ghastly, it could be comical, as we might consider it a typical political blunder. As a pre-emptive war, the invasion was to sacrifice some Iraqis for the sake of peace. Even if we concede, for the sake of argument, that this was not just a pretext but a genuine motivation for the Western meddling into Iraqi affairs, it obviously did not work. Regardless of its effectiveness, the very idea operated on an implicit assumption that the life of the sacrificed 'they' was inferior to ours; their sacrifice for the sake of security affirmed an implicit ontological distance between them and us: they could/should be sacrificed on the altar of peace, but not us. Yet, peace proves a recalcitrant divinity, averting her eyes from the site of blood. Hopes of achieving peace by sacrificing are falsified in Aristophanes' homonymous drama in a passage that stresses the incompatibility of peace with sacrifice and evokes for us, (post-)moderns, gruesome twists of fate:

TRYGAEUS [preparing a sacrifice to Peace] To the SERVANT
Take the knife and slaughter the sheep like a finished cook.

SERVANT
No, the goddess does not wish it.

TRYGAEUS
And why not?

SERVANT
Blood cannot please Peace, so let us spill none upon her altar.

In what is now southern Iraq, the Sumerian civilization offered us the first anti-war poem written by the Sumerian priestess Enheduanna in approximately 2300 BCE.[12] Enheduanna's poem describes the wilderness that war effects, indicates as causes or, at least, as inherent features of war the 'spirit of hate, greed and anger', and presents war as a 'dominator of heaven and earth', a god of such an unlimited abode. And she ends her poem with a question: 'Who can explain why you go on so?'[13]

Mainstream works in peace studies try to answer this question. But, despite being well meaning, they 'fail to acknowledge in substantive ways the historical, cultural, political, and economic asymmetries that persist and give rise to violent outbreaks and military aggression' (Darder, 2014, p. 93). Amartya Sen's response to such issues is that 'an enlightened attitude to war and peace must go beyond the immediate' to seek underlying 'deeper' causes. In looking for such causes, 'The economics of deprivation and inequity has a very plausible claim to attention' (Sen, 2008, p. 8). To the material conditions we may add (yet, in my view, in a complex relation that protects us from de-materializing the causes of war) 'the two pillars of enunciation: the racial and patriarchal foundation of knowledge without which the colonial matrix of power would not have been possible' (Mignolo, 2010, p. 120). Another set of causes we may extrapolate from the philosophical dialogue of Enrique Dussel and Karl-Otto Apel. Dussel's liberation ethics diagnoses in the globalized world a failure to respond to the height of the Other's demand. Apel believes that this failure is accomplished through a further failure of this world to meet the demands for self-consistency that are essential to self-critical rationality (Barber, 1998, p. 135). Indeed, are we not familiar with constant double standards and partial sensitivities? In turn, causes of violence may not be disengaged from responses to suffered violence: as Sen remarks, 'The tolerance of terrorism by an otherwise peaceful population is another peculiar phenomenon in some parts of the contemporary world, where many people feel that they were very badly treated in the past.' Violence is often tolerated as a 'retaliation for past injustices' (2008, p. 13). As for the fundamentalist blind violence and cruelty for which there can be no excuse or political offset, so many (and diverse) analyses are being deployed in current discourse that there is no space or reason here to delve into all this.

Complexity rather than simplicity helps us explain violence, a complexity that, to my mind, should seek causes at both the material and the symbolic levels: 'Poverty and inequality are importantly linked with violence and lack of peace, but they have to be seen together with divisions in which other factors, such as nationality, culture, religion, community, language and literature, play their parts' (Sen, 2008, p. 12). Some of the latter, though, are often singled out as the main cause of a conflict, risking a de-materialization or de-politicization of how we conceive conflict. Reductive explanations constitute, in my view, another great injustice often suffered by people who have been wronged in material/political ways and who expect, at least at the more symbolic level, recognition of the suffered injustice. In turn, reductive explanations may stir animosity and resentment, thus becoming possible causes of further tension themselves.

An even deeper cause of war (or at least toleration or justification of war in a complex interplay with the causal dimension) that remains mostly overlooked relates to a naturalization of war that works as an alibi for not striving for true peace. It relies on a specific anthropological self-understanding, our descriptions of our supposed 'nature', our twisting the constructed wilderness into natural and locating it in a supposed 'inside', that is, in the so-called 'beast within ourselves'. This conception of human nature has even contributed to considering humanity at war with the natural world too. It justifies treatments of the environment as a competitive wilderness in need of human taming and subjection. At first glance, this conception of human nature supposedly acknowledges the animality and naturality of humanity in close connection to the natural world (consider here Hobbes' 'homo homini lupus', Roman in origin, as a metaphor that likens human mutual cruelty to that of a wolf and shortens the human's distance from animality). Yet, ironically, instead of being a concession to a naturalist view, the assumption of a belligerent human nature and its naturalization of war reached the extreme point of inserting such a distance between the human and the natural that the world of nature could only be seen as antagonistic and in need of mastering. Hence I take issue with the view that 'questions related to the nature of humanity ... lose their relevance' (Mignolo, 2010, p. 124) in our times.[14] Supposedly, history 'teaches us that war is inevitable and that to strive

idealistically for lasting peace in the realm of real politics is dangerously naïve'
(Zammit, 2014, p. 77).[15] This empirical reading of the inauspicious record of
recurrent wars is grounded in accounts of human nature that couple it with an
anthropological constant of aggression. By contrast, 'Even if there are enough
histories of war to occupy every corner in all present and future archives, there is
still not one iota of evidence to suggest that the inevitability of war is an objective
fact imposed by the logical structure of reality' (ibid., p. 87). In other words, it is
the endorsement of the myth of wilderness *qua* natural rather than constructed
that has accompanied and supported the ontological citizenship granted to war.

Peace's dwelling place

HERMES
So that I don't know whether you will ever see Peace again.

TRYGAEUS
Why, where has she gone to then?

HERMES
War has cast her into a deep pit.

TRYGAEUS
Where?

HERMES
*Down there, at the very bottom. And you see what heaps of stones he has piled
over the top, so that you should never pull her out again.*

Aristophanes, Peace

Trygaeus mobilizes the citizens of various Greek city-states to excavate and
exhume Peace from the pit. With collective, maieutic efforts, she comes out
from that 'tomb' as if (re)born and is significantly accompanied by Opora and
Theoria.[16]

And in the here and now? Can a polycentric capitalist world be peace's dwelling
place? No, because such a world is not 'a de-colonial world'. The polycentric
capitalist world does not dispense with 'the colonial matrix of power and the
colonial and imperial differences regulating the field of forces in the modern/
colonial world' (Mignolo, 2010, p. 124). A de-colonial cosmopolitanism shall be
'the becoming of a pluri-versal world order built upon and dwelling on the global
borders of modernity/coloniality' (ibid., p. 117). Here, global borders evoke

contact zones where different people meet. In most contemporary postcolonial theory, these zones are considered sites where the promise of better politics may materialize. The underlying faith in plurality that singles out the global border as the possible abode for peace invites, in my opinion, one of Iris Young's questions. Young doubted whether Europe has shown any signs of recognizing its past. We may adapt this insight and apply it to powerful collectivities beyond Europe, those that are also typically designated as Western up to the global imaginary of the 'global city', the contact zone, the pluriversal global border. 'Colonialism was not just a vicious process of modernization, but a system of slavery and labor exploitation.' What are the signs that European people and states (or the de-colonial 'cosmopolitans' of a pluriversal global border) 'have responded to a call for accountability with gestures of contrition and reparation?' (Young, 2005, p. 157).

Through our framework so far, let us ask the questions: What is our world,[17] the hardly surprising world of today, the one supposed to host peace? From what genealogy has it emerged?[18]

It is a world that 'becomes increasingly dominated by an economic system that concentrates wealth and power in the hands of a global ruling class that is served by selectively porous states' (Borg and Grech, 2014, p. 9). In a world of limited vision and privatized hope (Papastephanou, 2009) where most utopian urge is directed at consumption and escapism, the recourse – especially of young people – to simplistic and pernicious 'ideals' is predictable, though surely not justifiable. Consuming irresponsibly, success and profit at all costs, the domination of resources and human bodies are some of the violent neo-liberal ideologies that 'have [taken] their toll on society's understanding of intimate human relationships as well' and constitute 'a threat to peace' (Gerada, Mercieca and Xuereb, 2014, p. 189).

Mobilizations such as The Occupy movements that are so often utopianized by both the global media and part of the academic world, despite their overall importance, do not always keep up the high-minded agency. Their intervention in some world problems reflects an account of conflict resolution that is too conventional and mainstream and too ignorant of the stakes of the specific context that hosts their particular intervention. Trite romanticizations and fashionable platitudes damage their efforts despite the best intentions. It would have been so much better to be more cautious and make pause for thought, investigation and interrogation regarding those issues before acting. As for academic textuality, even when declaring cosmopolitanism as an ideal to be pursued, it often fails so glaringly to enact this ideal. The texts in question frequently deconstruct themselves and performatively undermine the very cosmopolitanism they are preaching about.

Sometimes, public intellectuals conveniently criticize pathologies or events that appear safely distant in the past and to which they (and their current collectivities) had no direct relation. For instance, they rightly criticize the old Athenian society for the position of women, the racism of slavery, etc., but they fail to do so regarding more recent historical events within their own societies. Consider the racist treatment of Seretse Khama of Bechuanaland by the 'progressive' Labour government of Clement Attlee in 1951. Khama was a tribal leader of Bechuana, which was then a British protectorate. He married a white woman from London, and this was considered a provocation, given the colonial spirit of the times. Having banned interracial marriage under the apartheid system, neighbouring South Africa could not afford to have an interracial couple ruling just across their northern border. As Bechuanaland was then a British protectorate (not a colony), the South African government immediately exerted pressure to have Khama removed from his chieftainship. To maintain peaceful and harmonious relations with South Africa and secure the financial profit from those relations, the then Labour government of the UK betrayed the principles for which the just concluded Second World War had been fought.[19] It exiled Khama and his wife from Bechuanaland. I have not seen this fact stated anywhere in texts that (at times appropriately, at times self-righteously) condemn older realities. Depriving a family from their abode on racist grounds as late as 1951 (and this was done by the supposed bulwark of 'freedom' and 'peace' and by its 'progressive' party) does not come up in current discourses to complicate the uniform narrative of liberalism. It is a liberalism that is easily shocked by, say, ancient distinctions between the Greek and the barbarian (unquestionably shocking, nevertheless), but remains unaware of what has been (and is being) performed in its name and for profit-bearing pacification. Intellectuals sometimes fail to see how the principles betrayed then are precisely those that their 'near and dear' (collectivities such as the scientific communities, the various internet communities, the states/governments that pay their salaries and still profit from old and new exploitations, etc.) are still betraying. Quite often, academic criticism effects just psychic discharge and secures for the critic the image of the progressive, but deep down shows no real awareness of true political stakes, of the resilience of old mentalities, priorities and structures that effect a world lacking hope and lacking vision.

Can peace dwell in a predatory world without justice, in a world of double standards and states of exceptions that compromise the universality of law, in a world of *Realpolitik* where acquisitive and power-hungry mentalities hold sway?

Our world, the unsurprising world of today, also contains peace education. S. A. Cook (2014) gives a very rich and detailed account[20] of how peace is understood in the theoretical context of peace education. Yet, radical critique of the existent, radical self-questioning and awareness of the need for radical redirection do not surface at all in that account. All the self-reflective turn to the real is exhausted in realizing (in the multiple senses of the word[21]) its global possibilities of interconnectedness, as if oppression cannot occur when people are side by side. Thus, reflection becomes domesticated, as it remains unaware of the role that a deeper discontent with current realities and with the lip-service to discursively hegemonic ideals such as tolerance, diversity and respect should play.

Can peace inhabit a world that cannot even begin to spell politics? For, how knowledgeable of politics is a world in which many scholars, politicians and international referees tend to view some global problems (e.g. of some conflict-ridden areas) as easily reducible to the cultural differences of the parties involved without noticing the stakes of international right that make such conflicts primarily issues of violation of justice? Can a world-public 'spell politics' when its comprehension of politics seems typically to restrict itself to speaking in a politically correct fashion about others, yet without considering how various others have been (or are being) treated and without knowing the ethico-political debts that such treatment has created? How conducive to peace can this lack of knowledge be? How knowledgeable of politics is a world in which, despite all the fashionable talk against racism, it still remains unknown that the first genocide of the twentieth century was committed by Germany in 1904–7 against the Herero and Nama tribes (Kössler and Melber, 2004) in the black African space that is now part of Namibia?

The lack of knowledge of such political events and their stakes would not have been so significant if the events in question had been just archived historical givens, non-informative about the wilderness of our world. But as late as the 1990s and in the first years of the twenty-first century, the descendants of the Herero tribe who suffered all that loss have claimed compensation from Germany in order to be able to buy some of the lands for cattle that they had been deprived of as a side-effect of that genocide. What the United Nations decided (one wonders: has it not decided yet?) on the Herero complaint has not found a word in our quickly disseminated world press or in our Peace Education discourses. As far as it concerns the German political response to Herero claims for reparations, all that the Herero got from the German government was a verbal apology by one minister in 2004. As for the German public (its public, intellectuals and scholars notwithstanding, largely ignoring the issue), the whole story helped it become more politically correct: the city of Munich offered a 'nominal' appeasement in an intriguingly pacifying way. Instead of taking real measures (economic compensation, various reparations) of true ethico-political implications, it renamed a street from 'Lothar von Trotha Straße' (that was commemorating the man who ordered the genocide) into 'Herero Straße' as late as 2006.[22] Like the Herero case, other political issues that concern powerful countries also fail to attract the attention of Peace Education and, politically, to inform large publics. Such is also the case of Britain having created destructive 'facts-on-the ground', a literal wilderness, on the Diego Garcia island[23] about which little is known to broad publics, let alone discussed by them or practically dealt with through reparations.

Peace education and its initiatives often deal with various conflicts and world problems without exploring the political history and stakes of these problems. They rely on sensational or easily digestible accounts of historical facts, ask too few questions and use crude and shallow summaries. On their part, educators do not seem willing to investigate and speak 'of the silenced histories of violence and oppression' (Darder, 2014, p. 94). Such failures at the theoretical level make common cause with a global school reality. 'As agents of the war industry, schools also function effectively to block critical engagement with the dehumanizing brutality of aggression and the grand profits it affords' the involved global parties (ibid., p. 92).

As secret accomplices, institutional and scientific discourses hardly address the constructed wilderness promoting a pragmatic pseudo-consensus. Reflecting a pseudo-peace mentality, various instances of pseudo-consensus are concocted by negotiators whose only concern is to gloss over an injustice instead of undoing it. They fail to see that a hastiness to move on is part of the problem rather than its solution. The facile talk about peace that operates within international initiatives often privileges a crude negotiation framework. It involves reductive and simplistic accounts of conflicts as supposedly resulting from psychological issues in need of psychoanalysis. Facile approaches to some problems of international right reduce such 'crises' to psychological stances of the conflicting parties towards one another. It is assumed that the 'enemies' just do not like each other because of their fear of one another (real, imagined or exaggerated by the global negotiators and 'educators'). To help the conflicting communities 'grow out' of the psychological basis of their problem, intervening parties tend to make them an 'object' of psychoanalysis in a sweeping and totalizing way that obfuscates and misses those truly political dimensions of the conflict that touch upon global justice. It turns on those involved, bestows upon them the power and positive self-image of the peacemaker and mobilizes libidinal energies of rescuing the 'damsels in distress' (the conflicting parties) from their supposedly self-inflicted immaturity and inability to join the apparently conflict-free world of advanced states. It overlooks ethico-political stakes that have to be dealt with on the part of the intervening strong party in great transcendence of old habits. It exhausts itself in a merry celebration of a supposed overcoming of identities, as if belonging were the only obstacle to peace, as if the exploitation of the world and much conquest had not occurred due to profit-seeking rootless elites and complex socio-economic-political structures.

Certainly, there are more thoughtful approaches and there are undercurrents that challenge current global vogue. They are important to bear in mind in order to resist a possible (and gloomy) homogenization of the world of today. But the problem is precisely that those various voices remain inoperative or barely discernible in the maze of global communication.

Homelessness

Our world also hosts radical theoretical subversions of the search for peace's home or for a peaceful home. Global justice is often treated as easily deconstructible or as a residue of Kantian, obsessive visions of perpetual peace. Thus, deconstruction and deconstructibility sometimes become weapons, polemical tools, for undermining the other's claims to justice, but never for questioning one's own claims to relativizing justice. In this way, deconstructive operations often contribute to the perpetuation, rather than to the undoing of, injustices. Yet, neither is justice so easily deconstructible nor is one's recourse to time-honoured mindsets of sophistry as unnoticeable as it so far seems.

Can peace dwell in a world where even philosophy tends now to legitimize conflict[24] indirectly by asserting that we live in an imperfect world where disorder may be celebrated as redemptive, where we are all refugees as the language that constructs us is never a true home, and that, by extension, true peace might be *the* refugee *par excellence*?

The issue about the limited human potentiality in an imperfect world underpins much postmodern discourse. It directs it not only to accepting the homelessness of peace but even to giving onto-anthropological permanence to such homelessness. Thinkers who have never experienced the true state of exile celebrate it figuratively. It will come as no surprise if they start to explore the space that is purportedly opened by the supposedly *endemic* homelessness of peace ('endemic' is being used ironically and in a deliberately paradoxical manner, since the term etymologically involves 'having a stable home'). They glorify the figure of the refugee and its rootless potentialities, unable as they are to distinguish the ontological space of the precariousness of articulated order (and homelessness/lack of permanent residence of meaning) from the political space of a people deprived of home through acts of violence. Deep down, a reason for this inability to discern nuance is, in my view, an unspoken, though operative, conception of the natural inevitability of conflict. Instead of de-naturalizing war and the constructed wilderness to which the operation of naturalization offers an alibi, much current theory surrenders the hope for peace. It treats peace as an obsessive order. It sees it as a last vestige of the modern fascination with revolutionary optimism or of a longing for wholeness, harmony and consensus in a dissonant world that renders all this naïve and futile.

The underlying assumption of those who welcome this view may be that the postmodern debunking of grand narratives is a/the recipe for peace, that war and conflict are brought about by such narratives, particularly those spurred by modern optimism. Certainly, modern optimism is not only untenable within the confines of a constructed wilderness, as this chapter argues, but it is even dangerous in its implicit, hegemonic assumptions for reasons that are well known and into which we need not delve. But those who give in unquestioningly to the postmodern 'promise' fail to notice that, if thought through to its ultimate implications, the wholesale incrimination of order, consensus, perfectibility and utopia leads to a deconstruction of the very search for peace's 'home'. The glorification of the figure of the refugee as a general condition for all of us and, by implication, of notions such as peace may render the question about peace's 'home' expendable and thus declare peace a 'refugee' par excellence. Such are in my view the implications of Sharon Todd's book *Toward an Imperfect Education* (2009). The book critiques the assumed goodness of humans that underwrites the idea of humanity and explores how antagonistic human interactions such as conflict and violence are a fundamental aspect of life in a pluralistic and imperfect world. As for the faith in the debunking of grand narratives mentioned above, suffice it here to refer to the fact that Alain Badiou has already exposed the grand narrative character that this faith ironically has acquired and his vehement critique of some postmodern tenets (Badiou, 1999, p. 31).

The philosophical idioms that I have criticized render the very question about the dwelling of peace expendable, obsolete, meaningless, a residue of old metaphysics, an unsophisticated longing for abode, rootedness and stability. If the authority of such approaches derives mainly from their academic currency then, perhaps, the answer to them might be a deliberate and thoughtful obsolescence. Critiquing such philosophical idioms as mostly new liberal self-exculpating tactics, we may realize that the state of refugee is not ontologically determined/determining for peace. It is rather a condition constructed by the constantly (re)created wilderness in which we live. So long as human beings continue to find 'naturalizing' or 'ontologizing' paltry excuses for the wilderness they create and perpetuate, true peace will remain an exile. Like Sophocles' *Antigone*, true peace is hypsi-polis (aspiring to the best imaginable polis) and for this reason, it will remain a-polis (homeless) in our wild world of today.

Conclusion

The causes of war along with the perpetuation (or exculpations) of injustices may range from material ones related to profit up to more symbolic ones related to a naturalization of the created wilderness. Lack of attentive care to the contextual aspect of world problems and to their complexity proves that, even when intentions are good, an uneven or limited cultivation of intellectual and ethical virtues blocks the required nuance in understanding and critiquing various realities.

Perhaps the paradox of peace is that, in the world of today, its cause may not be promoted by the irenic talk that follows the contours of the existent without changing it, like a caress. It may be promoted by the confrontational words that hammer the existent, by the cynic and sarcastic idiom that transfers *polemos* from the battlefield to the philosophical language game. 'Unveiling the world requires us to acknowledge the crimes against humanity – genocide, slavery, colonization, incarceration and impoverishment' (Darder, 204, p. 94). In my view, it requires more than just acknowledging them. It requires radical redirection, more imaginative ways out of the current situation and more ability to go beyond established metonymies of atrocities. A true unveiling of the world also presupposes that we retrieve the non-thematized issue or the as yet overlooked, though pending, moral debt. It can use an idiom that destroys the lame excuses for the current situation, de-naturalizes alibis and de-beautifies a world that sees itself, despite indications to the opposite, as the best possible or as requiring facile solutions. Possibly, unveiling the world requires an acknowledgement of its wilderness as constructed and a dose of *contemptus mundi*, even an averted, horrified eye. Perhaps that was why, in *Peace*, Trygaeus turned to the audience and dystopianized it by addressing it in a way that evokes an interplay of transcendent and immanent gaze: 'How small you were, to be sure, when seen from heaven! You had all the appearance too of being great rascals; but seen close, you look even worse.'

Notes

1 http://www.thelatinlibrary.com/tacitus/tac.agri.shtml
2 For my somewhat different and *en passant* reference to Calgacus's words, see Papastephanou (2014a).
3 The term 'metaphoricity' refers here to the power of wilderness as metaphor, its various and rich functions as metaphor, its quality as metaphor, let us say, metaphor being one of the properties of the semantic role of wilderness. The term 'metaphoricity' is widely used by philosophers like Paul Ricoeur, Judith Butler and Jacques Derrida.
4 All references to this comedy here will be drawn from the English translation of the text that is open access at the following link: http://classics.mit.edu/Aristophanes/peace.html
5 Deriving from *pangere*, to put together something that has been broken, and sharing its root with that of 'the group *paciscor, pactum, pactio* whose meaning is "agreement, compromise taken between two opponents"', the Latin *pax*, peace, was tightly connected to *bellum*, war. Its meaning is, in its essence, negative: peace corresponds to the end of a violent conflict reachable through victory in a battle or an agreement. 'The concept of pax animi (the serenity and peacefulness of a person) was also present, although with minor relevance' (Bartolucci and Gallo, 2008, p. 4).

6 The word 'criticality' involves a play between being critical in the sense of critiquing and being critical in the sense of finding oneself in an urgent situation where action is needed.

7 In any case, Kant believes that he can avoid the implications of the dose of natural wilderness that might be relevant as an obstacle to peace by emphasizing that the political task of peace could be accomplished even by a 'nation of devils' (Kant, 1992, pp. 112–3). The 'why' and 'how' of this (and issues of plausibility) go beyond the scope of this chapter.

8 The Atlantic Charter was a pivotal policy statement issued in 14 August 1941 that, early in World War II, defined the Allied goals for the post-war world. It was drafted by the leaders of Britain and the United States, and later agreed to by all the Allies. The eight principal points of the Charter included the statement that 'all people had a right to self-determination'.

9 I use 'Western mind' here despite the fact that there had been some dissenting voices even then, voices that one may describe as 'undercurrents of thought'. But those voices did not gain enough popularity to suffuse the popular attitude to colonialism in a way that would have real effect or would matter and make a difference in the consequences of colonialism on those who suffered them. Thus, they do not change the fact that a general mindset was, indeed, operative in the designation 'West' and provided all sorts of rationalizations of expansion and of 'constructed wildernesses'. As a relevant thought experiment, let us ask: What was the difference made by dissenting voices in the overall situation of colonialism and slavery? Even now, how many lay people or experts know of philosophers who opposed the *terra nullius* logic or Grotius' 'ius gentium'? Samuel Pufendorf was to some extent such an exception to the generality of the 'Western mind', but is it accidental that too few people in the world know of him? Likewise with James Otis who was, indeed, another admirable exception in being an early opponent of slavery in America, sadly unknown though. Certainly, they contributed to a theoretical preparation of a better future in some specific respects. But, this did not have direct effects on the situation that, say, slaves generally confronted. There is no space in this chapter for discussing the risk of using undercurrents as facile self-exculpations of the West (that is, as supposed proof that things were not too bad after all because there had been critical voices). Here let me only explain that there is a kind of self-exculpation of the West in the act of always stressing the dissenting voices, even in cases where those voices did not manage to make any difference to those suffering the consequences of Western 'peaceful' interventions. Besides, the reader should bear in mind that the phrase 'the Western mind' to which this endnote corresponds, is not a blanket generalization because it refers to the 'they already evoked by Calgacus but renewed in each new case of constructed wilderness. That is, it refers to those who had the power to act and had acted

in ways that produced the constructed wilderness and to those masses that had passively tolerated (and even profited) from colonialism.

10 As I explain in Papastephanou (2009, Chapter 2), in Homer, when the Gods wish to avert their eyes from the cities in war, they turn them to the ideal extremes and edges of the world: the Ethiopians in the far south and the Hyperboreans in the far north. What is utopian about Zeus's averting his eyes from the scenery of the Trojan War and turning to the Ethiopians? By imagining a disapproving and dismissive withdrawal of divine attention, human beings express discomfort, guilt about the wars they unleash and a deep knowledge of the fact that it is possible to act better and that war is not inevitable.

11 http://en.wikipedia.org/wiki/Gay_bomb

12 The poem's title is: **Lament to the Spirit of War** and reads as follows:

> *You hack everything down in battle ...*
> *God of War, with your fierce wings*
> *you slice away the land and charge*
> *disguised as a raging storm,*
> *growl as a roaring hurricane,*
> *yell like a tempest yells,*
> *thunder, rage, roar, and drum,*
> *expel evil winds!*
> *Your feet are filled with anxiety!*
> *On your lyre of moans I hear your loud dirge scream.*
> *Like a fiery monster you fill the land with poison.*
> *As thunder you growl over the earth,*
> *trees and bushes collapse before you.*
> *You are blood rushing down a mountain,*
> *Spirit of hate, greed and anger,*
> *dominator of heaven and earth!*
> *Your fire wafts over our land,*
> *riding on a beast,*
> *with indomitable commands, you decide all fate.*
> *You triumph over all our rites.*
> *Who can explain why you go on so?*

http://voicesinwartime.org/category/tag/lament-spirit-war

13 http://voicesinwartime.org/category/tag/lament-spirit-war

14 There is no space here for expanding on this and for defending my view in detail. For more, see Papastephanou (2014b).

15 Clive Zammit refers to this view but, rightly in my opinion, he does not endorse it. Instead, he deploys a very apposite critique of it.

16   Opora and Theoria make on us their own interesting interpretive demands, but this goes beyond the confines of this chapter.

17   The 'is' of this question should not be read in the metaphysical sense that it acquires in specialized idioms of metaphysics. It refers to the sociopolitical constructed reality that invites our critical attention. Such attention was usually described by Theodor Adorno and other Frankfurt School theorists as 'a critique of the existent'. For this reason, this constructed sociopolitical world will be henceforth signified in the chapter as 'the existent'.

18   Certainly, social theory and other fields have a more complex explanation for the current situation than the one that can be provided or sketched here. However, the aim of this chapter is not to give detailed overviews or full argumentation but, rather, to evoke deep theoretical connections through indications and suggestibility.

19   This should not obscure the fact that the Conservative government that followed the Labour party in the British government betrayed the principles for which the War was fought even more glaringly and remorselessly.

20   The following are gleanings from Cook's account. All are amenable, in my view, to Antonia Darder's following criticism: 'A liberal formulation of peace education' is still 'detached from conditions of human suffering and gross inequalities that are experienced by the majority of the world's population' (Darder, 2014, p. 93). 'Like multiculturalism, peace education views tolerance, respect for difference and appreciation of the rights of others as productive of peace' (Cook, 2014, p. 493); 'peace education has been designed to promote understanding and enactment of non-violence, human rights, social justice, world-mindedness, ecological balance and environmentalism, meaningful participation, and personal peace' (ibid.). Peace education also comprises 'diversity education, violence prevention and conflict resolution' (ibid.). 'Peace education should combat violence on three levels: peacekeeping, peacemaking and peacebuilding' (ibid.). Peace education emphasizes 'the interdependence of all people within a global system; the connectedness and diversity of universal human attributes, values, knowledge, curriculum subjects, aspects of schooling, humans and their environment; and the privileging of multiple perspectives before settling on a viewpoint' (ibid.). All in all, it feels like all the expectations of peace education are exhausted at the communicative level of how we view or speak about others, as if their material conditions of existence are irrelevant to peace and make no serious demands upon us regarding diachronic and synchronic ethical debts.

21   'To realize' denotes to attain a heightened consciousness of a state of affairs, a reality, etc.; to understand or be aware of something; to 'cause something to become real' (http://www.merriam-webster.com/dictionary/realize); to 'achieve something, such as a goal, dream, etc.' (http://www.merriam-webster.com/dictionary/realize). In its multiple semantic operations, 'to realize' also denotes to

obtain something, to introduce it into the real, to make something happen and to acquire some effect (e.g. to realize a possibility, a plan, etc.).

22 http://en.wikipedia.org/wiki/Lothar_von_Trotha The street had been named 'Lothar von Trotha' in 1933 by the Nazi authorities. It took 70 years after the collapse of Nazism (and millions of recurrent passers-by) to view another name on the street, one commemorating the victims of von Trotha. And that happened only after the stirring of the issue by Herero themselves and their claims. Significantly, the Herero claims, as I have explained, were far more material and made more demands on the German public than the renaming of a street. The renaming allowed the German public to uphold the morally convenient self-image of the now politically correct 'cosmopolitans' without stressing the 'tax-payer' too much.

23 http://en.wikipedia.org/wiki/Diego_Garcia I refer to Wikipedia for reasons of quick and easily accessible information. There is no space in this chapter for discussing the Diego Garcia issue but only for mentioning it.

24 To acknowledge the importance of dissent without normalizing conflict, I draw a distinction between conflict and controversy: a conflict-free world would not be a controversy-free world, so, a commitment to resolving conflicts does not necessarily affirm appeasement or an obsessive sense of order.

References

Badiou, A. (1999). *Manifesto for Philosophy*. Trans. Norman Madarasz. Albany: State University of New York Press.

Barber, M. D. (1998). *Ethical Hermeneutics: Rationality in Enrique Dussel's Philosophy of Liberation*. New York: Fordham Press.

Bartolucci, V. and Gallo, G. (2008). 'Beyond Interdisciplinarity in Peace Studies: The Role of System Thinking'. http://www.di.unipi.it/~gallo/Papers/Interdisciplinarity%26Peace.pdf

Borg, C. and Grech, M. (2014). 'Introduction'. In C. Borg and M. Grech (Eds), *Lorenzo Milani's Culture of Peace*, pp. 1–12. New York: Palgrave Macmillan.

Cook, S. A. (2014). 'Reflections of a Peace Educator: The Power and Challenges of Peace Education With Pre-Service Teachers'. *Curriculum Inquiry*, 44 (4): 489–507.

Darder, A. (2014). 'Peace Education in a Culture of War'. In C. Borg and M. Grech (Eds), *Lorenzo Milani's Culture of Peace*, pp. 91–6. New York: Palgrave Macmillan.

Gerada, M., Mercieca, C. and Xereb, D. (2014). 'Peace and Sexuality – Two Reflections'. In C. Borg and M. Grech (Eds), *Lorenzo Milani's Culture of Peace*, pp. 187–94. New York: Palgrave Macmillan.

Kössler, R. and Melber, H. (2004). 'The Colonial Genocide in Namibia: Consequences for a Memory Culture Today From a German Perspective'. *Ufahamu: A Journal of African Studies*, 30 (2–3): 17–30.

Marshall, J. D. (1980). 'Thomas Hobbes: Education and Obligation in the Commonwealth'. *Journal of Philosophy of Education*, 14 (2): 193–203.

Mignolo, W. (2010). 'Cosmopolitanism and the De-colonial Option'. *Studies in Philosophy and Education*, 29: 111–27.

Papastephanou, M. (2009). *Educated Fear and Educated Hope: Utopia, Dystopia and the Plasticity of Humanity*. Rotterdam: Sense Publishers.

Papastephanou, M. (2013). 'Utopian Education and Anti-utopian Anthropology'. *International Education Studies* 6 (2): 22–33.

Papastephanou, M. (2014a). 'On Education, Negotiation, and Peace'. In C. Borg and M. Grech (Eds), *Lorenzo Milani's Culture of Peace*, pp. 77–90. New York: Palgrave Macmillan.

Papastephanou, M. (2014b). 'To Mould or to Bring Out? Human Nature, Anthropology and Educational Utopianism'. *Ethics and Education* 9 (2): 157–75.

Sen, A. (2008). 'Violence, Identity and Poverty'. *Journal of Peace Research*, 45 (1): 5–15.

Todd, S. (2009). *Toward an Imperfect Education: Facing Humanity, Rethinking Cosmopolitanism*. Boulder, CO: Paradigm Publishers.

Young, I. (2005). 'De-Centering the Project of Global Democracy'. In D. Levy, M. Pensky and J. C. Torpey (Eds), *Old Europe, New Europe, Core Europe*, pp. 153–9. Verso: London.

Zammit, C. (2014). 'Responding to the Call of Peace: In Memory of a Future that Might Have Been'. In C. Borg and M. Grech (Eds), *Lorenzo Milani's Culture of Peace*, pp. 77–90. New York: Palgrave Macmillan.

2

A Gramscian Analysis of Passive Revolution and its Contribution to the Study of Peace

Joseph Gravina

Introduction

This chapter considers peace from the perspective of Antonio Gramsci's conceptual re-elaboration of Vincenzo Cuoco's idea of passive revolution. It opens by giving a definition of peace that is somewhat different from that commonly and implicitly found in ordinary discourse. A more qualified understanding of peace is proposed. In relation to this, the chapter defines the concept of passive revolution and applies it to some concrete historical cases.

Rather than analysing peace and its absence in relation to issues between nation states or between the First and Third worlds, the chapter considers a number of cases from Italian and European history that were 'peaceful' or were followed by periods of supposed 'peace'. The chapter argues that what we had in these cases was a 'Passive Revolution' that, despite appearances to the contrary, did not result in peace as understood here. What the cases in question fundamentally involved is the adaptation of political and social structures to capitalist economies at various stages. The cases considered are the Italian *Risorgimento*, industrial developments in Italy in the twentieth century (during both the Fascist *ventennio* and post-World War II) and European institutionalized integration in the European Union (EU). The political and economic processes that occurred at the time seemed justified as attempts to defend or bring about stability and 'peace' during times of change. The Piedmontese, Fascists, Christian Democrats and European bureaucrats of an integrated Europe all claimed to be struggling to achieve peaceful stability. The common and much more basic theme in these ventures, however, is the adaptation of political and social structures to capitalist needs. An important role in this strategy was played by the education system, 'normalizing' and 'pacifying' what otherwise might have been conflict-ridden times of change. In each case referred to in this chapter, the powers that be produced a seminal educational reform that complemented and, hence, reinforced the passive revolution in question.

Peace and passive revolution

Mainstream media, education and discourse often define peace as the mere absence of violent conflict. This understanding of peace may allow 'mechanisms of domination [the ability to control the activities of others] and exploitation [the acquisition of economic benefits from the labour of those who are dominated]' to persist. (Olin Wright 2009, p. 107) This chapter on the other hand, defines peace as not merely the absence of violent conflict, but as the absence of violence together with the existence/coming into being of relations of justice and equity.

'Passive revolution' is understood to refer to developments both within a society and in the international sphere that are piecemeal, gradual and frequently deemed 'peaceful', especially in relation to their outcomes and aftermaths. These developments generally involve the adaptation of earlier political and social structures to new realities, rather than their abolition. The process of change involved in a passive revolution contrasts with more radical and abrupt changes, typical of active revolutionary upheavals. This essay considers passive revolution in its Gramscian redefinition. The concept did not originate with Gramsci. Yet, in the words of Buci-Glucksmann, Gramsci 'remoulded and enriched' the concept of Passive Revolution 'to the point of being completely transformed' (Buci-Glucksmann 1980, p. 314), reflecting the openness and undogmatic character of his thought. The concept as elaborated by Gramsci contributed 'to the extension of the Marxist problematic of bourgeois revolutions … [i.e. to Marxist] theoretical efforts to understand the "transformations that create the political conditions of capitalist domination"' (Callinicos 1989, in Callinicos 2010, p. 494). In his *Prison Notebooks*, Gramsci links the concept of 'passive revolution' to other notions 'besides domination', like 'leadership', 'war of position and manoeuvre' and 'consensus and dominance' (rather than opposition) (Q8: 48, 86). Passive revolution need not entail peace as as it is understood in the chapter. Indeed, passive revolution has often been characterized by unequal relations and inequities, and hence is inimical to peace as this is understood in this context.

The Risorgimento: State formation, geopolitics and social class

Focusing on Italy from the mid-eighteenth century to the Congress of Vienna in 1815, rivalries between different European states created the right conditions for Italian unification, especially in relation to the eventual curtailment of Bourbon and Austrian hegemony over the peninsula. The French revolution of 1789 had sparked these conditions. It inspired, ten years later, the short-lived Neapolitan revolution. In his *Saggio Storico Sulla Rivoluzione Napoletana del 1799*, Cuoco noted how this democratic revolution in Naples failed because it did not reflect Neapolitan reality. This 'revolution without a revolution' was simply part of the spatial extension of the French revolution on Italian soil through French occupying forces. Being top-down, it was difficult for it to gain popular support; indeed, it led to a contradiction between the needs of wide sectors of the population (including the poorest ones) and those of the minute new democratic leadership that were supposed to give these sectors representation. The Neapolitan Republic failed.

A successful attempt to change the political geography in the Italian peninsula had to follow a different logistic. Eventually, the central role in state formation on the broader peninsular canvas was performed by the small monarchy of Piedmont, coinciding with the rise to political prominence of Camillo Benso di Cavour. The task was extremely complex. Piedmont had to push the Austrians out of northern Italy, where they had many followers (including in Piedmont itself),[1] defeat and invade the Bourbon monarchy in the South (a feat achieved thanks to indirect and not-so-indirect British help and manoeuvring) and unite different cultures and communities in one political state. In political terms, the goals of the *Risorgimento* seemed to have been successfully accomplished. The unification of Italy came into being.

Gramsci, however, compares the *Risorgimento* to the French Revolution in order to highlight the differences between the two, differences that may be understood in terms of the distinction between 'revolutionary renewal' and mere 'renewal' (See Voza 2004). In Piedmont, the Liberals supporting Cavour were not revolutionary Jacobins; they believed in a top-down, monarchy-led state. In the process of unification, old landed classes maintained an active political role even if they did not retain their traditional dominant role.

The official narrative of the *Risorgimento* is one of liberation and unification of a people who shared essentially the same national identity. Even the educational reforms that preceded unification and were implemented after it – the 'Casati

Law' named after the Piedmontese Minister of Public Instruction Gabrio Casati – seemed progressive and enlightened. Gramsci himself later praised the reform and the educational curriculum that resulted for its positivistic aspects, and for its emphasis on science and hard facts, which he deemed essential to overcome a folkloristic culture. According to the official narrative, the *Risorgimento* involved independence from 'reactionary' regimes (the Bourbons and the Austrians) and the subsequent state-building, which, with the exception of a few forays against a few brigands in the south, was largely 'peaceful'. Reality was much more complex. The Piedmontese monarchy did annex the other territories and create a political unity (characterized by an uneven economic geography). Yet, while direct Austrian and Bourbon influence ceased, the classes that had wielded economic and political power (with the partial exception of the clergy) were not to be estranged from the politico-economic set-up that came into being following unification. The political upheaval that was Italian unification, was a 'passive revolution', creating 'an institutional framework consonant with capitalist property relations' (Morton 2007, p. 66), which involved continuity beyond the ruptural process of state formation and the establishment of stable conditions for capitalism. While the political and social institutions adapted to reflect the needs of dominant or emerging classes, many sectors (with the partial exception of the church) of the previously dominant groups were accommodated within the new set-up. If in France the bourgeoisie had broken the suffocating hold of the aristocracy, in the Italian case, as in Germany, the aristocracy retained its political presence. Everything had to change, but at the same time everything (or quite a lot) had to remain as it was. Revolution-restoration became a straightjacket: in Buci-Glucksmann's words, a 'blocked dialectic as opposed to a dialectical supersession' (1980, p. 315). This impasse exposed 'the "passive" aspect of the great revolution' (Q10: 9), with change carried out legalistically and in small doses. The process achieved 'peace' but not as 'peace' is understood in this chapter, that is, in terms of equity and justice. Entire social sectors were excluded and marginalized. The educational reform did not lead to or abet political emancipation.

That the popular masses were left out of the process of unification is testified, according to Gramsci, by the absence of any genuine bottom-up revolutionary upheavals (Q3: 40). Where fervour was manifested, it was either in favour of the previous rulers (e.g. the Bourbons in the South) or fervour that clamoured for socio-economic changes, for example, the distribution of lands rather than unification as such (which the new rulers were not willing to undertake). The Piedmontese regime was willing to resist and quell both types of resistance.

Regarding the former, the South was 'pacified' once 'brigands' were defeated, a bloody process of what, for a time, was military colonization. 'Brigands' were wiped out, but not the mafia, or the local aristocrats and notables with whom the Italian state would establish a *modus operandi*. Those who wanted socio-economic change, those who were traditionally excluded in economic, political and cultural terms (peasants, urban poor, etc.) did not, on the whole, experience any improvement to their lot with the *Risorgimento*. Rural and urban masses still suffered depravation. The South was condemned to perpetual underdevelopment.

The Risorgimento and its aftermath then, as a passive revolution, did not achieve peace. Indeed, the passive revolution in question was meant to quell the possibility of a radical change in relation to the masses who were materially deprived, minimizing the possibility of revolution while retaining 'progressive' and 'enlightened' rhetoric. For some time, this guaranteed internal 'peace' as this is commonly understood (i.e. the absence of violence on a large scale) and stability, particularly to the propertied classes (be they aristocrats, landowners or bourgeois).

Given the development of industrial capitalism particularly in the North-West however, as well as the several crises that occurred in agriculture (including a long-stretching crisis hitting the share-cropping system and the agricultural proletariat employed in the technologically primitive Po basin, and at the same time the small allotment peasantry in the South), new social conflicts would in due course emerge, social conflicts that the Establishment of the day would consider a threat to 'peace' as it understood it. These conflicts would involve the industrial bourgeoisie of the North, the landed aristocracy of the South, the State and the army and, in its own way, the church on the one side, and industrial workers as well as politicized sectors of the artisan classes and the peasantry, on the other. This would in time require another sort of pacification, involving other passive revolutions. In neither case was peace in the long run achieved.

Capitalist consolidation in Italy – Fordism and Fascism

Sometime after the *Risorgimento*, large-scale industries started to develop in some parts of Italy (and in these only). Fordist mass-production industry was introduced in Italy, primarily in the North, something that influenced social relations and the post-*Risorgimento* 'pacification'. It was a time of change and crisis. As in other parts of Europe, the introduction of mass-production industry would weigh non-complementary social relations in the balance. Some of these realities had survived political unification and prolonged their presence therein, along with parasitic and semi-feudal strata of society that thrived on them. At the same time, industrial relations of production and conditions created class consciousness in the nascent proletariat. Worker resistance surfaced in the late nineteenth and early twentieth centuries. Originally, the response of the powers that be was violent. The Savoyard State did not back off from using soldiers against workers and the industrial poor. An infamous case is that of General Bava Beccaris ordering his soldiers to fire on demonstrators protesting against the price of bread in Milan in 1898. In recognition, Beccaris was awarded The Great Cross of the Order of Savoy by King Umberto. There were also measures aimed at social appeasement, particularly from Catholic quarters. Cases in point are the *Casse Rurali*, credit cooperatives for small farmers that were especially active in the Veneto region. This notwithstanding, worker militancy continued to increase, culminating in the *Biennio Rosso* (the Two Red Years 1919–20), where tensions in industry and agriculture reached boiling point. This led to the occupation by workers of some factories in 1920. The powers that be had to resist. This took the form of suppression of worker takeover on the one hand, and a supposedly radical readaptation of the state, on the other. Organized labour was challenged by a corporative counter-revolution featuring policing and a fascist *coup d'état* in 1922. Yet, rhetorically, the coup had the trimming of a revolution – *la Rivoluzione Fascista*.

The Fascist takeover was another case of passive revolution, a change that co-opted actors from the previous regime (including the monarchy itself and the army), and that eventually led to pacification rather than peace. Labour was not merely attacked violently, as when workers' organizations were defeated and destroyed, but also co-opted and neutralized. Corporativism, promoted by industry and supported by the fascist policy of autarky, was an important aspect in this drive, apparently incorporating labour in political and work practice hierarchies. Change, supposedly meant to benefit the people, was being imposed from the top. While it made some gains for those in the lowest echelons of society, the interests of the powers that be (large-industry, land-proprietors, etc.) were guaranteed. Though appeasing sectors of the country, these measures did not achieve equity or address unequal economic, political and cultural relations in a radical and fundamental way. On the cultural-political sphere, the Fascist regime even achieved peace with the Catholic Church, with the signing of the 1929 Lateran Pacts. The overall result was that the country was 'pacified' for twenty years. Labour and Catholic opposition was apparently tamed. 'Peace', meaning the absence of violent resistance, as the word is normally understood, was by and large achieved. Peace in the way in which it is understood in this chapter, on the other hand, was not.

Passive revolutionary changes, as had already been the case with the Piedmontese unification effort, required the state's institutions to contribute towards the 'peaceful' enactment of such change. As with Italian unification, the Fascist passive revolution was also intertwined with educational 'reform', one that reflected and abetted the pacification that was sought following the Fascist takeover in 1922. In 1923, during his twenty months as Mussolini's minister of public instruction, the philosopher Giovanni Gentile promoted a reform that regulated the status of teachers and heads of school, and made notable changes to curricula. This reform, while involving broad sectors of the population, did not lead to popular emancipation or empowerment. The secondary school *ginnasio-liceo*, established with the aim of promoting future leaders, was separated from the inferior secondary school meant for the commoners. In teacher training, as well as in other areas, Gentile opted for a humanistic and philosophical approach instead of a technical or pedagogic one. Six years later, following the Lateran Pacts, the state introduced the obligatory study of the Catholic religion in state schools. Bishops gained the right to appoint or dismiss teachers of religion as well as to select textbooks. Positivist aspects of post-Unification pedagogy were eliminated.

Extending the concept of passive revolution to post-war Republican Italy and economic integration in Western Europe

Even the demise of Fascism during the Second World War and its aftermath could be described in terms of a passive revolution. The Fascist State collapsed. Yet, not all those that supported Fascism, benefited from it or enjoyed some form of cultural, economic or political standing, fell with the regime. There was continuity in state restructuring. Fascist collaborators in the bureaucracy, judiciary, army and police kept their place. Anderson (2009) notes that till 1960, 62 out of 64 fascist prefects, and all 135 of the country's police chiefs, were still in office. Torturers of the regime were acquitted, and the Fascist Republic of Salò's fighters were declared legitimate belligerents. The Lateran Pacts between Mussolini's government and the Vatican were confirmed. The Roman Catholic

Church contributed heavily towards the electoral defeat of the Socialist and Communist parties.

Those who wielded economic power in the Italian manufacturing industry, who had supported Fascism from its infancy and during its heyday, did not merely retain their grip on the country's economy, but began to expand. Factors pertaining to the international conjuncture of the immediate post-war period had assisted economic growth, including labour problems faced by British firms and the suspension of imports from former war allies, that is, from Japan and Germany. The Italian manufacturing industry began to export a host of goods, and FIAT, Pirelli and Falck consolidated their pre-war industrial leadership. State-controlled banks supported industry. The domestic market sustained 'national' industry and provided it with avenues for consolidation and growth. The state helped FIAT with a 40 per cent tariff and quota imposition on imported vehicles during the 1950s.[2] The American government provided a 10-million dollar loan from the US Export – Import Bank and 30 million dollars from the Marshall Plan grants (Eichengreen 2007, p. 115, n. 66). By the 1960s, there was an industrial boom. The real change in the basis of profit was from building the Fascist war machine to transforming a primarily agricultural economy into a consumer-based one.

But what about the classes that did not enjoy cultural, political or economic hegemony? A respectable degree of welfare was enacted. Working-class representatives could claim to have made some major gains. Most families could afford new electronic appliances (refrigerators, electrical cookers, etc.) and a family car (generally, a FIAT 500). Yet, the situation did not entail peace, if by this one understands that unequal relations and exploitation ceased to exist.

As with the two cases of Passive Revolution previously considered, post-war changes led to education reform. Mass-production industry was accompanied by a mass education system. In 1962, a law was enacted that made secondary school obligatory for all children up to the age of fourteen. This doubled the student population and implemented the right to free schooling for all sanctioned in the Italian Constitution by article 34. Yet, the reform had important limits in relation to its emancipatory potential. Three years after the Secondary School Act, in 1965, Minister Luigi Gui tabled a bill on university reform. The parliamentary commission responsible for implementing the details took three years to deliver its results, and was then overcome by the crossfire of baronial power represented by the rectors on one side, and the anti-privilege demands of students, on the other.

Despite the social advances, many industrial workers felt unjustly deprived in relation to the returns that they believed they were entitled to from the wealth that was being generated. FIAT did not buy out FIAT workers, especially the young southern immigrants of the 1960s. These were on the forefront during the capital–labour conflict at the end of the decade. A combative industrial working class protested the injustice done to a class that had not benefited equitably from industrial growth, a point conceded by Prime Minister Mariano Rumor who oversaw the capital–labour crisis that led to the promulgation of the Workers Charter protecting employment rights. (Rumor 1991) By the 1970s, the reformist and radical wings in the labour front parted company. The Italian Communist Party (PCI) and CGIL, the largest union in Italy, faced the upsurge of the new working-class youth challenging low wages and oppressive conditions in the industrially advanced North-West. The workers' mainstream political and syndicalist organizations, which by then were integrated into the establishment, were 'disconcerted by spontaneous outbreaks of militancy or unexpected forms of struggle' (Anderson 2009, unnumbered). The Red Brigades were one among a host of armed groups attacking representatives of the state and the economy. Post-war pacification was failing. The bourgeois state reacted by implementing stringent anti-terror legislation.

On the educational front, at the end of the 1960s, students in alliance with workers forced a crisis-hit government to accept their claims. Tristano Codignola's 1969 law opened the doors of the university to the working classes. The generation benefiting from open doors in the secondary school in 1962, now gained the same opportunity with regard to the university. At the time, this seemed a major victory for the working classes. In due course, it would turn into a means of embourgeoisification.

It would be in the 1980s that another nation-wide 'pacification' would occur. This involved, among other features, Bettino Craxi's taming of PSI and furthering the PSI-DC alliance, huge losses suffered by worker militancy and the dumbification of the masses by Berslusconi's *Mediaset*. But consideration of these themes and events falls outside the remit of this chapter.

In the three examples considered here, we can unearth a basic commonality in what otherwise might be interpreted as separate chronicles. With passive revolution understood as a stopgap and counter to popular activism, we can unearth a pattern in the three events, particularly in relation to education. The reforms and events discussed were accompanied by high expectations among sectors of the social formation actively involved in the separate events (*Risorgimento*, Fascist 'revolution' and the anti-Fascist Republic) including radicals, liberals and communists in some cases. In all cases, expectations of radical social changes – changes that would help eliminate inequality and permanently bring social injustice to an end – were deluded. Instead, what one had were examples of passive revolution to counter popular agitation. In the three cases, the need of achieving the goals the hegemonic powers set is clearly evident. These hegemonic powers used, among other things, reforms in the educational system to achieve their ends. Taking their cue from Gramsci, reforms in formal education were intended to build a civil society that served to counter opposition or crisis. Even when these educational reforms sounded progressive and inclusive, they were, on the whole, anything but critical of the 'peace' that was achieved in each case.

Passive revolution at a European level

In earlier sections, Passive Revolution was considered in relation to the coming into being of the Italian state, and in relation to the consolidation and growth of Italian industry in the twentieth century. In what follows, the concept is applied to the European continent. The discussion concerns post-war reconstruction and growth, its crisis (starting from the late 1960s and early 1970s) and the expansion of European economic integration.

Official rhetoric often presents the coming into being of the European Union as the idealistic brainchild of people like Konrad Adenauer, Robert Schuman and Alterio Spinelli. As the official version of the story goes, the setting up of what later became the European Union led to more than 50 years of peace on the continent, ensuring that there would no longer be conflict among nations that had previously butchered each other. Reality was/is much more complex and much less idealistic. The passage from war to peace (in the popular sense of the term) brought about the alignment of democratic politics and capitalism. Streeck argued that this was possible only because of the Cold War, and that it was bolstered by economic growth. In the long run, it would lead the working classes 'to accept a free-market, private-property regime' (2014a, p. 40).

By the 1950s, the conditions of capitalism in mainland Europe had changed to the extent that many national states could not cater for the new needs of their major capitalist industries on their own. The need was felt for a different, multi-national institution. The setting of the European Economic Community (EEC) addressed this need. If Fordism was considered by Gramsci as a sign of hegemonic leadership by the United States, this post-war resurgence was its reiteration.

The EEC was politically agreeable to the United States since it kept under control chauvinistic nationalism, especially in former colonial nations that were temporarily weak. It was also economically agreeable since it facilitated capital accumulation and transboundary investments with its uniformity of regulatory regimes. This blocked individual nations from going their own way and adopting protectionist measures. Not only was the United States favourable to the coming into being of such a union, but Gill and Law trace the origins of Europe's post-war reconstruction and eventual integration back to the: 'outward expansion of emerging (American) social forces' as they internationalized the principles and forms of the New Deal, in terms of a 'Fordist capital-intensive, mass consumption accumulation' (1994, p. 96). This was externally projected by means of exports and/or foreign direct investment in manufacturing and extraction.

The EEC changed its name and characteristics a number of times as it became, in the words of Arrighi (2000), something comparable to a multinational company, a transnational institution with local franchises in different countries, some of which are more important than other franchises. Growing integration at the continental scale in the 1970s broadened markets beyond relations within national frontiers. For some time, along with gradual economic integration, the idea of a social Europe started to gain ground; a European set-up that did not merely seek to create better structures for capital and resources, but was also concerned with the rights, dignity and well-being of those in the lowest echelons of society. Economic progress had to be coupled to improvements in employment conditions and the standard of living of most members of society, including the weakest ones. This, in many cases, coincided with and was a continuation of the Keynesian/welfarist tendencies that were popular in a lot of nations in the post-war period (Streeck 2011). Indeed, the European Community seemed to be initially bent on resisting the first neo-liberal experiment on a major scale in Europe: Thatcher's reforms in Britain. It seemed that things in Western Europe were as near to peace (as understood in this chapter) as they could be. This idyllic period however, did not last. As things turned out, what the period had witnessed was state intervention aimed at guaranteeing a capital–labour compromise that, though giving something to the latter, secured the interests of the former. This was not the stuff of active revolution, although it guaranteed some material improvement to working-class people. With the 1980s and the 1990s, the tide began to turn decisively. Competitiveness and warfarism started replacing the idea of a social Europe. State welfare provision had to be sacrificed or sidelined because of international competitiveness. Poverty and social exclusion started to raise their heads. Peace as defined in this chapter became a more distant ideal.

A major development of an institutional passive revolution and adaptation to the demands of mobile, transnational capital was the Maastricht Treaty of 1993, which established the European Union (EU). The Treaty followed up on the Single European Act (SEA) of 1987 that formalized the establishment of the Economic Monetary Union (EMU) and the Single Market as established by Article 8A of SEA. This posited the EU as 'an area without internal frontiers in which the free movement of goods, persons, services and capital is ensured'. EMU facilitated the free movement of capital, 'harmonising' monetary policies and enforcing budget discipline on member-states. This top-down, macro-territorial framework meant rigid reinforcement of exchange and interest rates. According to Lipietz (1997), this curbed the EU's peripheral economies' ability to flexibly respond to challenges that affected their competitiveness.

This market-oriented drift was also reflected in the educational sphere. As a European Commission (2000) study reported, education policymaking across Europe changed. From an earlier emphasis on cultural, and social and economic welfare, policy was increasingly promoting a higher education that affirmed a stronger 'responsiveness to the changing demands of economic life and the workplace by focusing education and research on required new skills and technologies'.[3] Education became increasingly workfarist. Agreements like the Bologna Accords reflect this new tendency.

That the many gains the working classes made in Europe in the past are being eroded and that what occurred in the post-war years was not peace as understood in this chapter but Passive Revolution, is evidenced by what happened during the last economic crisis. A small elite of technocrats working within the folds of the Troika (European Central Bank, European Commission and International Monetary Fund) managed the 'recovery' through finance-regulated mechanisms; they preferred this to regulating finance itself (Gallino 2012, pp. 126–7). Other sectors of society had to foot the bill.

European integration, then, was another case of passive revolution. Former national state structures were changed and altered in a top-down fashion. At the same time, the interests of those whom these national state structures had protected were guaranteed. Regarding those in the lowest echelons of European society, for a time Europe waivered the notion of a 'Social Europe'. Yet, this project faltered over time. That the European project turned out to be a Passive Revolution, rather than a bottom-up project, became evident when the democratically unaccountable European Central Bank (and the European Commission) started to oversee state budgets and determine wage policies from a top-down supranational vantage point. Resistance to these losses has been sporadic and up to now not very effective. With women attracting relatively lower pay and youth ready to work flexibly, these two sectors were strategically put up against older members of the working class who attempted to cling on to employment protection clauses that date back to the historic compromise between capital and labour during the immediate post-war and Cold War crises. Meanwhile, the extended crisis forced more citizens to ask for protection against the market as inequality rose; political structures seem unable to offer such protection. Education, at least at an official formal level, has generally reflected and abetted such passive revolution rather than nurturing critical vibes that help analyse its limits and possibilities. Investment in vocationally instrumental training, for instance, has increased while that in the humanities has declined.

Conclusion

This chapter considers how passive revolution, masquerading as peace, characterized the birth and consolidation of a national capitalist economy (the *Risorgimento* and twentieth-century Italy), as well as the superseding (of certain aspects) of the nation state in Europe, exemplified by the creation of what today is the European Union. These passive revolutions were successful, they changed what for the dominant and burgeoning classes required to be changed and retained what had to be retained. Peace, however, was not achieved (though there were instances where this ideal was to an extent embodied in measures and outcomes). These passive revolutions were accompanied by educational reforms and practices that, even when apparently progressive, abetted these processes and, hence, the hegemonic exercises they involved.

Notes

1   Intellectuals and landowners, primarily members of the Milan aristocracy, supported Austria. Lombard and Veneto peasants formed part of the Austrian military forces that crushed the 1848 rebellion in Vienna.

2   Regarding FIAT, the British protected the company's leadership accused of being Fascist accomplices.

3   Study retrieved on 28 October 2012, from http://eacea.ec.europa.eu/education/ eurydice/thematic_studies_archives_en.php.

References

Anderson, P. (2009). 'An Invertebrate Left. London Review of Books', 31/5, 12 March. Retrieved 10 September 2014, from http://www.lrb.co.uk/v31/n05/ande01_.html.

Arrighi, G. (2000). 'Globalization and Historical Macrosociology'. In J. Abu-Lughod (Ed.), *Sociology for the Twenty-First Century. Continuities and Cutting Edges*, pp. 117–33. Chicago, IL: Chicago University Press. Retrieved 16 June 2011, from http://www.alpcub.com/arrighi.pdf.

Bernardi, U. (2005). *Veneti*. Treviso: Canova.

Bohle, D. (2006). 'Neoliberal Hegemony, Transnational Capital and the Terms of the EU's Eastward Expansion'. *Capital & Class*, 88: 57–86 (Spring). Retrieved 4 November 2014, from http://search.proquest.com.ejournals.um.edu.mt/docview/20 9697166?accountid=27934.

Buci-Glucksmann, C. (1980). *Gramsci and the State*. Translated by D. Fernbach. London: Lawrence & Wishart.

Burgio, A. (2010). 'La dialettica dell'egemonia nelle rivoluzioni passive del XX secolo'. Retrieved 15 September 2014, from http://prcrho.altervista.org/index. php?option=com_content&view=article&id=187:il-conetto-di-rivoluzione-passiva-in-gramsci&catid=34:nazionale-lombardo-provinciale&Itemid=28.

Callinicos, A. (2010). 'The Limits of Passive Revolution'. *Capital & Class*, 34 (3): 491–507.

Coriat, B. (1997). 'Globalization, Variety and Mass Production: The Metamorphosis of Mass Production in the New Competitive Age'. In J. Rogers Hollingsworth and R. Boyer (Eds), *Contemporary Capitalism: The Embeddedness of Institutions*, pp. 240–64. UK: Cambridge University Press. 1st digital printing edition of 2005.

Coutinho C. N. (2007). 'L'epoca neoliberale: rivoluzione passiva o controriforma?' Retrieved 25 August 2014, from www.gramscitalia.it/html/coutinho.pdf.

Dunford, M. (2006). 'Industrial Districts, Magic Circles, and the Restructuring of the Italian Textiles and Clothing Chain'. *Economic Geography*, 82: 27–59. Retrieved 2 October 2009, from www.lse.ac.uk/collections/.../whosWho/.../a.c.../mdeg03.pdf.

Eichengreen, B. (2007). *The European Economy Since 1945: Coordinated Capitalism and Beyond*. Princeton, NJ: Princeton University Press.

European Commission (EC) (2000). '"Two Decades of Reform in Higher Education in Europe": 1980 onward'. Brussels: European Commission.

Gallino, L. (2012). *La lotta di classe dopo la lotta di classe: Intervista a cura di Paola Borgna*. Bari: Laterza.

Gill, S. and Law, D. (1994). 'Global Hegemony and the Structural Power of Capital'. In Stephen Gill (Ed.), *Gramsci, Historical Materialism and International Relations*, pp. 93–124. Cambridge: Cambridge University Press.

Gramsci, A. (1975). *Quaderni del carcere*. Edited by V. Gerratana, Vols. I–IV. Turin: Einaudi.

Harvey, D. (1990). *The Condition of Postmodernity: An Enquiry into the Origins of Cultural Change*. Cambridge, US: Blackwell.

Harvey, D. (2011). *The Enigma of Capital and the Crises of Capitalism*. London: Profile Books.

Howson, R. (2011). 'From Ethico-Political Hegemony to Post-Marxism'. In Marcus E. Green (Ed.), *Rethinking Gramsci*, pp. 167–76. Abington, Oxon: Routledge.

Jessop, B. and Sum, N.-L. (2006). *The Regulation Approach and Beyond: Putting Capitalist Economies in their Place*. Cheltenham: Edward Elgar.

Olin Wright, E. (2009). 'Understanding Class: Towards an Integrated Analytical Approach'. *New Left Review*, 60 (November–December): 101–16.

3

Breathing Peace, Relating with the Other and the Maternal

Simone Galea

Introduction

This chapter discusses the relevance of an ethics of sexual difference in thinking about peace. It draws on Luce Irigaray's philosophy of the maternal and her concept of breathing, to argue that one needs to understand oneself as different from others (rather than as fundamentally similar, as one may intuitively assume) to be able to approach and relate ethically to them, and, hence, attempt to achieve ideals like peace. These differences, through which one can conceive oneself, are various and have several dimensions, including social, national, ethnic, religious and sexual dimensions. The chapter considers the last-mentioned dimensions. In conceiving oneself as sexually different, however, one runs the risk of thinking the difference through a phallocentric logic that has reduced women in particular, to an economy of the same. Through this logic, femininity has been understood from a masculine point of view and women have been negated, even in the ways through which they conceive their feminine selves as sexually different subjects. This has been evident in many areas, even in a lot of characterizations of peace, as will be discussed in the first part of the chapter.

The chapter addresses the question of how we can re-conceptualize the feminine as a sexually different 'other', and how this can open up our thinking about relations with various different 'others'. It draws on Irigaray's notions of the maternal and of the sharing of breath (and the space between two different individuals this involves), and reflects on the implications this has for pedagogical relations and for the teaching of peace in particular.

Women and peace

Women's relations with peace are complex. Women have been described as prime victims of war, suffering from gender-based violence and exploitation. Most violence is gender based in that women suffer physical, psychological and sexual harm simply because they are women; they do not have their own rights recognized and their bodies frequently become 'a battleground over which opposing forces struggle' (UN Women 2002, p. 10). Though women themselves have at times actively participated in war (especially to safeguard themselves, their interests and those of their families), they still remain the main victims of war-related violence, experiencing trafficking, sexual slavery and exploitation. Even in times of peace, when conflicts have supposedly come to an end, women continue to suffer violence, exploitation and increased domestic violence. The UN report on Women, War and Peace (2002) notes that in the aftermath of conflict, there is a tendency towards an increase in sexual violence against women and in prostitution, even after peacekeeping forces arrive, and this includes violence perpetrated by UN personnel. These aspects of war are frequently ignored when war is characterized as the mere absence of violent conflict.

Nevertheless, women have actively contributed to bringing about peace and resolving conflicts. The UN strategic results framework on Women, Peace and Security (2011),[1] while recognizing the importance of protecting the rights of girls and women in conflict, and of preventing violence against them, calls for an increased participation of women in the various national and international fora aimed at bringing about peace. It is argued that increased representation of women in peacekeeping organizations and activities will ensure that their issues and interests will be represented. This seems to indicate the need of having a gender perspective in the characterization of peace, a view upheld by both egalitarian[2] and maternalist feminists.[3]

Egalitarian feminists contend that bringing the gender perspective into peace initiatives addresses the violence brought about by patriarchal relations that subject women to particular oppressive experiences. Maternalist feminists hold that women participate differently in the building of peace in comparison to men, and have their own distinctive interests. Women, especially through their association with the maternal, are considered to be more morally inclined to speak and act against war. Their caring role as mothers can inform their visions about peace. This is evident in various contexts. The silent protests of the mothers of the Plaza de Mayo are a concrete example of how maternal values of love and caring could help subvert the violent operations of a patriarchal state. Their organization into silent marches in protest against their children's disappearance during the Argentine Dirty War challenged the state-propagated, dominant image of the 'good' mother as one who is devoted to the private sphere of the family rather than being actively involved in bringing about political changes (Taylor 2001). In the United States, both egalitarian and maternalist feminists contributed to a coalition of women protesting against the war in Iraq and the related 'War on terror' (Kutz-Flamenbaum 2011).

Both egalitarian and maternalist feminists, then, envisage women as 'subjects' of peace; women have to engage in peace and not merely be the beneficiaries of peace-related initiatives. Both perspectives, however, tend not to take into account the philosophical dimension that would explain how women's relations with peace are intimately tied to issues of conflict that arise out of patriarchal cultural arrangements (rather than simply patriarchal relations). In this regard, the chapter considers Luce Irigaray's ethics of sexual difference, claiming that recognition of sexual difference contributes towards a new paradigm concerning the ways in which human beings relate to one another. It later considers Irigaray's interpretations of the notion of the 'maternal' as a metaphor that symbolizes alternative ways in which humans can relate, of how they can be: 'autonomously connected'. The notion of 'breathing' is another metaphor that may contribute to persons enhancing their relations to one another, while developing their own autonomous growth. In addressing the notions of the maternal and breath, the questions of the participation of women in educational encounters as well as of the pedagogical relations in the teaching of peace that can be conceived with reference to symbolizations of the maternal will be addressed.

Irigaray and the question of sexual difference

Irigaray's philosophy considers the notion of sexual difference as crucial to understanding relations between human beings (1993a). One cannot address questions of peace without recognizing the differences between men and women, how these have been constructed and/or sustained in such a way that relegate women to an inferior position in society, and how they are related to various phenomena including peace and war (see Andermatt Conley 2006). Women are naturally socially and culturally positioned to contribute towards peaceful arrangements that recognize persons as different. Yet, this dimension has frequently been overlooked, even, ironically, in peacemaking initiatives. Irigaray attributes this to patriarchal relations and structures, and to the logic and assumptions imbued in them.

Patriarchal social and cultural systems tend to hinder women from constructing their own subjectivities, thus leaving them in a state of dereliction. In this regard, Irigaray refers to essentialist characterizations proposed by the predominant phallocentric order, that is, by a linguistic, social and thinking order that is based on predominantly masculinized world views, which are hostile to the creation of a feminine subjectivity (Irigaray 2002, 2013a). Women have failed to construct their own subjectivity. Consider surnames. These give one a legal and social identity, and are frequently inherited from the father. Hence, a woman has to articulate herself as an individual via a male-defined language (her surname), but not vice versa. In contrast, feminine genealogies are usually not named. The male is the master-signifier. This is just one example that provides evidence that women are subjected to social systems that are dominated by masculine frames of thought. One of the side effects of assuming the male subject as the master-signifier in sociocultural and political *milieu* is that the feminine and all that is associated with it is repressed. In one of her earlier works, Irigaray describes this position of women as 'being exiled in the house of our husbands' (Irigaray 1993b, p. 19), the 'house of our husbands' being the world that women have to inhabit and that is framed in patriarchal terms. No wonder, then, that women's perspectives and sensibilities are not included in the widespread characterization of peace.

One of the problems that have contributed to the fact that women have struggled to participate in the social symbolization of their own selves is that, since the Enlightenment, human subjects have been characterized in masculine terms even if this was not explicitly stated. (Irigaray, 1985). According to Irigaray, such patriarchal systems of thought work through universal and monolithic socio-symbolic systems. The male subject, then, is the universal master-signifier, that is, the source and origin of meaning in relation to humanity. These characterizations dominate forms of life, and impose a masculinized point of reference. Because conceptions of the subject are constructed in male terms, the feminine is always conceptualized with reference to and in comparison with the masculine subject. In considering the male subject as the norm and in recognizing him as a universal signifier, representations of the feminine (1) have always been conceived through male systems of thought; (2) have been devalued by the very representation of woman as that which is not male. She either has to identify with characteristics that are not primarily hers (to be 'human' as humans are characterized in predominant socio-symbolic systems) or else she falls short of the standards of what is human. The feminine subject can never have positions from where to speak and identify herself as a sexually different human subject.

An example of the workings of such patriarchal systems of thought is the ordinary characterization of human rights using generalized, universalized language. The rights that humans have, and their possible infringements and limits, are frequently characterized in terms that implicitly assume that the subjects of these rights are male. Irigaray, indeed, claims that in spite of its commitment to improve conditions of all human beings, the Universal Declaration of Human Rights – a key document in relation to peace – does not address the particular and specific realities of women (Irigaray 1994). The universal language of the Declaration does not reflect the inequalities, injustices and oppressions women frequently suffer because they are women. Indeed, as Bunch (1995) points out, because human rights were articulated by members of dominant groups, primarily members of a Westernized elite, and men, they were mostly concerned with the violation of the rights that mostly preoccupied them, especially those related to property, and to civil and political rights. Although these public rights are also an important aspect of women's lives, they do not cover concerns and experiences that are more peculiar to women, for example, rights that concern the private sphere such as food, shelter and work. Consider terms such as 'property' and its inclusion in this declaration of human rights. Irigaray asks whether it is possible to make sense of the article: '*No one shall be arbitrarily deprived of his property*', without taking note of the fact that, with regard to many women, even their own bodies are considered as the property of others, bodies that are exploited in advertisements, raped and abused in many other ways. Hence, the Declaration does not contribute to the advancement of all humanity as it purports to do. To be relevant to women's lives, it needs to be translated through the language of sexual difference.[4] Similar male-centred bias is often present in 'neutral' characterizations of peace. Peace is frequently represented as a cessation of fighting (often between men). Other factors that pertain more specifically to women, some of which were illustrated in the previous section, remain marginal.

Women, therefore, need to rethink their feminine selves in terms that are radically different from the dominant, universalist and essentialist ones proposed by the phallocentric order. An articulation of the feminine is not just beneficial to women. It can also bring about an alternative understanding of the ways in which human beings relate to one another. In what immediately follows, the consequences of a masculinized order for peace will be considered.

The makings of a hostile culture and the hospitable feminine

Irigaray claims that the imposition of a masculinized order has made our cultures inhospitable to difference, since this order seeks to imperialistically impose its universal 'single cultural horizon' on the 'other'. Patriarchal power includes 'the male's power as legal head of the family, of the tribe, the race, the State' (Irigaray 1993b, p. 192). This patriarchal power has negated women and all the world of their connections with what is natural.[5] The negation of women's articulation of their selves as subjects has brought about a breakdown not merely in the relations between the sexes, but also in relations between human beings in general. Patriarchal systems have brought about the destruction of life, peace and nature. One reason for this is the fact that these patriarchal systems have denied women the opportunity to express themselves properly and in a dignified manner, and especially mothers the opportunity to express properly their relations with their daughters (Irigaray 1993b). This has important consequences with regard to peace. Irigaray contends that the mother–daughter relationship is

> most fertile in regard to safeguarding life and peace [Yet, this] was destroyed [to establish] an order … that is linked to private property, to the transmission of goods from father to son, to the institution of monogamous marriage – which ensures that all property, including children, can be passed down the male line and to the establishment of social organizations open to men alone and designed for the same purposes. (Irigaray 1993b, p. 192)

She compares the inhospitable relations between persons that such a culture engenders to those of players on a chessboard. The movements of the players are not free; players can move only to allow antagonistic relations between them: 'Most of our cultures resemble chessboards in whose frames we apparently can move, but without our movements being really free, nor with a still-virgin space remaining in which we can meet outside of our respective chessboards, assuming that we can go beyond them' (Irigaray 2013a, p. 43).

The violence of such cultures is evident in their inherent oppositional character, where participants are always involved in a hostile opposition to each other. This paradigm has entered all spheres of life, with people considering antagonistic relationships between individual and individual, class and class, state and state as natural. Within such an architecture, the movements of participants are fixed and predetermined; they can never allow participants to support each other and to live in peace with different 'others'. The suppression or relegation of maternal relations, then, has had an effect that goes beyond the domestic spheres, one that affects the different levels of peace.

Through their association with their maternal aspects where they give life and rear children, women are highly equipped to provide an understanding of human relations that departs from the chessboard model (Andrematt Conley 2006). The recognition of the feminine in sociocultural contexts suggests different arrangements that allow differences to complement each other, rather than confront each other agonistically (Irigaray 2013a). In such an arrangement, 'peace governs' (Irigaray 2013a, p. 42) because the space of the 'other' to be other is respected. This is, hence, a culture that is open to differences, a culture of hospitality that allows the 'other' to be itself.

It is important at this point to note that Irigaray is not suggesting that one substitutes wholesale a sexually defined characterization of what it is to be human and of how to engage in human relations with another. What she seeks are ways to symbolize a feminine imaginary that is not tainted by the impositions of a patriarchal culture, a notion of the feminine that is not male-defined, nor understood through a binary logic that defines the feminine as inferior to the male. As part of her strategy, Irigaray notes that in spite of women being given fixed maternal spaces within masculinized cultures, and notwithstanding the fact that motherhood has been rendered a service that women perform for men, the maternal can be a very powerful symbolic space from where women can reinvent themselves and their relations with different 'others'. Her strategy is mimetic (Irigaray 1985a), drawing on traditional and conventional images of the feminine in order to rethink the maternal and associate it with more fruitful notions that give birth to new meanings. A case in point of her counter-symbolic strategy is her reading of the maternal as a hospitable space that is generative of differences. This is contrasted with phallocentrism, which is described as that order which *denotes the primacy and domination of one kind of subjectivity and the appropriation by that single model of all other possibilities* (Rozmarin 2013, p. 471).

The feminine and its association with the maternal symbolizes, and allows for, spatial arrangements that are open to plurality, where different 'others' coexist freely. Within the feminine exists the possibility that 'a woman can give birth to a child, and even to a child of another gender' (Irigaray 2013a, p. 44). The feminine, therefore, is a socio-symbolic space that is generative of difference.

Maternal relations make it possible for two different beings to coexist. What makes this possible is the creation of a space between two, which, in biological terms, is the placenta. This leads to another important notion, that of the third space.

The placenta is a biological third space that is produced with the intent of welcoming the other; it belongs either to both the child and the mother or to neither of them. Yet, relations between them are possible because of this space. The metaphor of a third space has important implications for peaceful relations between different beings. Take peace in relation to the social sphere, particularly with regard to the issue of immigration to Europe and the relations between different ethnic/religious groups. Frequently, the welcoming of the 'other' entails allowing this other to enter into one's culture and society on the condition that he or she becomes more or less like the host; the culture and/or society in question is considered to be the host's space and he or she has the right to set the rules. This 'welcoming' involves an assimilation process by which the one who is hosted is forced to negate his or her difference and become similar to the one who hosts. Irigaray, on the other hand, inspired by the placenta as a maternal configuration of the conditions of the coming and welcoming of the other, argues that a 'third space' is essential to establishing peaceful relations that do not entail that one dominates or forces the other into sameness – a space between different parties where none of the two imposes their way of thinking and living upon the other. This would be a space where different parties are related to one another, while their singularity is respected. The placenta concretely symbolizes this space in between individual human beings:

> Neither the woman nor the fetus could survive without this organ that secures both the existence of each and the relation between the two. Likewise, yet differently, sexuate belonging cannot assert itself or be kept and cultivated without a third, especially a spatial third, which does not belong to one gender or the other but happens through the between two, without it being possible for this third to be appropriated by or to one or the other gender. (Irigaray 2013a, pp. 44–5)

Breath

The mother's breath is another metaphor one can use in Critical Education and in conceiving peace. Breath, like the placenta, is very much a 'third space'. Even, breathing, particularly maternal breathing, symbolizes relations that are open to differences. The mother breathes autonomously. Yet, she is also capable of breathing in relation with an 'other', of having another person breathing within her. As Irigaray explains: 'The woman breathes in order to live but also in order to share to communicate, to commune' (Irigaray 2002, p. 86). Maternal breathing, then, 'holds a secret' of relating to 'others', a secret that can be unravelled to generate implications for peaceful relations. This 'other' for whom the mother breathes, is distinct from her. Successful breathing with this 'other' requires that the mother does not reduce 'the other' to her. Mother and child may share the same space through which they breathe, but they are not the same being and their breathing is not one. Moreover, in sharing breath the mother is not giving something of hers to another (unlike when she gives her milk or blood), but engendering autonomous breathing by another being. Breathing is *cultivated with* rather than being *given to* the 'other'. The mother's sharing of breath with others is what enables this other being to breathe autonomously (Irigaray 2013b). The relations that develop between mother and child are not intended to possess the 'other' but to engender another autonomous life; the mother's breath brings to life another being who is different from her.

Breathing, then, can become a metaphor for how peaceful relations may be established, between the sexes and between humans in general. As Deutscher (2002) explains, Irigaray is here suggesting a

> culture in which sexed subjects would be primarily oriented toward the other, as opposed to drawing on the other only to provide succour for their own identity. They would be turned outward toward the other, rather than being primarily fixed on whether the other is turned toward them. A new relation to sexed identity might facilitate this outward orientation, in Irigaray's view. She imagines a reconstruction of society. (Deutscher 2002, pp. 77–8)

Maternal symbolizations of breathing can also inform peace education. Zemblyas and Berkerman (2013) claim that peace education still lacks the theoretical foundations that would sustain and inform the ideas upon which it is grounded. Irigaray's metaphors of breathing and the maternal are useful in this regard: to theoretically conceive the pedagogical possibilities for the teaching of peace and to explain how teaching can be understood in the light of these maternal aspects. In what follows, I focus on teaching.

Teaching is not an unfamiliar practice to women. As mothers, women take and are frequently given the responsibility of rearing and educating their children, helping them to develop into adult and autonomous human beings. As professional teachers, many women would extend their domestic roles as teachers to the public sphere. Yet, in spite of their presence in educational institutions, women have not always been successful in challenging patriarchal and regulatory agendas, being often subjected to regulative practices that train them into authoritarian forms of teaching (e.g. teaching to the test or adopting an uncritical attitude to dominant ideas). The feminization of teaching, on the other hand, might provide a useful space where teachers, men and women, can challenge such practices, and it can foster spaces that allow individuals involved in teaching and learning contexts to manifest their differences (Griffiths 2006). What Griffiths is suggesting here is using the feminine and feminized aspects of teaching to subvert an 'economy of the same' that is imbued in a mainstream educational system that conceives human beings as if they were homogenous. The concept of feminised teaching can draw on maternal understandings of relations and on the concept of the third space, which allow people to flourish in their differences. Regarding peace, this would entail that one does not merely teach *about* peace but, rather, conceive peace as a practice through which different people generously relate to each other, even if they have diverging views or their relations of power are unequal. Moreover, it suggests that individual students arrive at their own characterization of peace in an autonomous manner. This is particularly important in relation to the metaphor of motherly breathing.

In breathing, the foetus is dependent on the mother to breathe. Yet, the foetus is not the mother; it is a separate being that dwells within a space within the mother. Although the offspring is sustained by the mother, it is not her replica. The mother's breath is shared with, rather than transposed to, an 'other'. This analogy may serve important pedagogical purposes, particularly in relation to the teaching of peace. Irigaray's differentiates between pedagogy considered as the transmission of knowledge and pedagogy that entails a more open exchange between participants: 'The first model of transmission or instruction is more parental ... more hierarchical, the second more horizontal, intersubjective. The first model risks enslavement to the past, the second [one which is symbolized by the mother's breathing] opens up the present in order to construct a future' (Irigaray 1996, pp. 45–6).

In terms of teacher–student relations, the second model suggests that, although the teacher is in a position of authority and seeks to teach peace, her ideas should be shared rather than simply transposed. In breathing peace through teaching, the teacher cannot impose her conceptions of peace on her students. She should create a space where education occurs. Metaphorically, the teacher ought to breathe the life of education onto others, with the aim of having them eventually able to breathe on their own. The student's ideas about peace need not necessarily reflect the ideas of their teacher/s. The teacher, like the mother, is in close connection with another who is in the process of gaining autonomy; he or she is aiming to develop his or her students' 'autonomous breathing' and helping them develop their own thinking about peace. As for the students, they may develop their own concept of peace in relation to various variables. Peace may, then, have different meanings depending on the sociopolitical, historical and personal contexts through which it is lived. Peace cannot be lived through an imposition of a universal concept that has to be taken up by everyone. The different rhythms and intensities of breathing, as well as the unique modes by which individuals breathe, symbolize the different ways through which peace can be experienced. It involves a critical practice whereby different views are heard and taken into account.

Shortcomings of Irigaray's characterization of peace and sexuality

Irigaray's philosophy of sexual difference has been criticized on some important counts. Mahadevan, for instance, criticizes what she takes to be Irigaray's claim that women and feminine communities are inherently 'peace loving', arguing that bonding between women does not necessarily lead to their engagement in peaceful actions (Mahadevan 2013, p. 71). Women have been initiators of violent actions, and in this regard, Mahadevan refers to their engagement in Nazi and Fascist organizations during the Second World War, and to their more recent involvement in extreme Right organizations. These are examples where women do not hesitate to use and promote violence, even against other women. Mahadevan is correct in highlighting the anything but peaceful cases in which women are the protagonists of violence. Yet, one may still hold that these are antithetical to the motherly model Irigaray promotes, which, after all, is only a model she puts forward – a model that is more inclusive and fecund than the dominant phallocentric models and characterization of society generally adopted in mainstream discourse.

Another criticism levelled at Irigaray refers to her predominantly heterosexist account of relations between human beings. Her ethics of sexual difference is, indeed, based on the idea that it is openness to sexual difference that paves the way for an openness towards 'the other' in general, even if 'the other' is the one who is racially, culturally and religiously different. She clearly states that 'in a multicultural society sexual difference should be placed at the foundation of democracy' (Irigaray 2000, p. 140). Various commentators claim that this does not adequately address other kinds of relations, especially multicultural relations, and the role these play in fostering peace relations. Stone (2006), for instance, claims that her heterosexist conception of difference cannot address other kinds of differences, especially intersectional ones where differences between different individuals and/or groups cannot be simply understood in terms of sex but, rather, through some complex interrelation between race, culture, religion and other variants: 'Irigaray cannot ... acknowledge deep differences between women but considers them to differ only as particular members of a common kind. She therefore regards sexual difference as more fundamental than other differences such as race' (Stone 2006, p. 7).

Another shortcoming of Irigaray's characterization is that at times she seems to assume that relations of peace are ones where conflict is avoided as much as possible. For example, in speaking about the importance of cultivating spiritual and physical breathing between man and woman, she states: 'Without the cultivation of breathing, in each person and between them, man and woman are ... thrown back upon death. And they remain in perpetual conflict concerning who, of the two, best assures the survival of the human species' (Irigaray 2002, p. 77)

Irigaray's notion of peace seems to assume that people need to consensually agree on certain issues in order to have good relations with one another; it seems to presuppose that people that hold diverging or conflicting views will inevitably end up breaking the relations between them, that conflict is fundamentally inimical to peaceful relations between different others. This is an assumption that is also found in a lot of mainstream peace education, as Zembylas and Bekerman testify (Zembylas and Bekerman 2013, p. 197). Conflicts and disagreements, however, particularly conflict in the classroom, need not be inimical to peace. Conflict and disagreement can be fruitful and productive. Indeed, as Todd (2009) indicates, conflict, particularly conflict in the classroom, is actually necessary for a democratic and pluralistic exchange between people, to foster peaceful relations that are truly respectful of differences. Developing ethical relations with others does not simply entail respecting adversaries but also being able to develop what Todd calls 'the unstable space of conflictual consensus'. There are educative moments of disagreement where one generously acknowledges difference through an encounter with the other. With respect to the teaching of peace, one should not avoid conflict or seek to enforce a consensus with the intent of creating a seemingly peaceful environment. Welcoming others and responding to their otherness ought not to lead us to disregarding differences or silencing divergences and disagreements. Indeed, Irigaray's own conceptualization of the third space may enhance such discrepant encounters in a peaceful environment; the metaphor of breath may symbolize the possibility of communication between different parties, groups, societies and cultures – even conflicting ones – where listening and compassion are essential to the teaching of peaceful relations. This would lead to what she herself calls an 'awakening' (Irigaray 2002, p. 79) – that is, the realization that the different 'other' can never be known, nor possessed; and that an encounter with the 'other' is not an unproblematic territory where different views reach consensus.

Conclusion

Irigaray criticizes the dominant characterization of peace and many peace initiatives because they tend to exclude women's concerns and needs. She also claims that these reflect a phallocentric logic that is based on predominantly male world views. Irigaray's insistence on referring to the feminine in conceptualizing relations with the 'other' draws our attention to the implications that such symbolizations can have on the teaching of peace, and particularly the pedagogical relations that can be developed in engendering peace in the classroom. Irigaray uses the maternal and the mother's breath as metaphors that are relevant to conceptualizing peaceful relations. Through her breath, the mother sustains the life of another being, yet this being is autonomous. This relation can be understood as an analogy that suggests possibilities for how different others can be engaged with in a truly peaceful manner.

Notes

1   http://www.un.org/womenwatch/ianwge/taskforces/wps/Strategic Framework_2011-2020.pdf.

2   Egalitarian feminism advocates women's liberation and militancy in terms of
    equality between males and females, frequently considering differences in roles and
    characterization of males and females as artificial, distorting and oppressive.
3   The type of feminism that assigns an emancipatory and liberatory function to the
    roles of mothers and care-givers which women have traditionally played.
4   Even when such rights have been recognized, as in the 'Beijing Fourth Conference
    on Women' in September 1995 (UN 1996) and in the 'Beijing Declaration and
    Platform for Action', the commitment towards women's progress and participation
    in all areas of life cannot be taken for granted. Although the Conference and
    Declaration drew attention to the fact that human rights are still recognized as
    universal and relevant to all human beings, women and girls continue to suffer
    injustices related specifically to the fact that they are women. This has given rise
    to the need to identify rights that arise out of the particular experiences of women
    and to recognize sexual difference as an essential aspect in thinking about women's
    rights as an aspect of human rights.
5   Irigaray also frequently associates the feminine with nature because of women's
    maternal dimension.

References

Andermatt Conley, V. (2006). *Ecopolitics. The Environment in Poststructuralist Thought.*
    Taylor and Francis. e-library

Bunch, C. (1995). 'Transforming Human Rights from a Feminist Perspective.' In
    J. Peters and A. Wolper (Eds), *Women's Rights, Human Rights. International Feminist
    Perspectives*, pp. 11–17. New York: Routledge.

Deutscher, P. (2002). *A Politics of Impossible Difference. The Later Work of Luce Irigaray.*
    Ithaca: Cornell University Press.

Griffiths, M. (2006). 'The Feminization of Teaching and the Practice of Teaching'.
    Educational Theory, 56 (4): 387–405.

Irigaray, L. (1996). *I Love to You. Sketch for a Felicity within History.* New York:
    Routledge.

Irigaray, L. (2000). *Why Different?* New York: Semiotext(e).

Irigaray, L. (2002). *Between East and West.* New York: Columbia University Press
    (first French edition 1999).

Irigaray, L. (2013a). 'Toward a Mutual Hospitality'. In Claviez Thomas (Ed.),
    *The Conditions of Hospitality. Ethics, Politics and Aesthetics on the Threshold of the
    Possible*, pp. 42–5. New York: Fordham University Press.

Irigaray, L. (2013b). 'To Begin with Breathing Anew'. In A. Holmes and Skot Lenart
    (Eds), *Breathing with Luce Irigaray.* London: Bloomsbury.

Irigaray, L. (1985a). *This Sex Which is Not One.* New York: Cornell University Press (first French edition 1977).

Irigaray, L. (1985b). *Speculum of the Other Woman.* New York: Cornell University Press (first French edition 1974)

Irigaray L. (1993a). *An Ethics of Sexual Difference.* New York: Cornell University Press (first French edition 1984).

Irigaray L. (1993b). *Sexes and Genealogies.* New York: Columbia University Press (first French edition 1987).

Irigaray L. (1994). *Thinking the Difference: For a Peaceful Revolution.* London: The Athlone Press.

Kutz-Flamenbaum, R. V. (2011). 'Recruiting or Retaining? Frame Perception in the Women's Peace Movement'. In *Critical Aspects of Gender in Conflict Resolution, Peacebuilding and Social Movements.* Published online 2011, pp. 191–218. http://dx.doi.org/10.1108/S0163-786X(2011)0000032012.

Mahadevan, K. (2013). 'Feminist Solidarity in India: Communitarian Challenges and Postnational Prospects'. In Bailey Tom (Ed.), *Deprovincialising Habermas*, p. 71. New Delhi: Routledge.

Rozamarin, M. (2013). 'Living Politically: An Irigarayan Notion of Agency as a Way of Life'. *Hypatia*, 28 (3): 469–82.

Stone, A. (2006). *Luce Irigaray and the Philosophy of Sexual Difference.* New York: Cambridge University Press.

Todd, S. (2009). *Toward an Imperfect Education.* Boulder: Paradigm Publishers.

UN (1996). *Report of the Fourth World Conference on Women.* Beijing. 4–15 September 1995. New York: United Nations.

UN (2011). The UN Strategic Results Framework on Women, Peace and Security. http://www.un.org/womenwatch/ianwge/taskforces/wps/Strategic Framework_2011-2020.pdf (accessed 13 October 2014).

Zembylas, M. and Bekerman, Z. (2013). 'Peace Education in the Present: Dismantling and Reconstructing some Fundamental Theoretical Premises'. *Journal of Peace Education*, 10 (2): 197–214.

4

The Limits of Exogenous Initiatives in Peacemaking, Focusing on Iraq after the US Invasion

Arsalan Alshinawi

Introduction

A stable Iraq, in the middle, between Turkey, Iran and Saudi Arabia, not far from Israel – all of them regional powers with conflicting interests and positions in international relations – holds notable importance, not only in a region like the Middle East, but also far beyond. Iraq has access to the Persian or Arabian Gulf; strategic waterways for global oil transportation in one of the most energy-rich areas. It is known to have the world's fourth-largest proven oil reserves, and, according to many estimates, may possess huge still-undiscovered deposits, the largest extractable in the entire region.[1]

In 2003, in line with a major pillar of the US foreign policy targeting states branded as threats to world stability, the regime of Saddam Hussein was toppled in large-scale military operations by the United States-led multinational coalition forces.[2] The United States did not merely topple Hussein's regime, but sought to bring about a change in the country's political and economic *modus operandi*. Political and economic ideas, beliefs, procedures and transformations were imposed upon a nation and a social formation from outside through the use of military force – a clear case of exogenous initiative, that is, an initiative that originates from outside an organism, body or structure, which, however, causes drastic change to occur within the organism, body or structure in question. The official purpose of the military intervention was to turn Iraq into 'a beacon of good governance' for its authoritarian neighbours, helping in spreading democratization in the region and possibly abetting an accord between the Israelis and the Palestinians in the 'troubled Middle East'.[3] The mission announced by the American president was to 'build a decent and democratic society' and transform the area into 'a place of progress and peace'.[4]

In 2014, Prime Minister Al-Maliki had relinquished power in light of a security situation best described as disastrous. Al-Maliki had led the first government that took office in 2006, after the permanent constitution was approved in a referendum in 2005. His eight years of tumultuous rule were marred by the most severe internal fighting in the country's modern history. In what has become one of the world's 'top' unstable countries in Failed States Index (an index produced by Foreign Policy magazine and the Fund for Peace), the scale of humanitarian emergencies in Iraq was reported in 2008 by the Red Cross as 'among the most critical in the world'. After huge losses of life and property on both American and Iraqi sides, the US army began withdrawing in 2009. This withdrawal was completed by the end of 2011. As noted by Toby Dodge, the 'story' of the role of the United States in Iraq has turned out to be tragic, complicated and befuddling.[5]

In 2016, less than five years from the official withdrawal of the last American soldier, many parts of Iraq, including the northern oil-rich city of Kirkuk (long claimed as an integral part of the semi-autonomous region of Kurdistan), are out of the control of the central government. Much of the north and the west, together with the strategic city of Mosul, are overrun by fighters of the Islamic State (IS). A proto-state has been carved out by the *Al-Qaida* offshoot insurgents who proclaimed an Islamic Caliphate on both sides of the border with Syria, where also they have seized vast territories.

This article considers the limits of exogenous change, by focusing on the difficulties of implementing such a change in the concrete scenario of Iraq. It seeks to make a contribution to the academic and public understanding of the limits of exogenous initiatives of peacemaking in a country like Iraq, a contribution that might be used by critical educators committed to promoting peace in different *fora* and educational sites. It configures the key obstacles that stand in the way of reconciliation and peace in Iraq as seen by the Iraqi people in their real-life situations; difficulties that were heightened after the country adopted a new constitution following the toppling of the Hussein regime. Apart from consulting literature in the area, I drew relevant information from personal experience and observations, especially from direct contact and engagement with people in Iraq during a field study in the summer of 2013. Here I could probe local perceptions and insights in detail. The publications cited include magazines, newspapers, journal articles and monographs, as well as government documents. Though focusing on Iraq, the insights gained may, with good judgement and proper adjustments, be applied in some other scenarios.

Exogenous peace

Exogenous change refers to that type of change which originates from outside a system, and changes the latter radically. It is the opposite of endogenous change, that is, change that is generated in or originates from the system itself. In this chapter, exogenous change in relation to societies, in particular to a society that has definite characteristics (Middle Eastern, ethnically and religiously mixed though predominantly Arab and Muslim, one where religious and at times tribal allegiances are very strong and where the Shia–Sunni divide runs very deep, oil-rich, which was run by a dictator whose rule embodied some features that one might term secular and modern), will be considered. The arguments in favour of exogenous change in such a situation could be various. One may argue that exogenous change is needed if elements within the system to be changed cannot themselves bring about the change in question. In the case of societies, exogenous change could be envisaged because members within that society do not have the cultural, political, economic or military means to bring about the required change in this democracy, which was the official goal envisaged for the exogenous change in question. Or else, in a rather paternalizing manner, one may argue that members of that society, or sufficient members of that society, are so enmeshed in the latter that they cannot see the need to bring the changes that would suit them. Shortcomings of exogenous change that are normally highlighted include the top-down approach this involves; those who are supposed to benefit from the change have to 'suffer' such change, even if this is supposed to occur for their own good.

In the case that is considered in this chapter, that is, post-Saddam Hussein Iraq, the shortcomings of this top-down approach involve both the actual process of change and its simplistic representation in intellectual circles, media, public opinion and even scholarly circles. Relating to the latter, there was both trivialization and dramatization in the mass media as well as in some scholarly interpretations of the regime change that was being theorized in the case of Iraq. These interpretations were largely shaped by Western ideas, experiences and perspectives, rather than by the ideas, experiences and prospects of the people on the ground.[6] Such shortcomings were noted even by some Western agencies, like the German Development Institute, which in 2012 observed that conceptual and empirical knowledge on state-building in fragile countries is still very limited and is first-world centred, noting that the current body of research and evaluation documents does not yet provide urgently needed information that does not suffer from such limits.[7] In the case of Iraq, studies that captured the details of the individual case being studied – the challenges for taking real steps towards peace and the implications of the dramatic changes that would be unleashed after the external invasion in the internal sociopolitical order – were conspicuous by their absence.

These shortcomings were not just evident in the theoretical field. Since the exogenous change occurred, the effects have been felt on the ground by the Iraqi people.

Peacemaking in Iraq since 2003: A statement of the central problematique

In 2003, the United States attacked Iraq, supposedly to topple its dictatorial regime and introduce democracy. In the United States, many opinion makers, members of educational institutions and academics rallied blindly behind their president,[8] who claimed to have embarked on a mission to 'build a decent and democratic society' in Iraq and to transform the area into 'a place of progress and peace'. The perceptions of many Americans were mostly shaped by media constructs and representations, rather than by academic examination or reliable information from the people directly involved.[9] Sites where education is supposed to occur – both formally and informally – were conspicuous by their failure to produce critical thought in relation to this exogenous initiative.

Having won the war against Saddam Hussein's army easily, the next task the United States faced was achieving a peaceful and democratic aftermath. After occupying the whole country, the United States became directly responsible for ruling 25 million people and taking charge of the country's administration, security and infrastructure.[10] However, contrary to the US government's predictions, after removing from power the strongest dictator in the region, foreign troops were not regarded as liberators, but as occupiers. They had to confront unrelenting armed rebellion, with violent clashes between different groups and factions, overwhelming divisions in state and society, and far-reaching dysfunction in various government institutions, including the military and police force. Comprehensive stabilization and wholesale transformation, as well as plans for 'replacement regime' – all of which required massive long-term political, military and financial resources – became extremely difficult.[11] With more than 150,000 forces on the ground, the United States was incapable of halting the massive violence, looting and infrastructure breakdown.[12]

Following the initial phase when the reign of Saddam ended, Iraq witnessed a long phase of gunfire attacks and suicide bombs, which injured or killed many thousands of combatants and civilians. Indeed, it was when 'Operation Iraqi Freedom' was over that the coalition forces suffered nearly 95 per cent of their total casualties.[13] The civilian toll averaged around 13,000 deaths each year from 2003 through 2005. It went up to nearly 30,000 in 2006. (These figures are according to *Iraq Body Count*, a British-based NGO that runs an online database of civilian deaths.[14]) According to the *UN High Commission for Refugees*, more than two million Iraqis fled the country, mostly to Syria and Jordan, while an additional 1.9 million have become displaced within Iraq itself.[15] The standard of living and quality of life became terribly low, while oil production, the foremost source of income,[16] went down.[17] After two wars and more than a decade of sanctions, Iraq suffered from an insufficiency of infrastructure and shortage of skilled labour. It also lacked investment. The oil industry,[18] a possible lifeline for the economy, has been considerably constrained, requiring billions of dollars to fix field development and exports.[19] According to various US government agencies, multilateral institutions and other international organizations, the costs of long-term reconstruction of Iraq could reach $100 billion or even more.[20]

The United Sates embarked on finding systematic and effective ways to stop further social fragmentation, prepare for some kind of self-rule and lay the foundations for stable government with established structures and mechanisms.[21] The US occupation forces needed to rebuild a post-conflict-failed state, something that is considered (both inside the academy and outside) as crucial for stability and functioning of the economy.[22] Between 2003 and 2007, the United States directed and supervised initiatives and activities designed towards reconstructing Iraqi state institutions based on neo-liberal development paradigms that became dominant in the West during the 1990s. These advocate democracy and market-economy as essential means for rehabilitating public authority, restoring order and bringing about improvement in society.[23] The United States also needed to introduce a 'social contract' between the state and its citizens, ensuring the rights and liberties of the latter.[24] Priority was given to drafting a new constitution after the United States annulled the existing one.

This constitution was meant to be the guarantor of sovereignty and unity, and the most appropriate legal instrument for political compromise within the state. The remaking of the constitution signified the most fundamental and critical act of political reconstruction in post-conflict regeneration, and is discussed in detail later in the chapter.[25] The limits of the constitutional set-up of the post-Saddam Iraq will be taken as an example of the limits of the exogenous peace initiative that is being considered in this chapter.

The crisis of the constitution

Iraq's first constitution came into effect in 1925 under the auspices of the British military occupation forces. It created a constitutional monarchy and remained in effect until 1958, when a republic was established after a military revolt that overthrew the Hashemite Kingdom. Interim constitutions were adopted in 1958, 1963, 1964, 1968 and 1970. Between December 2003 and March 2004, the Iraqi Governing Council (IGC), established by the US-led Coalition Provisional Authority (CPA) as the provisional government of Iraq, appointed the Transitional Administrative Law (TAL) to draft the post-Saddam Hussein constitution.[26]

Following the war, the United States had annulled the existing constitution, with all its rules and regulations. Paul Bremer was appointed by the American president as the 'presidential envoy to Iraq,' subject to the 'authority, direction and control' of the secretary of defense. As the country's chief executive authority, he was permitted to rule by decree. Bremer was the holder of the 'most powerful foreign post held by any American since Gen. Douglas MacArthur in Japan'.[27] He can also be compared to General Lucius Clay who administrated the American zone in Germany after the Second World War.[28] Bremner banned the Ba'ath party in all its forms, dismantled the Iraqi Army and played a leading role in the formation of the IGC and the TAL.[29] Governance transition and sustainable peacemaking required the re-establishing of public institutions, and the reform of legal codes, judiciary, police and penal systems. Most importantly, it required remaking the constitution.

From the perspective of the United States, the constitution had to reflect both the ideal for which the United States fought the war (democratization) as well as express the aspirations of the people (the Iraqis) whose fundamental law it would be. Hence, the writing of the constitution was a sensitive exercise where the future rights and interests of all groups in society were implicated.[30] As a study by the US Institute of Peace on constitution making in 2003 concluded, the successful outcome of the constitution-making process in countries such as Iraq is dependent not only on the final document, but also on the path through which it is produced and adopted. If properly organized and given adequate attention and resources, the constitution and its drafting could become transformational ventures for the society in question.[31]

The Iraqi constitution drafted by members of the Iraqi Constitution Drafting Committee was approved in a referendum in October 2005, a few days before the first government of Iraq led by Al-Maliki took office in May 2006. The new constitution was supposed, in the words of the National Assembly speaker, to 'bring settlement and stability' to the people of Iraq, who needed to 'come together to build a new nation'.[32] Things on the ground, however, have been markedly different.

Many critics claim that the way in which the constitution was drafted was 'hasty'. Saad Jawad, for instance, claims that the document has created more problems than it solved, pointing to the myriad of confusions and divisions underlying the constitution's drafting process, and to the vagueness and ambiguity that hinder its application.[33] Jawad also notes that in 2005, 'the people' of Iraq voted and approved an incomplete and badly written draft, not realizing that the document would deepen Iraq's misery. He also points to overwhelming external interventions in the process leading to its adoption, despite international agreements like the Hague and Geneva Conventions not giving a foreign power the right to impose a constitution on an occupied country.[34] The absence of Iraqi constitutional expertise was also a limiting feature, as was the sidelining of Sunni Arab representation, something that contributed to the precarious situation in the subsequent years. The latter aspect is considered more deeply in the following section.

The Sunni–Shia divide

The American constitution starts with the words 'We the People. ...' The assumption behind the phrase is that despite the differences between the different signatories and the parties they represent, there are fundamental unifying features that make them a 'people'. When the document was drafted, this unity was cemented by the war these people and the groups they represented were at the time fighting against the government of the United Kingdom. The constitution of Iraq was also supposed to represent a 'people' that exist over and above the religious, ethnic, regional and, possibly, tribal differences that characterize different sets of Iraqis. Yet, only someone with a superficial knowledge of Iraq and its history could think that it would be easy for Iraqis coming from different backgrounds to come together and 'as a people' write and ratify a constitution embodying collective aspirations. Iraq is a heterogeneous country, in both religious and ethnic terms. Even if we consider the major religious and ethnic groups – Muslim and Arab – sharp divisions exist along the Shia–Sunni lines. Unlike what was the case for the colonies that were to become the United States in 1776, Iraq in the late twentieth and early twenty-first centuries was not governed by a distant monarch, but by a dictator associated with one ethnic-religious group and despised by the other.

Iraq is an Arab-majority country. It, however, also includes other ethnic minorities, most notably the Kurdish minority. In religious terms, apart from the majority of people following the Muslim religion, Christian (of various denominations), Yazidi and Mandanean communities also exist. The Muslim majority is decisively split. According to most sources, including the *CIA's World Factbook*, the majority of Iraqis are Shia Muslims, around 65 per cent while Sunnis represent about 32 per cent of the population. Though Shias form the major group, what is Iraq has traditionally been ruled by Sunnis. Saddam Hussein was the last Sunni Muslim to rule the country. After the independence of Iraq in the 1950s, the Shia majority remained under the rule of the Sunni minority. Their oppression continued under Saddam Hussein's (largely Sunni) Ba'ath Party. The Ba'ath suppressed their aspirations, especially of those in relatively more depressed areas in the south. Sunni members occupied the top posts in government, security and the army.[35] Some Shias founded the theocratic *Al-Dawa* party, dedicated to the establishment of a Shia Islamic state in Iraq. The party was banned and membership made a capital offence by Saddam's regime. The latter also ruthlessly crushed a Shia rebellion in the early 1990s, following the First Gulf War. Public commemorations of Shia rituals were prohibited, hundreds of Shia clerics were imprisoned and assassinated, and thousands of Iraqi Shia families were deported to Iran. The toppling of the Hussein regime helped the rise to power of the Shias. The appointment of Al-Maliki as prime minister turned Iraq into the first Arab-majority country to be ruled by the Shia followers since 1171, when the Shia Fatimids in Egypt were overthrown by Salahiddin, a Sunni of Kurdish origin and the founder of the Ayyubi dynasty.

This divide in Iraq, like similar divisions in other parts of the Muslim world, is visibly interrelated with the wider regional Sunni–Shia conflict. This conflict has widened notably, especially during what became known as the 'Arab Spring', and later as the war raged in Syria between the Sunni and the Shia *Alawis*.[36] The two variants of Islam are associated with two countries in particular – Saudi Arabia and Iran – countries that have deep-rooted tensions between them concerning security, economic, energy, religious and geopolitical issues.[37] These regional powers have become actively involved in advancing sectarian interests and helping sectarian allies in a 'regional cold war'.[38] Iraq lies across what is known as the Shia Crescent extending from Lebanon through Syria and Iraq to the Gulf, and to Iran and further east. Iraq has, in the words of a veteran Iraqi journalist, Nasrawi, become an 'arena for the Saudi-Iranian tug-of-war'.[39] With a Shia government in Iraq, Iran moved on to forge a larger Shia alliance in the region, an alliance that is essential for its strategic aims. Saudi Arabia, on the other hand, was determined to confront Iran's hegemonic aspirations, aspirations that it sees as a threat to its national interest, and to its historical and self-proclaimed position in the Muslim world.[40] With regard to Iraq, it worked to keep close connections to Sunni tribes and religious figures, using its 'traditional cheque-book diplomacy'. Funds and other aid for the Sunni rebels in Iraq are coming from sources in Saudi Arabia and from other predominantly Sunni Gulf states.[41]

The differences between the Shias and Sunnis in Iraq intensified following the toppling of the Saddam Hussein regime. The Shias wanted a leading share in the power that had been denied to them for centuries. This was evident even in visible terms. The fortified block-houses in the Green Zone and much of the rest of Baghdad that houses the government, together with checkpoints, prisons and police stations, became decorated with Shia banners, posters and religious figures. The first elected prime minister of Iraq following the US Invasion, Nuri Al-Maliki, was the secretary-general of *Al-Dawa*, a Shia Islamic Party, one of the main parties in the religious-Shia United Iraqi Alliance. The Sunni community, on the other hand, as the deputy speaker of parliament pointed out, would 'not accept power in the hands of the Shia'.[42] After the Kurds and leading Shia figures and clerics assumed important roles and functions, Sunni groups revolted against the government and against security forces, demanding a larger share of power and more access to government, wealth and religious authority. The Sunni, as Ali Abel Sadah (Baghdad-based writer for both Iraqi and Arab media) pointed out, were fighting against marginalization and alienation by the Shias. In this fight, they started showing higher levels of religious and sectarian identification, representation and institutionalization. The involvement of *Al-Qaeda* led to suicide bombings of Shia shrines and mosques.[43] Armed Sunni fighters first embattled foreign troops before hitting Shia neighbourhoods and ordinary Shia civilians, with thousands being abducted and murdered. The Shia militants, particularly after their holy sites came under attack by the Sunni, fought back in revenge, entering a killing spree that ran into deadly cycles. The backlash among both communities was strong, with human bombs in streets, markets, hospitals, offices, weddings and funerals inflicting heavy civilian casualties.[44]

A major contentious issue was the status of many former affiliates of Saddam's Ba'ath party, in what has become known as the de-Ba'athification enforced by the Shia government against (mostly Sunni) Ba'athists and Saddam sympathizers. The Ba'th party had already been made illegal by the Americans, another case of external imposition. A more thorny issue was the degree of regional autonomy. They are resenting the constitution, as currently worded, claiming that it puts in danger all those who had served in the government of Saddam and that it fails to guarantee the rights of all citizens. Above all, they claim that it undermines national unity by enshrining federalism, which most Sunnis oppose. Contrary to the Shias and Kurds, who are firmly in favour of decentralized governance with more regional autonomy, the Sunnis are against a constitution that does not comprise a set of fundamental principles or established precedents according to which a unitary, centralized and strong state (preferably Sunni-led) is governed. Many are disputing the concessions granted to the Kurds on the issues of federal government, natural resources and Kirkuk.[45]

This section presents only what is just an aspect of the complex scenario that is Iraq. It is a scenario that ought to have constituted the backdrop in relation to which any initiative aimed at bringing about change should have been considered. Those who sought to bring about exogenous change, however, seemed to have been unaware of these complexities.

The result

The result of the exogenous US initiative was neither peace nor pacification. Even when groups got round a table to discuss the building of a stable and peaceful nation, their efforts proved fruitless. The United States was unable to persuade or cajole important groups to fully, or even less than fully, cooperate with one another to form a stable government.[46] This was very evident in relation to the drafting of the constitution. The Americans could not resolve the disputes on several divisive issues in the remaking of the constitution between the local political elite, tribal leaders and representatives of different communities. The slump into terrible bloodletting became deeper, endangering safety, well-being and health of the whole population, and undermining territorial integrity and national unity.[47]

Many in the West had thought that differences could be settled by wiping clean the slate that was Saddam Hussein's power apparatus, existing institutions and about 1,000 years of Sunni rule, and by getting different representatives of different groups round a table to agree to a common text. After months of painstaking negotiations and weeks of deadlock, the Sunnis refused to accept the constitution deal, despite warnings of the danger of possible greater sectarian discord that would result from their refusal. They protested against becoming relegated to the fringe during the draft-writing. They also felt that their objections and concerns were being ignored by the Shias and by the Kurds, and that the ruling Kurd–Shia coalition determined to force through an agreement and avoid at all costs delays that would have cut into preparation time for the referendum.[48]

The hasty process by which the constitutional document was drafted by Shia and Kurd experts was completed under pressure from the United States. The task of preparing a draft constitution was given to a Constitutional Committee appointed by the Transitional National Assembly. It was obligatory, according to the TAL, for the Constitutional Committee to complete its work by 15 August 2005. The draft had to be submitted to a national vote by 15 October 2005.[49] Reports from Baghdad confirmed that consensus was elusive and the first deadline to submit a draft copy to the Transitional Assembly was missed.[50] Most negotiating parties were aware that they were still far from any final agreement on some of the constitution's most important prescriptions when the Committee was effectively dissolved and replaced by an *ad hoc* body (referred to as the Leadership Council) of no more than six members who continued to negotiate the constitution's final terms until three days before the referendum date.

The constitution was submitted to parliament without the support of Sunni leaders. The latter argued that it was drafted by the United States and not by the Iraqi people, and questioned the legitimacy of a document that was supposed to defuse inter-sectarian tension and unite the country, but which they considered to be inimical to their interests. The charter was rejected by the fifteen Sunni representatives on the seventy-one-member constitution committee, and last-minute concessions did not win over most of the Sunnis, or allay their fears. None of the fifteen Sunni members of the drafting committee signed it, and only three attended the signing ceremony, which was shunned by the vice-president, a Sunni, citing illness. The office of a Shia prime minister was reported confirming that the document would go before voters, even without the approval of the Sunni deputies.[51]

Sunni leaders and politicians were enraged at the lack of adequate compromise in negotiations, and they claimed that there was no real effort to bring them on board. They urged the UN, the Arab League and international organizations to intervene. Sunni tribal chiefs and religious scholars' associations mobilized thousands in Sunni areas, including some who carried pictures of Saddam, in protests against the government, chanting for the unity of Iraq. They were reported to be urging followers to vote against the constitution, accused of using abusive language riddled with anger when addressing the angry Sunni population and inciting reprisal against the Shias.[52]

Not merely was the text of the constitution unacceptable to many Sunnis, but the result of the countrywide referendum also came against their will. They had hoped to exercise a veto provision designed to protect minorities (the possibility of veto by the majorities of three or more governorates was originally written into the interim legislation, to ensure that the permanent constitution would be acceptable to the Kurdish minority), and they could have achieved this had they rallied two-thirds of the voters in three of Iraq's eighteen provinces to vote against it, the three provinces that included Sunni majorities. This would have resulted in the constitution's rejection. A two-thirds rejection vote in three of the country's eighteen provinces would also have required the dissolution of the Assembly, fresh elections and the recommencement of the entire drafting process. The constitution was, however, approved after 'No' votes greater than two-thirds were recorded in two provinces where Sunnis had the majority, but not in the third. In the latter, the two-thirds threshold was not reached.[53]

Conclusion

What were then the overall effects of exogenous change in Iraq, an exogenous change that was officially triggered by high ideals like democracy, freedom and peace? Thirteen years after the US Invasion and regime change, and following three rounds of elections, the country has become neither more democratic nor more secure. Nor has it achieved peace. Iraq is one of the most unstable countries in the world. Violent attacks have escalated, much the way of the previous year that saw the highest death toll since the grisly civil war in 2006 and 2007. With much of western and central territories falling under the control of the IS, the country is breaking apart. A stable system of administration could not be formed, with the writing, approval and amendments of the constitution a major bone of contention. Exogenous change has been anything but successful.

The structural, legal and political failings of the Iraqi constitution, for which both US officials and Iraqi politicians bear responsibility, have demonstrated how the ill-conceived US experiment or exogenous initiative has failed. Representatives of Sunni Arabs, Shia Arabs and Kurds have failed to find solutions and agreeable to all of the three major groups; their distinct ethnic and sectarian identity, and their historical accounts and memories, have served to bolster their claims. These aspects were barely taken into consideration when the exogenous initiative in question was conducted. The position of the Sunnis, mostly in the resource-poor areas in the west and centre, appears to be the primary barrier to any sort of unifying constitution. The handing over of additional power to provinces dominated by Kurds in the north and Shias in the south, and more regional autonomy, means a greater share of oil revenues to Shia and Kurd areas where the largest oil reserves lie. Sunnis oppose the constitution for what they perceive as a wide division of power between the federal government and regional governorates that diminishes their rights and fortunes, leaving them marginalized and poor, and for dividing the country into semi-autonomous regions that allow Iran to exert greater influence over the Shia south and the Shia government. The rise of the often-brutalized Kurds and Shias, the Sunni revolt and the war with the Shias have been the major stumbling blocks for the return to peace and stability. The sectarian variable, which helped in no little way to the dramatic capitulation of many parts of the country to IS, appears capable of plunging the country into civil war and leading to the eventual break-up of the country. The effects of the American exogenous initiative in Iraq have had repercussions that spill beyond this country. The foreign intervention has put a Shia government at the helm of an Arab country, for possibly the first time since the early days of Islam. This has altered the extremely complex, local setting or context, in an already highly heterogeneous country like Iraq, with many ethnic, religious and linguistic groups sharing the same national space. It has also deepened historical external and internal divisions in the whole region.

The establishment of formal democratic procedures, then, do not necessarily amount to progress or peace, especially where national sovereignty and unity, fundamental prerequisites for stable governance, exist only on paper. In spite of what has become the biggest relief and construction in US history – of a magnitude not undertaken since the time of Germany and Japan after the Second World War – the future remains uncertain, exposing more than a decade of failed US foreign policy in Iraq. The war, which gave unfiltered insights into the complex combination of considerations driving US foreign policy, reveals the blind spots of the American perspective. Arguably a watershed in the study of international relations and diplomacy, the case of exogenous change in Iraq could for some years to come set research agendas on a number of subjects, theory and practice.

The course of upheavals in Iraq shows the importance of the internal setting, unique to each country or region, the result of a particular constellation of historical and geographical factors, which projects for each society a trajectory that only that society can follow. It underlines the strength and resilience of forces of continuity or resistance to change, and brings into question the validity of exogenous action. They derailed endogenous change, which on the contrary ought to have allowed and strongly nurtured/propagated a gradual move to more equitable economies and fair societies. The failure of change in Iraq calls for a reconsideration of the scope and direction of the US foreign policy, and for a critical review of definitions and prescriptions of democracy, democratization and peacemaking in the whole region, and outside the West. Could some of these shortcomings have been avoided had education in the United States and elsewhere – in both formal and informal sites – fostered minds that could see the possibilities and, more importantly, the limits of the exogenous projects that the political elite in the United States was promoting?

Notes

1   Luft, G. (2003).

2   Boot, M. (2005). 'Reality Check in Modern Imperialism'. In G. Rosen (Ed.), *The Right War? The Conservative Debate on Iraq*, p. 93. Cambridge: Cambridge University Press.

3   Record, J. (2010) *Wanting War: Why the Bush Administration Invaded Iraq*. Potomac books Inc., p. 110.

4.   *The New York Times* (8 September 2003).

5   Dodge, T. (2005). *Inventing Iraq: The Failure of Nation Building and a History Denied*. New York: Columbia University Press, p. 216.

6   Mullerson, R. (2013). *Regime Change: From Democratic Peace Theories to Forcible Regime Change*. Mullerson: Martinus Nijhoff Publishers.

7   Grävingholt, J., Leininger, J. and Haldenwang, C. (2012). *Effective State-Building? A Review of Evaluations of International State-Building Support in Fragile Contexts.* German Development Institute. Denmark: Ministry of Foreign Affairs.

8   Boot, M. (2005). 'Reality Check in Modern Imperialism'. In G. Rosen (Ed.), *The Right War? The Conservative Debate on Iraq*, p. 93. Cambridge: Cambridge University Press.

9   A Lexis–Nexis search of the '*New York Times*' coverage in a one-year period (March to March) showed 1,848 articles concerning Iraq in 2006–7 and 1,350 in 2007–8. http://www.truth-out.org/news/item/22570-the-iraq-war-forgotten-in-plain-sight (accessed on April 2014).

10 Hippler, J. (2005). 'Nation-Building by Occupation? The Case of Iraq'. In J. Hippler (Ed.), *Nation-Building – A Key Concept of Peaceful Conflict Transformation*, pp. 81–97. London: Pluto Press.

11 Ward, C. J. (2005). 'The Coalition Provisional Authority's Experience with Governance in Iraq. US Institute of Peace's Iraq Experience Project' (Special Report 139, May) and Katz, M. N. (2010). 'The U.S. and Democratization in Iraq'. Washington, DC: Middle East Policy Council (14 October).

12 Katz, M. N. (2010). 'The U.S. and Democratization in Iraq'. Washington, DC: Middle East Policy Council (14 October).

13 'Operation Iraqi Freedom and Operation Enduring Freedom Casualties'. *iCasualties* (Retrieved 2 August 2014).

14 The figures available on different types of casualties vary, with information on both military and civilian loss of life not always precise and consistent.

15 This was confirmed by the *Internal Displacement Monitoring Centre*.

16 Crude oil export revenues accounted for over two-thirds of Iraq's GDP in 2009, see 'Inter-Agency Information and Analysis Unit, UN, Various Reports'.

17 Dodge, T. (2013). *Iraq: From War to a New Authoritarianism*. London: Routledge.

18 Donovan, T. W. (2010). 'Iraq's Petroleum Industry: Unsettled Issues'. Washington, DC: Middle East Institute (April).

19 Skibiak, N. (2010). 'Political and Legal Obstacles in Iraq'. Washington, DC: Middle East Institute (April).

20 Donovan, T. W. (2010). 'Iraq's Petroleum Industry: Unsettled Issues'. Washington, DC: Middle East Institute (April).

21 Record, J. (2010). *Wanting War: Why the Bush Administration Invaded Iraq.* Potomac books Inc., p. 110.

22 For example, Mallaby, S. (March/April 2002), 'The Reluctant Imperialist: Terrorism, Failed States, and the Case for American Empire'. *Foreign Affairs*; Fukuyama, F. (2004). *State Building. Governance and World Order in the 21st Century*. Ithaca: Cornell University Press; and Rodrik, D. (2008). *One Economics, Many Recipes: Globalization, Institutions and Economic Growth*. Princeton: Princeton University Press.

23 For a summary and critique, see Paris, R. (2004). *At War's End: Building Peace after Civil Conflict*. New York: Cambridge University Press.

24 Jawad, S. N. (2013). 'LSE Middle East Centre Paper Series/01'. London: The LSE Middle East Centre.November.

25 See, for example, Fukuyama, F. (2004). *State-Building: Governance and World Order in the 21st Century*. Ithaca: Cornell University Press and Paris, R. (2004). *At War's End: Building Peace after Civil Conflict*. New York: Cambridge University Press.

26 The TAL, signed on 8 March 2004 by the Iraqi Governing Council and coming into effect on 28 June 2004 with the official transfer of power to a sovereign Iraqi government, was principally drafted by a ten-man committee with advice from US and UN officials.

27 Kakutani, M. (2006). 'A View From the Center of the Iraq Maelstrom'. *New York Times*, 12 January.

28 Bremer, P. (2006). *My Year in Iraq: The Struggle to Build a Future of Hope*. Simon & Schuster.

29 Jawad, S. (November 2013). 'LSE Middle East Centre Paper Series/01'. London: The LSE Middle East Centre.

30 Krtitz, N. (2005). 'Constitution-Making Process: Lessons For Iraq. US Institute of Peace's Iraq Experience Project' (Special Report 132, February). Samuels, K. (2006). 'Post-Conflict Peace-Building and Constitution-Making'. *Chicago Journal of International Law*, 6 (2): 1–20 (winter).

31 http://www.usip.org/publications/constitution-making-process-lessons-iraq (accessed August 2014).

32 http://edition.cnn.com/2005/WORLD/meast/08/27/iraq.main/.

33 Jawad, S. (November 2013). LSE Middle East Centre Paper Series/01. London: The LSE Middle East Centre.

34 Jawad, S. (November 2013). LSE Middle East Centre Paper Series/01. London: The LSE Middle East Centre.

35 Nakash, Y. (2007). *Reaching for Power: The Shi'a in the Modern Arab World*. Princeton: Princeton University Press.

36 Though estimates vary considerably, there are around one and a half billion Muslims in the world, and between 10 and 20 per cent are Shia, minorities in a Sunni homeland in most countries, but the majority in Iraq, Bahrain and Azerbaijan, in addition to Iran.

37 Wehrey, F. (2009). Saudi-Iranian Relations since the fall of Saddam: Rivalry, Cooperation and Implications for US Policy. RAND Corporation. See also http://www.aljazeera.com/indepth/opinion/2013/11/iraq-saudi-arabia-between-rock-hard-place-20131128638344586.html

38 Nakash, Y. (2007). *Reaching for Power: The Shi'a in the Modern Arab World*. Princeton: Princeton University Press, and the Iraq Institute for Strategic Studies publications (mostly in Arabic). http://www.iraqstudies.com/

39   http://www.aljazeera.com/indepth/opinion/2013/11/iraq-saudi-arabia-between-rock-hard-place-20131128638344586.html

40   http://www.aljazeera.com/indepth/opinion/2013/11/iraq-saudi-arabia-between-rock-hard-place-20131128638344586.html

41   http://www.al-monitor.com/pulse/originals/2013/10/iraq-sunni-leader-incitement-shiites.html#

42   http://www.independent.co.uk/news/world/middle-east/the-shia-are-in-power-in-iraq--but-not-in-control-8523280.html

43   Vows to destroy the American Empire are laid out in the ideological manifesto of the group *Al-Qaeda* in Iraq, which carried out many of the worst attacks, assassinations and beheadings.

44   See the Iraq Institute for Strategic Studies publications (mostly in Arabic). http://www.iraqstudies.com/

45   Jawad, S. N. (November 2013). LSE Middle East Centre Paper Series/01. London: The LSE Middle East Centre.

46   Katz, M. N. (2010). 'The U.S. and Democratization in Iraq'. Washington, DC: Middle East Policy Council (14 October).

47   Jawad, S. N. (November 2013). LSE Middle East Centre Paper Series/01. London: The LSE Middle East Centre.

48   Jawad, S. N. (November 2013). LSE Middle East Centre Paper Series/01. London: The LSE Middle East Centre.

49   See the Iraq Institute for Strategic Studies publications (mostly in Arabic). http://www.iraqstudies.com/

50   http://www.theguardian.com/world/2005/aug/29/iraq.rorycarroll2

51   http://edition.cnn.com/2005/WORLD/meast/08/27/iraq.main/

52   See the Iraq Institute for Strategic Studies publications (mostly in Arabic). http://www.iraqstudies.com/

53   http://www.washingtonpost.com/wp-dyn/content/article/2005/10/25/AR2005102500357.html

References

Boot, M. (2005). 'Reality Check in Modern Imperialism'. In G. Rosen (Ed.), *The Right War? The Conservative Debate on Iraq*, p. 93. Cambridge: Cambridge University Press.

Council of the European Union (2004). EU-US Declaration of Support for the People of Iraq. Dromoland Castle, 26 June, 10001/04 (Presse 187). http://www.consilium.europa.eu/uedocs/cms_data/docs/pressdata/en/er/81246.pdf

Dani, R. (2008). *One Economics, Many Recipes: Globalization, Institutions and Economic Growth*. Princeton: Princeton University Press.

Dodge, T. (2005a). *Inventing Iraq: The Failure of Nation Building and a History Denied.* New York: Columbia University Press.

Dodge, T. (2005b). *Iraq's Future: The Aftermath of Regime Change.* London: Taylor & Francis.

Dodge, T. (2013). *Iraq: From War to a New Authoritarianism.* London: Routledge.

Donovan, T. W. (April 2010). 'Iraq's Petroleum Industry: Unsettled Issues'. Washington, DC: Middle East Institute.

Evans-Pritchard, A. (2003). 'Fury as Chirac Threatens New EU States'. *Daily Telegraph.* http://www.telegraph.co.uk (18 February).

Fagan, P. W. (2009). *Iraqi Refugees: Seeking Stability in Syria and Jordan.* Washington, DC: Institute for the Study of International Migration.

Fukuyama, F. (2004). *State Building. Governance and World Order in the 21st Century.* Ithaca: Cornell University Press.

Gordon, P. H. and Shapiro, J. (2004). *America, Europe, and the Crisis Over Iraq.* New York: McGraw-Hill, Brooking Institution.

Hippler, J. (2005). 'Nation-Building by Occupation? The Case of Iraq', in J. Hippler (Ed.), *Nation-Building – A Key Concept of Peaceful Conflict Transformation.* London: Pluto Press.

Jawad, S. (November 2013). 'LSE Middle East Centre Paper Series/01'. London: The LSE Middle East Centre.

Katz, M. N. (2010). 'The U.S. and Democratization in Iraq'. Washington, DC: Middle East Policy Council (October 14).

Krtitz, N. (2005). 'Constitution-Making Process: Lessons For Iraq. US Institute of Peace's Iraq Experience Project' (Special Report 132, February).

Luft, G. (2003). 'How Much Oil Does Iraq Have?' Washington, DC: Saban Center for Middle East Policy, Brookings Institution.

Military Reform Project (2002). 'The European Union's "Headline Goal" – Current Status'. Washington, DC: Center for Defense Information. http://web.archive.org/web/20120309144841/http://www.cdi.org/mrp/eu.cfm (May 23).

Mokbel, H. (September 2007). 'Refugees in Limbo: The Plight of Iraqis in Bordering States'. Middle East Report 244, pp. 10–17.

Mowafi, H. and Spiegel, P. (2008) 'The Iraqi Refugee Crisis: Familiar Problems and New Challenges'. *Journal of the American Medical Association*, 299 (14): 1713–15.

Nakash, Y. (2007). *Reaching for Power: The Shi'a in the Modern Arab World.* Princeton: Princeton University Press.

Nasr, V. R. (2007). *The Shi'a Revival: How Conflicts within Islam Will Shape the Future.* New York: W. W. Norton & Company.

Pape, R. (2005). *Dying to Win.* New York: Random House Publishing Group.

Paris, R. (2004). *At War's End: Building Peace After Civil Conflict.* New York: Cambridge University Press.

Record, J. (2010). *Wanting War: Why the Bush Administration Invaded Iraq.* Potomac books, Lincoln: University of Nebraska Press.

Samuels, K. (2006). 'Post-Conflict Peace-Building and Constitution-Making'. *Chicago Journal of International Law*, 6 (2):1–20 [winter].

Scott, Z. (2007). 'Literature Review on State-Building'. Department of International Development, University of Birmingham.

Skibiak, N. (April 2010). 'Political and Legal Obstacles in Iraq'. Washington, DC: Middle East Institute.

Ward, C. J. (May 2005). 'The Coalition Provisional Authority's Experience with Governance in Iraq'. Special Report 139, *The Iraq Experience Project*. The US Institute of Peace.

Wehrey, F. (2009). *Saudi-Iranian Relations Since the Fall of Saddam: Rivalry, Cooperation, and Implications for US Policy*. Santa Monica, CA: RAND Corporation.

5

Critical Peace in the Digital Era
of Austerity and Crisis

Nicos Trimikliniotis and Dimitris Trimithiotis

Introduction

In a historical juncture characterized by socio-economic crises and geopolitical turbulence, we cannot but question the foundations of the kind of peace diagnoses, recipes and remedies developed to date. We need to assess the relevance, adequacy and effectiveness of the technologies of peacemaking developed in the last fifty years. This chapter aims to re-evaluate some of the prevalent and broadly accepted scripts for resolving ethnic/state, politico-religious and other sociopolitical conflicts. Most of these 'scripts' belong to the so-called 'liberal peace model'. This model will be problematized and challenged. The chapter also includes our contribution to reinventing peace models that could possibly lead to transformation.

The chapter is divided into four sections. We will start by providing a rudimentary framework for a critique of Liberal Peace and of the dominant paradigms of conflict resolution. We will then illustrate how a critical–sociological reconstruction of 'peace' can allow us to envision critical peace, not only or primarily as an abstract concept developed by specialists, academics or think-tank laboratories, but also as conceptualizations of potentialities-in-the-making, based on social action, social imaginaries and praxis of struggling subjects. The chapter will also offer an examination of aspects of peacemaking and reconciliation, as well as of their couplet-opposites, which lead to escalation of conflict, violence and wars. Finally, an agenda will be proposed based on a number of new challenges and issues, focusing on digital technology.

On the meaning of peace: A critical engagement

'Peace' is not merely the 'absence of war' (Creighton and Shaw 1987). 'Peace' is not a vague concept. There are different degrees, dimensions and levels of 'peace'. The extension of the term 'peace' in particular historical, social, political, economic and cultural contexts may entail different sociopolitical actions that range from stopping a slaughter that is taking place, to separating communities with no communication so as to create a minimum of contact, to what can be referred to as reconciliation (Ehrlich et al. 2013).[1] Theories of peace do not just emerge in a vacuum. Nor do they involve a mere play of concepts.[2] The way different social, political and cultural groups envision the world must be properly situated, embedded and lived, in order to produce relevant theories on conflict, resolution, reconciliation and peace. This is a process that involves 'substance, commitment and creativity' (Sitas 2004).

The particular location and context from which peace initiatives are born, as well as possible policy implications for their 'export', generate specific forms, processes and conflict resolution, management or accommodation strategies. For example, our eastern Mediterranean location, overshadowed by the post-Ottoman settings in the Middle East and by the role of British colonialism, breeds specific dynamics into the societies that constitute the region. Different levels of sophistication of social structures and various forms of coexistence and the legacy of several wars and conflicts have created – over thousands of years – devices, knowledge systems, that can only be considered in Braudelian terms. They have created, for instance, the mechanisms of coexistence and non-assimilation of different forms of minority existence, spiritualities and social materialities that a Western-made, laboratory-produced, conflict-resolution model would fail to capture. Other contexts will have their own specifics.

Alternative envisioning: Towards critical peace

Envisioning critical peace is certainly an ambitious project, especially if pursued historically, globally and regionally. In the context of the current multifaceted crisis (economic, political, social, crisis of hegemony, etc.), we are witnessing various alternatives to sponsored peace packages. The collapse of the post-Cold War promise of the projected 'liberal triumph' that we are witnessing in different forms, is producing virulent fundamentalisms, violence and conflict zones, which are spreading and threatening in different ways the so-called 'stable and secure zones'. This, however, is stimulating and promoting survival strategies wherever there is a collapse of order, nation states and welfare state. There may be local variants of global phenomena, which are intertwined and interconnected to wider transnational movements and phenomena. It is (should be) also stimulating alternative peace models and processes. These alternative peace processes have not been systematically studied, understood and connected in terms of their potentialities to be viable alternatives. Alternative peace processes start by engaging critically peacemaking strategies that operate within a neo-liberal framework. This is what we do in what follows.

Peacemaking instruments of the neo-liberal era

Most of the current peacemaking concepts, instruments and paradigms were developed within specific historical contexts, mostly in the 1990s and 2000s. The dominant paradigms adopted by peace promoting institutions – governmental and non-governmental – have certain characteristics in common. First, they are generally informed by an economic model that is neo-liberal in essence. Second, they were/are mostly conceived within particular geopolitical and spatial contexts – the Western/northern traditions and hemispheres. They were/are then imposed on some non-Western regions in conflict. Third, they tend to overlook the 'internal' consequences suffered by 'pacified spaces' as a result of invasive practices that often ignore, orientalize or romanticize the 'other'.

In the geographical areas where the 'liberal peace' model has been applied, often by force, as in Libya, Iraq, Afghanistan, Lebanon, Israel/Palestine, Sri Lanka and various Latin American countries, it is failing to achieve the basic goal of 'order' and to bring about standards of stability, development and hope for the people affected. Indeed, in many cases, forced 'liberal peace' processes are causing new forms of conflicts with unprecedented violence. In an age characterized by socio-economic crises, geopolitical turbulence and uncertainty, (Bauman's 'liquid times', Bauman 2006), various forms of violence and ethnic/religious/state-related conflicts, have been part of the geopolitical re-engineering happening in different parts of the globe.

Different societies deal with conflict, polarizations and divisions differently. This, however, does not exclude the fact that they are also influenced by one another. Ideas and social processes 'travel' or 'migrate' and influence other contexts, but they do so in different and unintended ways. There is neither consensus as to the 'best route', nor one 'toolkit' that ought to be copied and applied universally. The adaptation of imported models of conflict resolution, peace and reconciliation are often closely connected to political, economic and cultural agendas in a world system based on hegemonic relations. This should not lead one to idealize 'indigenous recipes' or processes. In a world ridden with gross competition and inequalities of wealth and power, geopolitical and social contestations, fragmentations and contradictions at all levels, there is no quick-fix toolkit – be it indigenous or imported – for conflict zones and default-lines, particularly at times when the hegemonic structure of the world seems to be shaking. No social science can promise to fix that. However, a great deal can be done once the liberal peace model and its derivatives are theoretically dismantled and rejected. Then, we can begin to properly envision the alternatives generated by Critical Peace.

'Critical peace' requires that we fundamentally reconsider what is generally perceived as successful peace building, peacekeeping and 'restoring' societies torn by war, conflicts or other violence in mainstream circles. 'Critical peace' requires that we reconsider what was considered to be state of the art in successful peace building and peacekeeping and in 'restoring' societies torn by war, conflicts or other violence. The development and increasing usage of new social media, and the issues relating to the processes of securitization, surveillance and digitalization in war and peacemaking, the various peace management and peacekeeping missions, as well as the contestations and potentialities these have unravelled, open up new terrains of struggles in the search and meaning of peace.

This approach also requires that we think anew peace building and peacekeeping in ways that actually transform the thinking and practice of peace-seeking in the world. At the core of this rethinking is the need to locate 'peace' within the processes of transformation struggles, which generate new socialities, that is, people and groups coming together, developing social links and creating communities. (see Trimikliniotis 2015) – hence, the importance of drawing insights form fields like sociology. With the exception of some works (Creighton and Shaw 1987; Yuval-Davis, Anthias 1989; Mann 2005), most contemporary studies of collective violence and war are lacking in proper interfacing with sociological scholarship (Malešević 2010). Recent sociological studies, though, have produced interesting readings that can enrich the debates on peace, peacemaking and reconciliation, enabling one to see through, and go beyond, the liberal peace models of conflict resolution. Historical sociologists had an interest in dealing with such phenomena until the development of the specialized interest in ethnic-related phenomena, with the study of nations, nationalism, ethnicity, race and racism. The fields of inquiry of Sociology itself, which have traditionally been underdeveloped fields, have expanded and deepened.

Sociology, particularly the coming into being of *critical conflict sociology* is an essential ingredient that can open up ways of seeing, thinking and acting in this direction. Despite the enormous growth of research and knowledge at the technical level as well as in the variety of approaches, including critical approaches, what is still missing from many critiques is *social self-reflexivity* to develop specific thinking, and contextualized policies and frameworks in the post-austerity-and-crisis era. This requires that we think anew peace building and peacekeeping in ways that actually transform the thinking and practice of peace-seeking in the world.

People engaged in peace initiatives ought also to ask themselves what the sociological underpinnings for the consolidation of the ethic of reconciliation are (Sitas et al. 2008).[3] In this chapter, we argue that tackling this question is vital with regard to how deeply divided societies deal with conflict, particularly with regard to how particular societies deal with a violent and divisive past. Such an endeavour will not only enhance academic knowledge but may also have an impact on policy with regard to peace and reconciliation processes, both in a particular society and in intra-societal terms. A sociological enquiry into conflicts, wars and peace and reconciliation processes requires a deeper insight into societal forces at place, examining closely the network of relationships, mechanisms and processes promoting justice, and addressing the root causes of possible enmity, contestations and differences. Yet, it cannot limit itself to analysing one society only, as though particular societies may exist in a vacuum.

Challenges ahead: A research agenda for critical peace

First, Critical Peace has to take into consideration the global scenario. In this regard, a number of challenges lie ahead for Critical Peace as we need to rethink peace within the context of a world that has aptly been described as being 'out of joint' (Wallerstein 2014). 'Critical Peace' must take into account the new reality of the world political stage: a reality where the old hegemonic order is being challenged, something that is bringing about critical transformations relating to the role of intentional actors in the shaping and evolution of conflicts.

Following the liberal triumphalism expressed by Fukuyama who announced a world of managerial capitalism as the end of history, we are witnessing the result of a world disorder, long-term disequilibrium and long-drawn processes of the demise of American hegemony. The kind of peace and democracy offered by the liberal peace packages is crumbling, as are neo-liberal economic solutions. The political structures devised to support them are increasingly being seen as illegitimate, irrelevant and undemocratic, and have failed to resolve ethnic, religious, political and social conflicts in various parts of the world, especially in those that Wallerstein calls 'semi-peripheral' and 'peripheral'. Even in the so-called 'core', though (e.g. within the EU, Portugal, Italy, Ireland, Spain, Greece and Cyprus), people are facing severe strains and the kinds of turbulence usually experienced by the countries outside the core (especially former colonies of world empires).

Then there is the challenge of conceptualizing power-games in regional contexts. Conflicts involve multiple sets of other conflicts, riddled with local, regional and international contradictions. With the transformations in the architecture of the global, the roles of global, regional and national forces in different regions, the fault lines, the frontiers and the terms of contestations are also being transformed (Gindin and Panitch 2012). Each situation must be closely scrutinized and properly understood in its specific historic and geographical context, and in relation to processes of political and social formations. Conflicts involve a condensation of local and global factors, which cannot be flattened out in a one-dimensional reading but must be understood as a systemic totality. They must be read as *a local problem within the global/regional context.* Consider the Middle East. The region is witnessing popular revolts against unpopular and undemocratic regimes. It is also witnessing the resurfacing of age-old conflicts between ethnic, religious and secular, as well as proxy wars between regional powers. Regarding the latter, the declining US hegemony in the region has increased regional rivalries. The latter have redefined the fault lines in regional geopolitical, energy and security contestations. Three poles are emerging: Iran, Saudi Arabia and Turkey, each with its own allies. The three are diversely related to the United States, to NATO and to Russia. Then, there is also Israel. Apart from the big regional and global forces (US/NATO, Iran, Turkey, Russia, etc.), there are contestations between various factions, ethnic groups, army factions and/or Muslim organizations. The intersections arising from these confluences are producing new forms of opposition and throwing up various contradictions. The forces that will take over different areas in the region will not necessarily be secular-democratic.

Another factor that Critical Peace should consider is the transnational and transterritorial challenges that involve transformations and a multiplicity of contestations that are not confined to particular national territories. Al-Qaeda and IS are two such transnational phenomena. The interplay and shift between deterritorialized networks (Hardt and Negri 2000, 2011) has generated assertive regional forces as a reaction. (Cases in point are the roles played by Iran and Saudi Arabia, and their backers, in Iraq, Syria and elsewhere in the Persian Gulf and Middle East.) These reactions normally aim to reterritorialize if not 'recolonize' a territory – a reloaded, redefined and reshaped imperialism. Whether these initiatives constitute a 'new imperialism' as Harvey has it, or a decentred and deterritorialized imperial network redefining sovereignty in a crisis of world systems (Wallerstein 2006), or a reconstituting of the imperial chain, only time will show.

Issues of peace and conflict today also involve transnational and transterritorial variables. The current hydrocarbon issue, for instance, is one. In the era of the 'hydrocarbon-man' (Shaffer 2009, p. 60), energy and water have a notable geopolitical significance. They influence contestations and peace arrangements. The Middle East and North Africa are good examples. Here, we have conflicts related to energy and water that involve a regional/global order, and cannot be understood through the utilization of the traditional centres of territorialized power.

Another challenge that Critical Peace cannot avoid relates to the new security agendas that are constantly being devised in response to the crises-ridden global order. An example of this is the latest EU policy, *The European Agenda on Security*. (Yet, this is a common pattern developing in different parts of the globe, be it the EU or the USA/Mexico border, the South African border or Australia.) This, essentially, involves a process of securitization that produces 'solutions' based on extending further the logics of surveillance, repression and militarization, and on extending the role and funding of agencies of repression (despite the lip-service to fundamental rights, transparency and democratic control).[4] The focus is supposedly on counterterrorism, border control and cybercrime. Yet, the primary goal is the containment of refugees and immigrants from reaching the 'core countries', using military, political and other devices, and preferably utilizing extra-territorial means. Even the Mediterranean 'migration crisis', by and large derived from the application of the interventionist 'liberal peace model' in North Africa and the Middle East, is addressed essentially in military terms (rather than conceived as a true humanitarian crisis). Peacemaking in this context is hence being distorted and subjected to the new security agendas.

In the current era of austerity and crises, Critical Peace should take into consideration new social questions that are cropping up even in the First World. The dramatic collapse of the welfare state, which has been in decline since the late 1970s and early 1980s (Esping-Andersen 1990) as part of 'the new social question' (Rosanvallon 2000), is resurfacing violently and with new terms in countries in the EU periphery such as Spain, Portugal, Italy and Greece (see Lapavitsas, 2012). The old structural adjustment programs (SAPs) previously imposed by the IMF on parts of the Third World, are now being imposed on the debt-ridden peripheral countries of the Eurozone, resulting in the drastic collapse of European welfarism, causing poverty, homelessness, mass unemployment, disintegration of the middle classes, closure of small businesses and destruction of the web of social security. Peace that is not conceived as the mere absence of violence cannot ignore such issues.

Digital socialities, peace and commons: Building alternatives?

A major player in the current peace/war dialectic is digitality. Critical Peace cannot ignore this player. For a long time, especially within media and communication research, there was an emphasis on a *digital divide* or, more pointedly, a *digital gap,* that is, on an almost unbridgeable chasm concerning access to digital media by different groups. This gap was frequently explained in terms of social, cultural and economic inequality. It was generally assumed that disadvantaged groups lack access to digital networks. Things, however, may not be as simple as these assumptions make out. Consider digital media in relation to borders and frontiers. Border zones are composed of different agents and actors in conflicting, hierarchical and dynamic interplay. They include both repressive information and control policies, and the practices of border-making, border-crossing and border-breaking. Studies have shown how disadvantaged groups, such as migrants and refugees fleeing war zones, use digital media and digital social networks in their border crossings, many of them with considerable virtuosity. Given this complexity, one must distinguish between those aspects of the digital space that are constitutive of new social dynamics and those that reproduce more traditional conditions: 'Digital space and digitization are not exclusive conditions that stand outside the non-digital. Digital space is embedded in the larger societal, cultural, subjective, economic, imaginary structurations of lived experience and the systems within which we exist and operate' (Sassen 2002, p. 369).

In this context, the notion of 'mobile commons' (see Trimikliniotis 2015) – goods available to more than one individual that are not spatially defined to one place – can be extended to capture the potentialities of digital technology in survival struggles, in wars, in conflicts as well as in peace building and peace activism. Often, the debates over the commons as well as their supposed *tragedy* are connected to land and property, agrarian and urban settings – the 'tragedy of the commons' being a situation where, within a system of shared resources, a number of individuals acting according to their own self-interest independently of each other in relation to some resource(s), exhaust the resource and thus act contrary to the common good of all users. While the predominant neo-liberal thought that has been hegemonic in academia for the past forty years encouraged such tragedy, there seems to be rethinking now, and not merely in radical or fringe fora.[5]

Regarding digital technology Jeremy Rifkin's work (2014) emphasizing collaborative commons in relation to technology is indicative of the swing in scholarly debates away from a neo-liberal paradigm. The link between collaborative commons and digitality is also made by numerous radical thinkers (Hardt and Negri 2000, 2011; Harvey 2003). In this regard, Alonso and Arzoz (2011) refer to 'digital diasporas as activist commons'. This fascinating combination of commons with the diaspora approach as proposed by Alonso and Arzoz (2011, p. 69) provides the frame whereby a political geography of migrants or minorities without, beyond or against States is created. Digitality, and the new knowledge forms it involves and transmits, then, are a vital organizing force that shapes the very concept of *mobile commons*, which are an essential acquisition resulting from the collective power to reshape the world of people on the move or people seeking to settle conflicts and seek reconciliation. Once the positive aspects of digitality have been emphasized, it is important that this is not seen as a somewhat miraculous manna sent from heaven to change the world (just as, negatively, it cannot be seen as the prelude to a world of total surveillance).

Conclusion

Problems relating to peace, reconciliation and peace education cannot be conceived in abstract terms (as in the liberal peace model). Social struggles must be examined within the specifics of their historical, political, ideological, cultural and social contexts. Critical Peace, however, cannot ignore global, regional, transnational and transterritorial variables.

Any attempt to 'read' these phenomena requires a significant reordering and re-referencing that injects the richness of theorizing from other perspectives than the Global North. Any effort to properly capture these processes requires a serious re-imaging of socialities; there is considerable thinking of this kind in the South and the East. Peacemaking must be read in the context of the modes of livelihoods, the socialities, solidarities and connectivities long experienced in the Global South, the East and what was thought of as the 'backward Rest' (i.e. that which is not in 'the West' or the 'Global North' Hall 1992). In these days of austerity, new socialities are being produced by the 'wretched of the earth'. 'Structural reforms' are made possible by listening in on what Sitas called the 'voices that reason' (Sitas 2004), that is, from the perspective of the ordinary lives. Contrary to the neo-Schmidtean and neo-Platonist readings of politics as the exception, reading 'ordinary lives' as resistance can illuminate how we construct notions such as 'peace' and reconciliation. The subalterns can and, indeed, do speak; they speak back, but, most importantly, they act and inscribe social struggles (Sitas 2004, p. ix). Digitality, and new forms of knowledge pertaining to this, may be a transformative force that can help in remoulding the world of people seeking to escape war, as those hoping to build peace.

Notes

1   A key task in post-war/post-conflict societies is 'reclaiming the social character of the reconciliation process, in opposition to legalistic discourses, focusing on punishment, and to business approaches focusing on "economic reconstruction"' (Ioakimidis 2015).

2   See Anthias and Yuval-Davis (1992); Yuval-Davis et al. (2006) and Sitas (2004).

3   A critical response to the abridged version of this work was elaborated in the form of a debate in *Current Sociology* 59 (5): 2012.

4   Communication from the Commission to the European Parliament, the Council, the European Economic and Social Committee and the Committee of the Regions, The European Agenda on Security, 28.4.2015 COM (2015) 185 final, see http://www.statewatch.org/news/2015/apr/eu-com-agenda-on-security-com-185-15.pdf.

5   The shift can be seen since the sardonic response by the legal scholar Carol Rose (1986), who insisted that rather than speaking of a 'tragedy' we ought to speak of: 'the comedy of commons'. Since then, the *International Journal of the Commons (IJC)* was established. See http://www.thecommonsjournal.org/index.php/ijc/index (accessed 21 August 2014). The 2009 Nobel Prize winner in Economics, Elinor Ostrom, emphasizes the benefits of having people collaborating and organizing themselves to manage common resources, rather than following the tragedy model (1990, 2002; Hess and Ostrom 2003; Ostrom et al. 2012; Rose 2011).

References

Alonso, A. and Arzoz, I. (2011). El 15M y la quintacolumnia digital. Comentarios para un laboratorio estrategico, Cybergolem. In *Teknocultura, Rivista de Cultura Digital y Movimientos Sociales*, 8 (2): 177–82.

Anthias, F. and Yuval-Davies, N. (1992). *Racialised Boundaries*. London: Routledge.

Bauman, Z. (2006). *Liquid Times: Living in an Age of Uncertainty*. Cambridge: Cambridge University Press.

Brewer, J. (2010). *Peace Processes: A Sociological Approach*. Cambridge: Polity Press.

Creighton, C. and Shaw, M. (1987). *The Sociology of War and Peace*. Dobbs Ferry, NY: Sheridan House.

Ehrlich, N., Marks, L. and Yuval-Davis, N. (2013). 'Introduction'. In N. Ehrlich, L. Marks and N. Yuval-Davis (Eds), *The Work of Avishai Ehrlich: Political Sociologist, Activist and Public Intellectual*, pp. vii–xi. Cambridge: Cambridge Scholars.

Esping-Andersen, G. (1990). *The Three Worlds of Welfare Capitalism*. Cambridge: Polity Press and Princeton: Princeton University Press.

Gindin, S. and Panitch, L. (2012). *The Making of Global Capitalism: The Political Economy of American Empire*. London: Verso.

Hall, S. (1992). 'The West and the Rest: Discourse and Power'. In S. Hall and B. Gieben (Eds), *Formations of Modernity*, pp. 275–95. Cambridge, MA: Open University and Blackwell.

Hardt, M. and Negri, A. (2000). *Empire*. Cambridge: Harvard University Press.

Hardt, M. and Negri, A. (2011). *Commonwealth*. Cambridge, MA: Harvard University Press.

Harvey, D. (2003). *The New Imperialism*. Oxford: Clarendon Press.

Ioakimidis, V. (2015). 'Editorial: The Two-Faces of Janus; Rethinking Social Work in the Context of Conflict'. *Social-Dialogue*, The International Association of Schools of Social Work (IASSW). http://social-dialogue.com/ (10 April 2015).

Jacklin H. and Vale, P. (2009). *Re-imagining the Social in South Africa: Critique Theory and Postapartheid Society*. Durban: University of Kwazulu-Natal.

Lapavitsas, C. (2012). *Crisis in the EuroZone*. London: Verso.

Malešević, S. (2010). *The Sociology of War and Violence*. Cambridge: Cambridge University Press.

Mann, M. (2005). *The Dark Side of Democracy: Explaining Ethnic Cleansing*. Cambridge: Cambridge University Press.

Rifkin, J. (2014). *The Zero Marginal Cost Society, The Internet of Things, The Collaborative Commons, and the Eclipse of Capitalism*. New York: Palgrave Macmillan.

Rosanvallon, P. (2000). *The New Social Question: Rethinking the Welfare State*. Princeton: Princeton University Press.

Said, E. (1978). *Orientalism*. London: Routledge & Kegan Paul Ltd.

Sassen, S. (2002). 'Towards a Sociology of Information Technology', *Current Sociology*, 50 (3): 365–88.

Shaffer, B. (2009). *Energy Politics*. Philadelphia: University of Pennsylvania Press.

Sitas, A. (2004). *Voices that Reason: Theoretical Parables*. Pretoria: University of South Africa Press.

Sitas, A. (2008) *The Ethic of Reconciliation*. Durban: Madiba Publishers University of Kwazulu-Natal.

Sitas, A., Latif, D. and Loizou, N. (2008). *Prospects of Reconciliation, Co-Existence and Forgiveness in Cyprus in the Post-Referendum Period*. PRIO Cyprus Centre Report 4/2007, 2008. Available at http://www.prio.no/upload/Prospects%20of%20 Reconciliation%20low.pdf.

Sitas, A. (2011) 'Beyond The Mandela Decade: The Ethic of Reconciliation?' *Current Sociology*, 59 (5): 571–85.

Trimikliniotis, N. (2013a). 'Can We Learn from Comparing Violent Conflicts and Reconciliation Processes? For a Sociology of Conflict and Reconciliation Going Beyond Sociology'. In C. Borg and M. Grech (Eds), *Lorenzo Milani's Culture of Peace, Essays on Religion, Education, and Democratic Life*, pp. 203–17. London: Palgrave Macmillan.

Trimikliniotis, N. (March 2013b). 'For a Sociology of Conflict and Reconciliation: Learning From Comparing Violent Conflicts and Reconciliation Processes'. *Current Sociology* 61 (2): 244–64.

Trimikliniotis, N. (2013b). 'Avishai Ehrlich, A Pessimist of Intellect but Optimist of Will: A Gramsci-inspired Sociology, An Interview by Nicos Trimikliniotis'. In N. Ehrlich, L. Marks and N. Yuval-Davis (Eds), *The Work of Avishai Ehrlich: Political Sociologist, Activist and Public Intellectual*, pp. 95–110. Newcastle upon Tyne: Cambridge Scholars Publishers.

Trimikliniotis, N. (2015). 'A Sociological Critique of Liberal Peace'. In O. P. Richmond, S. Pogodda and J. Ramovic (Eds), *Dimensions of Peace: Disciplinary and Regional Approaches*. New York, NY: Palgrave Macmillan.

Trimikliniotis, N. and Bozkurt, U. (2010). 'Rethinking Cypriot State Formation(s)'. *The Cyprus Review*, 22 (2): 87–110 [Fall].

University of Birmingham (1982). *The Empire Strikes Back: Race and Racism in 70s Britain.* London: Hutchinson in Association with the Centre for Contemporary Cultural Studies, University of Birmingham.

Väyrynen, R. (1991). *New Directions in Conflict Theory.* London: Sage Publications.

Wallerstein, I. (2000). 'Peace, Stability, Legitimacy, 1990 to 2025/2050'. In *The Essential Wallerstein*, pp. 435–543. New York: The New Press.

Wallerstein, I. (2006). *European Universalism: The Rhetoric of Power.* New York: The New Press.

Woodhouse, T. (June 1999). *International Conflict Resolution: Some Critiques and a Response*'. http://www.brad.ac.uk/acad/confres/papers/pdfs/CCR1.pdf.

Yuval-Davis, N. and Anthias, F. (1989). 'Introduction'. In N. Yuval-Davis and F. Anthias (Eds), *Woman-Nation-State*, pp. 1–15. London: Macmillan.

Yuval-Davis, N. (1997). *Gender and Nation.* London: SAGE.

Yuval-Davis, N., Kannabirān, K. and Vieten, K. (2006). *The Situated Politics of Belonging.* London: SAGE.

Part Two

Challenges to Peace Education

Dreaming of Peace in a Culture of War

Antonia Darder

In the name of peace
They waged the wars
Ain't they got no shame

—Nikki Giovanni[1]

Throughout my lifetime, thus far, the US government has been in a permanent state of war. Over a hundred overt military campaigns of varying degrees have been undertaken in the name of peace, and who knows how many covert operations have been launched. As a Puerto Rican child, my very identity from the beginning has been intimately intertwined with the legacy of war. My citizenship is the direct result of the Spanish-American War, which converted my country into a colony of the United States. In the year in which I was born, 1952, the United States was embroiled in both the Cold War and the Korean War. As a pre-teen, reports about the Cuban missile crisis and the action at the Bay of Pigs were interspersed with fears of nuclear war on the evening news. During my teen years, civil rights conflicts erupted on the national arena. I watched on television as members of the Black Panther Party were being shot in their home. Growing up in Los Angeles, I also found myself in the midst of the Watts Riots, and later, as a witness to violent police attacks on Chicana and Chicano activists, who had congregated at Laguna Park, after a peaceful march along Whittier Boulevard. As a young mother, I sang my babies lullabies which commingled with radio reports of the Vietnam War.

Beyond these war campaigns, US military actions over the last sixty years have also included participation in the First Indochina War; The Lebanon Crisis; the Cambodian Civil War; the Invasion of the Dominican Republic; the Invasion of Grenada; The Lebanese Civil War; the Action in the Gulf of

Sidra; the Contras (Counterinsurgency) attack of Nicaragua; the Bombing of Libya; the Iran-Iraq War; the Invasion of Panama; the Gulf War; the Somali Civil War; the Bosnian War; Operation Uphold Democracy in Haiti; the Bombing of Afghanistan and Sudan; the Kosovo War; the War on Terror; the War in Afghanistan; Operation Enduring Freedom in the Philippines, Horn of Africa and Trans Sahara; the Iraq War; War in North-West Pakistan; Yemeni Al-Qaeda Operations; the second Liberian War; the Haitian Rebellion; the Libyan Civil War; the Lord's Resistance Army Insurgency in Uganda and Southern Sudan; attacks near the border of Pakistan; and military operations in both Afghanistan and Syria. In each instance, the toll paid by the working and poor populations of these regions has been staggering, while the elite and powerful have filled their coffers, as US forces have bombed and killed predominantly poor people, bringing to mind Sartre's words: '*quand les riches se font la guerre, ce sont les pauvres qui meurent.*' (*When the rich wage war, it's the poor who die.*)[2]

The hidden curriculum of violence

Our schoolbooks glorify war and conceal its horrors. They indoctrinate children with hatred.

Albert Einstein[3]

Most of these military offensives remain obscure or unknown to the majority of US citizens – although not to the working-class men and women in the US military who soldier these offensives and to the families who have lost their children on foreign soil. Yet, despite this history of permanent war, students attending public schools are socialized to be deeply ignorant and detached from the realities of war, through a discourse that rationalizes military aggression in the name of victory, freedom and security at home. This veiled and fragmented perspective of war (and, thus, of peace) is carried out through both a hidden curriculum within schools that claims to be apolitical, neutral and objective, and a public pedagogy of the media that glorifies violence and conquest as virtuous human production. Negated, of course, is the obvious, wholesale human destruction in the interest of capital.

On the movie screen, sanitized or sensationalized illusions are created to simulate wartime action, with the hero (usually white, male and typically

'American') moving courageously through thick and thin to come out victorious. Seldom given much thought or 'air time' is the suffering of exploding bodies, or the devastation of the people or that of 'our soldiers' caught up in the melee of destruction. The audience, instead, is cleverly seduced into a gripping narrative of protagonists, in such a singular manner that everyone else becomes background noise for the epic stories of military brutality portrayed as triumph. In this way, war is normalized, habituated and conditioned into the psyche of viewers who are swiftly catapulted from passive observers to emotional participants in this brutal terrain of glorified wartime. Yet, there is actually no glory in war, save for the myth and spoils reaped by the wealthy who are seldom physically implicated in the dangerous action. Outside of the arena of war, even former soldiers are left starkly numb and become silent when questioned about the atrocities witnessed or perpetrated in their *theatre of war*,[4] when all consciousness of humanity was suspended and their *lean, mean, fighting machine* training was unleashed.

In the process of public schooling, students – particularly working-class students who historically have been both objectified and instrumentalized as reserve armies of the powerful – are exposed to a hidden curriculum that effectively and systematically alienates them from the suffering of others. Students learn, directly or indirectly, that the poor are so by their own making and, thus, empathy or money spent on the impoverished is not only resources wasted, but also, for us, deprivation of greater wealth. Concentrated wealth is normalized and naturalized as a legitimate goal to aspire for in our lives. Schools as political and moral agencies of the war industry also function to effectively block critical engagement with the dehumanizing brutality of aggression and the grand profits it affords to the ruling class. Similarly, the daily news media function as public pedagogical venues, which conveniently normalize and reinforce the necessity of war. Hence, the violence becomes twofold, in that the judgement of students is swayed against their own best interests, as they are initiated into a culture of permanent war. This points to an ideological formation that simultaneously obscures and underhandedly perpetuates conservative patriotic discourses and patriarchal exultations of hypermasculinity and military aggression – in both men and women – as equivalent to invincible power, sexual prowess and homeland protection. Or, at least, this is the case until the brutal casualties of young US soldiers begin to cross the class and colour divide of affluence, suddenly disrupting the Disneyland veneer of 'middle-class' existence. Such was the case during the Vietnam War, when televised body bags rolling down a conveyor belt held not only the children of the urban ghettos and barrios, but also the bodies of 'red-blooded American boys' of the suburbs. This was a historical moment in which people, across class and colour lines, finally began to take to the streets in an effort to end the war in Southeast Asia. We saw aspects of this phenomenon at work during the Occupy Movements, as formerly 'middle-class' or well-established people, who had lost their jobs and homes, took to the streets to shout in unison, 'We are the 99 percent!' – while others held signs with the words of the late rapper Tupac Shakur: '*They got money for wars, but can't feed the poor.*'[5] Not surprisingly, the voices of protestors in different parts of the country were muffled and bodies trampled in an effort to drown dissent, which exposed the sacrosanct bond between economic apartheid and perpetual war.

Peace: A critical moral imperative

We must have research for peace. … It would embrace the outstanding problems of morality. The time has come for [our] intellect … to win over the immoral brutality and irrationality of war and militarism.

—Linus Pauling[6]

The search or re-search for peace is often perceived as a one-dimensional affair, from which urban peaceniks or global peace movement activists garner intellectual authority. However, the landscape must be understood as far more complicated. On one side of the equation are justifications of advancing militarization made in the name of democracy and peace, where the ends justify the means. On the other side are liberal formulations of peace and peace education, also detached from conditions of human suffering and dreadful inequalities experienced by the majority of the world's population. As such, a critical discourse of peace seldom finds its way into mainstream public school classrooms, despite the presence of a Peace Movement in the United States that has persisted for over thirty years. This is the case because central to a critical politics of peace must be a radical moral imperative, the imperative to transform the contemporary hegemonic apparatus that commonsensically envisions war as essential to peace in the republic.

Even the lyrics of *The Star Spangled Banner*,[7] the national anthem of the United States, expose the hidden curriculum of a national psyche deeply entrenched in a steadfast commitment to the glory of war as essential to the free and the brave.

The United States' national anthem – which children are taught from a very young age to sing in school – at assemblies, at sporting events, along with the pledge of allegiance, contains lines such as the following:

> Whose broad stripes and bright stars through the perilous fight,
> O'er the ramparts we watched, were so gallantly streaming?
> And the rockets' red glare, the bombs bursting in air,
> Gave proof through the night that our flag was still there;

and:

> What is that which the breeze, o'er the towering steep,
> As it fitfully blows, half conceals, half discloses?

It also tells that
> their blood has washed out their foul footsteps' pollution.

These lyrics and national codes, not to mention violent or patriarchal scriptures from the Bible (i.e. Lev. 26:29 or Tim. 2:12 or Deut. 25:12), are bound to influence how children think, consciously or unconsciously, and how they behave in the world. Repetitive recitations shape a national collective psyche so as to uncritically accept the symbiosis of war and triumph, and an unflinching allegiance to biblical assertions. Through commonsensical reproduction in schools, churches and other public venues, such reified notions bypass consciousness, leaving an ethnocentric patriotic zeal and the savage inequalities that result unquestioned.

Accordingly, what should characterize critical peace education efforts is precisely a stalwart commitment to unmask such unexamined assumptions and to establish political relationships that nurture a deeply communal and emancipatory ethics of justice, liberty and human dignity – all essential to the dialectical exercise of peace in our personal and public lives. Given this critical commitment, a revolutionary practice of peace education attempts to strike at the root of the ideologies and conditions that perpetuate patriarchal fantasies of war and dominance. This signals radical peace initiatives that extend our political reasoning beyond dualisms, abstractions, absolutism or romanticized platitudes and dematerialized refrains, in order to unearth those critical questions of morality buried by the 'free-market' logic of neo-liberalism. A critical peace education demands that we contend with tough moral questions, with the hope that we might move closer towards more humanizing strategies and political solutions, as we struggle collectively to confront the exploitation and domination that preserve the structural roots of violence.

Towards this end, critical approaches to peace education unfailingly retain a dialectic connection to complex interrogations of both peace and violence. This is particularly important in that mainstream or liberal peace studies, although well-meaning and correct in many instances, often fail to substantively acknowledge the deeper historical, cultural, political, and economic asymmetries that persist (which give rise to orchestrated and spontaneous violent outbreaks in civil society), along with campaigns of military aggression in the United States and around the globe. What makes analysing such occurrences more complex is that not all forms of violence can be neatly standardized or distilled into simplistic or one-dimensional proclamations of peace, particularly when such meanings serve to protect ruling configurations of power and privilege.

This dynamic, Paulo Freire contends, is well evidenced where 'the dominant elites consider the remedy [for dissent] to be more domination and repression, carried out in the name of freedom, order, and social peace (that is, the peace of the elites)' (Freire 2005, p. 78).

Thus, they can condemn – logically, from their point of view – the violence of a strike by workers and can call upon the state in the same breath to use violence in putting down the strike. During the Occupy struggles, we witnessed this positivist logic of peace at work in state efforts to dismantle the movement's encampments within cities and on university campuses. The use of pepper spray against students at the University of California Davis[8] and the incarceration of hundreds of occupiers in New York and California were justified by rhetorical claims of their necessity in order to ensure security on the streets and peace on the campuses – messages carefully spun in unison by police, politicians, university officials and the media.

Hence, without thoughtful and grounded engagement with those moral questions associated with the disabling social and material conditions at work in the lives of oppressed communities, traditional Western notions of peace falsely obscure the impact of gross inequalities, by prescribing to a definition of peace that is apolitical, absolute, universal and devoid of concern for the existing societal institutional structures, policies and practices that ultimately provoke manifestations of violence or uprisings. Without interrogating empty notions of peace and war with a critical lens, the underlying truth – that oppressed populations are often thrust into episodes of violent dissent, not of their own making, but, rather, the outcome of an oppressive racializing economy that dehumanizes and strips them of dignity and political self-determination – remains hidden.

Making a peacefully just world possible

When the power of love overcomes the love of power the world will know peace.

—Jimi Hendrix[9]

In order to support the development of transformative peace approaches, educators must be willing to speak of the oppressive silences and historical violence that have remained shrouded by the hegemonic agents of the capitalist state. Unveiling the world requires us to acknowledge the profound historical crimes against humanity – genocide, slavery, colonization, incarceration and material impoverishment – and their enduring consequences upon populations. In so doing, we can potentially labour politically towards just forms of reparation and forge revolutionary practices of peace that can genuinely support the power of the commons.

This entails a critical pedagogy of peace that acknowledges openly that all power relationships among human beings are forged within contradictory terrains of struggle and thus, we require a fundamental political commitment to a revolutionary love,[10] anchored in an emancipatory ethics of self-vigilance, a commitment to global human rights, the collective exercise of dignity and respect, and an embodied solidarity across our differences. More specifically, as suggested above, a fundamental intent of critical peace education constitutes the integration of curricular content, classroom structures and pedagogical approaches that challenge the personal, collective and structural forms of violence at the heart of unbridled militarism, racism, class warfare, gender and sexual oppression and other forms of exclusion. But more importantly, we need a critical pedagogy that can forthrightly unveil, counter and transform a fundamental acceptance of the necessity of aggression and violence to resolve domestic and international disputes associated with geopolitical control of vital natural resources and global supremacy. Had this not been the case, the United States would never have become so bitterly embroiled for decades in calamitous wars and military campaigns in the Middle East and elsewhere.

Hence, educators and peace activists must be willing to raise complex and controversial questions – questions that turn common ideas of war and peace on their proverbial head. This requires that we grapple with the permanent realities of war in the United States and the ideological and structural policies and practices that inform this condition. However, in today's world, where the internationalization of capital has become even more concentrated and callous to human suffering, to do this is simply not enough. We must also work diligently to call for a necessary radical rethinking of peace education within US schools, communities, the nation and around the globe. This demands a perspective and practice of peace anchored in critical principles *and* grounded empirical knowledge[11] that can offer us groundbreaking insights into long-standing cultural, economic and political conditions, which underhandedly impede the progress of peaceful solutions. This is so in that the decolonizing logic required in breaking with hegemonic definitions of peace and war is fundamentally incompatible with the abyssal divide[12] of Western epistemology, which functions to render invisible all that exists outside its culture of domination.

This point, especially, is an ongoing concern, given the manner in which policies and practices within public schools – particularly within working class and racialized communities – are increasingly being utilized as convenient venues for military recruitment. This is clearly visible in the increasing establishment of Junior Reserve Officers' Training Corps (JROTC) programs in public schools,[13] where the military curriculum readily cultivates allegiances to an imperialist vision, while thwarting critical interrogations of pro-military views and their negative impact on both individuals and the larger society. In response, critical peace educators have employed counter-recruitment strategies within vulnerable communities to challenge ideologies and epistemologies of war and violence, as they surface in the everyday lives of students. Moreover, these educators also work to halt the long-standing US military occupation of public school campuses as recruitment sites – where often the only options for impoverished youth of colour are de facto military conscription, the underground economy or incarceration.

Similarly, it is imperative, as Henry Giroux rightly asserts in *The University in Chains*,[14] that important connections and useful critiques regarding the intellectual work of scholars within the corporatized university be made, given that the university functions more and more as an extension of the military – industrial complex. Such critical interrogation points to the ways in which neo-liberal university policies actively sustain the culture of violence and, thus, bolster a permanent economy of war. Through both covert and overt means, the political values and financial priorities of corporate rule have also sought greater control of student intellectual formation, the labour of academics and research agendas, in order to legitimate transnational military imperatives. With a keen eye on profit, control over resources and the use of working-class communities for warfare, the neo-liberal rhetoric of difference has functioned strategically to increase production, maximize commerce, and support the growing needs of US militarization and to sustain the growing financial impact of global violence.

In fact, a recent report entitled *The Most Militarized Universities in America* noted: 'Seventeen powerhouse research universities traditionally supporting the military-industrial complex rank in the top 100.'[15] Some included in this elite group are John Hopkins (#7), Penn State (#15), Georgia Tech (#26), Harvard, Stanford, the Massachusetts Institute of Technology (#47) and the University of Southern California (#21). The US government awarded over $3 billion last year to these schools alone – and rather than studying traditional weapons systems, these universities primarily carry out classified research on intelligence technologies, cyber security and big data analytics, which dramatically requires us to shift how we think of militarization, in the age of social media and increasing virtual existence. Also noteworthy here is the fact that most common academic concentrations for military workers are found in the STEM (Science, Technology, Engineering and Mathematics) field. The current tenacious focus on STEM in universities across the country must also be understood then in terms of the expanding militarization. Rather than relying on superficial interpretations of science as 'the new frontier', critical educators and peace advocates alike must question why the unbridled advancement of STEM today is the preferred area of 'career' choice, when 50 per cent of all STEM jobs do not even require a bachelor's degree.[16]

Key to a critical engagement of peace education is the need for a radically dialectical understanding of how local, regional, national and international conditions are inextricably linked to contradictory perceptions of peace and war. By moving across distinct educational terrains and diverse regions of political unrest around the world, what can become more evident is the manner in which students are socialized, from very early in their academic formation and socialization as citizens, to attach ideologically specific meanings to narratives of peace and war. Such narratives are, more often than not, linked profoundly to those specific power relations, cultural differences and class distinctions that shape students' social location within their own communities and the larger social sphere. To engage important differences requires that critical educators and peace activists remain true to a dialogical political process within their practice. This entails a pedagogy built on Freire's[17] precept of beginning, first and foremost, with the views that students bring to this work, so that commonalities, differences and contradictions can be fleshed out in the community, with an expressed emancipatory purpose of building together a more peaceful, just and loving world.

Of revolution and dreams

How poor is a revolution that doesn't dream.

Amilcar Cabral[18]

The reflections in this chapter have pointed to a variety of issues that must be engaged if we are to work towards a revolutionary understanding of peace. Central to this is our critical capacity to uncover the unexpected ways in which discourses on peace and war are inextricably linked to oppressive ideologies of power that manifest in the everyday. Through such grounded consideration, critical educators can move towards a pedagogy of peace studies that can engage with greater complexity what it means to teach for peace, particularly in light of domestic and global regions where suffering and poverty persist and values of dignity, liberty and critical democratic life seem to remain ever illusive. Given the difficulties under which we must labour to realize a critical peace pedagogy in public schools, it is paramount that critical educators and peace activists passionately and consistently grapple with the contradictions and tensions at work in domesticated notions of peace and war so that we can move beyond prescription, into the complex and murky waters of political domination, economic subordination and the repressive relations of production that incessantly disrupt the possibilities of peace, and from whence violence is born.

Given the very real potential for widespread human destruction, critical educators committed to a critical utopian vision of peace in the world must grapple deeply with a range of policy, curricular, pedagogical and sociological interpretations aimed at generating a robust critical dialogue about peace education locally, nationally and internationally. This demands political reinvention and creative practices of peace education that aim to radically dismantle the hegemonic paradigm of war, where violence is accepted as the predominate solution for resolving conflict. In its place, what is required is a revolutionary paradigm of peace situated *in the everyday*, where issues of human rights, social justice and ecological concerns rightly reframe domestic and international debates towards an emancipatory ethic of community that honours the preciousness of all life.

Nevertheless, we cannot ignore the fact that the culture of violence and war is so intensely reified and embedded within our psyches that it is often difficult for many, even the more radically inclined, to not fall prey to a disabling cynicism – where words of hope are quickly dismissed as impossible utopias or idealistic ramblings or romanticized ideals of fools. In this respect, the perspective offered here is well grounded in a profound belief in revolutionary possibility – a possibility that is born from our capacity to dream, as Cabral would attest 'a possible dream'.[19] In that all revolutionary possibility is born from the belief that, although incomprehensible in the present moment, we as human beings are capable of transforming the social and material conditions of our lives, constructing together more just and peaceful dynamics and structures of human existence – not as absolute or totalizing phenomenon, but, rather, as the outcome of our emancipatory labour.

Inherent in such a transformative paradigm of peace, then, is also an important political and pedagogical message – one that calls for a deep analysis of both historical and contemporary conditions, along with the civic courage and uncompromising commitment to revolutionary action, so that we, as educators and cultural citizens, may work both philosophically *and* practically *on the ground* to persistently challenge the oppressive culture of war in our society. And, by so doing, we can breathe life into an emancipatory ethics of peace and into a culture where policies and practices aligned to social justice, human rights and economic democracy can flourish in our schools, our communities, our societies and the world. Underlying this timely call is the recognition that through the power of collective political commitment, critical consciousness and the *power of love*, a democratic, just and peaceful world is possible.

Notes

1   From the poem 'The Great Pax Whitie' included in the recording, *Nikki Giovanni: Truth is on its Way*. The text can be accessed on Poetry Foundation website. See: http://www.poetryfoundation.org/poem/177829.

2   In Jean Paul Sartre (1951). *Le Diable es le Bon Dieu*. Fammarion et Cie.

3   In Jean Maalouf (2007). *If We See What They See: Peace According To…* Blomington, IN: AuthorHouse, p. 28.

4   According to the *Dictionary of Military and Associated Terms*. US Department of Defense (2005), 'theatre of war' is defined by the National Command Authorities or the geographic combatant commander, as the area of air, land and water that is, or may become, directly involved in the conduct of the war, its theatre of operations.

5   From Tupac Shakur lyrics, *Keep Ya Head Up*. See: https://play.google.com/music/preview/Tifjep6dmrenof7nemoxhen4uda?lyrics=1&utm_source=google&utm_medium=search&utm_campaign=lyrics&pcampaignid=kp-lyrics

6 In George Savage (2003). *War of Peace*. Toronto, Canada: Sound and Vision, p. 111.

7 See: http://www.usa-flag-site.org/song-lyrics/star-spangled-banner/

8 See: http://web.archive.org/web/20111224055409/http://edition.cnn.
   com/2011/11/20/us/california-occupy-pepperspray/index.html?

9 From a bumper sticker, available on Amazon, see: http://www.amazon.com/Jimi-
   Hendrix-Overcomes-Peace-Sticker/dp/B001AZLQ8O/ref=sr_1_cc_1?s=books&ie
   =UTF8&qid=1323205291&sr=1-1-catcorr

10 Darder, A. (2015). *Freire & Education*. Routledge: New York.

11 Carr, P. R. and Porfilio, B. J. (2012). *Educating for Peace in a Time of Permanent
   War: Are Schools Part of the Solution or the Problem?* New York: Routledge.

12 de Sousa Santos, B. (2007). 'Beyond Abyssal Thinking'. *Eurozine*. See: http://www.
   eurozine.com/pdf/2007-06-29-santos-en.pdf

13 See: http://www.rethinkingschools.org/archive/29_01/29_01_mcgauley.shtml

14 Giroux, H. (2007). *University in Chains: Confronting the Military-Industrial-
   Academic Complex*. New York: Routledge.

15 See: https://news.vice.com/article/the-most-militarized-universities-in-america-a-
   vice-news-investigation

16 Rothwell, J. (2013). *The Hidden STEM Economy*. Washington, DC: The Brookings
   Institution.

17 Friere, *op. cit.*

18 In Shor, I. and Freire, P. (1987). *A Pedagogy for Liberation*. South Hadley, MA:
   Bergin & Garvey, p. 186.

19 Ibid.

References

Carr, P. R. and Porfilio, B. J. (2012). *Educating for Peace in a Time of Permanent War:
   Are Schools Part of the Solution or the Problem?* New York: Routledge.

Darder, A. (2015). *Freire and Education*. Routledge: New York.

Dictionary of Military and Associated Terms (2005). US Department of Defense.

Nikki Giovanni (2004). 'The Great Pax Whitie'. see: http://www.poetryfoundation.org/
   poem/177829.

Giroux, H. (2007). *University in Chains: Confronting the Military-Industrial-Academic
   Complex*. New York: Routledge.

Maalouf, J. (2007). *If We See What They See: Peace According To ...* Bloomington, IN:
   AuthorHouse, p. 28.

Rothwell, J. (2013). *The Hidden STEM Economy*. Washington, DC: The Brookings
   Institution.

Sartre, J. P. (1951). *Le Diable es le Bon Dieu*. Fammarion et Cie

Savage, G. (2003). *War of Peace*. Toronto, Canada: Sound and Vision.

Shor, I. and Freire, P. (1987). *A Pedagogy for Liberation*. South Hadley, MA: Bergin & Garvey, p. 186.

Francis Scott Key. 'The Star-Spangled Banner'. see http://www.usa-flag-site.org/song-lyrics/star-spangled-banner (accessed 21 August 2016).

de Sousa Santos, B. (2007). Beyond Abyssal Thinking. *Eurozine*. See: http://www.eurozine.com/pdf/2007-06-29-santos-en.pdf

Tupac Shakur. 'Keep Ya Head Up'. See: https://play.google.com/music/preview/Tifjep6dmrenof7nemoxhen4uda?lyrics=1&utm_source=google&utm_medium=search&utm_campaign=lyrics&pcampaignid=kp-lyrics

https://news.vice.com/article/the-most-militarized-universities-in-america-a-vice-news-investigation

http://web.archive.org/web/20111224055409/http://edition.cnn.com/2011/11/20/us/california-occupy-pepperspray/index.html?

http://www.rethinkingschools.org/archive/29_01/29_01_mcgauley.shtml

7

The Myth of the Inevitability of War

Clive Zammit

Introduction: Western thought and the culture of war

Ancient Greek cities and settlements faced continuous threats of war, internal strife and natural calamity. Their survival and prosperity was never guaranteed. The 'permanent possibility of war', which Levinas (1969) considers a characteristic feature of Western thinking, clearly has its roots in the historical realities of the Greek ancestry of this tradition.

To mitigate these ever-present destructive forces, the ancient Greeks appealed to three sibling goddesses, *the Horai* – Eirene, Eumonia and Dike – who represented Peace, Good Law and Justice (Hesiod 1988). In the Greek mindset then, Peace, Good Law and Justice were the three essential pillars on which the survival and prosperity of their cities, and therefore civilization, depended (Athanassakis 1983).[1]

While, as descendants of this heritage, we still consider Good Law and Justice as essential to the well-being of our societies, it seems that the third sister, Peace, has been vastly overshadowed and largely forgotten. While Good Law and Justice remain among our highest values, our approach to peace is, by stark contrast, generally characterized by scepticism, if not outright cynicism.

Eirene has been relegated to the status of the fragile and reclusive sister who, as some myths would have it, Zeus had to rescue from earth and lift to the realm of the gods. In Eirene's absence, war has established its lasting hold on our world view.

The main objective of this chapter is to throw light on how, and to what extent, underlying semiological and linguistic structures and mechanisms shape our reality and condition our relations within it. It will analyse and expose linguistic structures that enable and support those shifts in value priorities which allow myths such as that of the impossibility of peace to acquire their tenacity. Exposing the power of such myths highlights the urgency of developing and adopting tools and strategies across all educational sectors which would impart the media and image literacy skills required for more informed and less passive consumption of the ever more ubiquitous media products and events.

By drawing on Wittgenstein's insights on the interactions of different discourses, and on Barthes' semiological analysis of first-order and second-order signification, I will argue that the emergence of the myth of the impossibility of peace is the result of a subtle hybridization of the two first-order discourses of History and Mythology from which a new Mytho-Historical hybrid discourse emerges.

The chapter presents the hypothesis that the tenacity of the belief that war is inevitable is based on the emergence of this second-order hybrid discourse, which constructs this reality and imposes it as a necessary fact. This hypothesis is supported by an analysis of the constitution of the discourses of Myth and History, from which this hybrid emerges.

While this piece does not present a formula for the averting of war and the establishment of world peace, it attempts to raise awareness of linguistic structures that support and empower the destructive discourse and mindset of war. Such awareness is a prerequisite that may enable our continued vigilance, identifying and exposing such myths, and thereby weakening their hold. It is an awareness that ought to be present in any pedagogic initiative aimed at achieving peace.

The multidimensionality of discourse: A Wittgensteinian perspective

Wittgenstein's *Philosophical Investigations* (2001) opens with a passage from Augustine's *Confessions* in which the saint relates his early memories of how he learnt the use of language. Wittgenstein's aim in quoting this passage is to highlight a very commonly held conception of language – that language consists mainly of names by which objects are pointed out, and that the process of learning a language amounts to learning the names of such objects and using these names correctly. Wittgenstein goes on to argue that such descriptions of language, which reduce its functions to one of pointing out objects or ideas merely by calling out their names, are simplistic and inadequate. In order to highlight the actual complexity of language and the multilayered discourses it enables and employs, Wittgenstein uses a number of analogies, the most popular being the language-game analogy. He also uses the analogy of language as the instrument panel in a locomotive cabin.

By drawing an analogy between language and games, Wittgenstein argues that the application of different sets of rules and modes of engagement allows us to use language to engage in and construct different types of discourses. Modification may create new types of discourse, in the same way that modifications in sets of rules give us the possibility to play different board games while still using the same board and pieces. In the same way that the same ball can be used to play a variety of ball games, the same words and sentences may be used to engage in discourses whose objectives can vary from merely pointing out objects to discussing abstract concepts and ideas. Shifts in the rules of engagement allow for the possibility of the same words and sentences to be employed in different 'language-games'. Wittgenstein notes that there are 'countless different kinds of use of what we call "symbols", "words", "sentences". This multiplicity is not something fixed, given once for all; but new types of language, new language-games, as we may say, come into existence, and others become obsolete and get forgotten' (2001, p. 10e).

Wittgenstein mentions numerous examples of possible 'language-games' such as 'reporting an event', 'making up a story', 'making a joke', 'giving orders, and obeying them', among others. Each of these language-games or types of discourses, such as historical discourse, religious discourse and scientific discourse, functions in accordance to specific rule variants that may not always be explicitly stated or made obvious. When engaging in historical discourse, for example, it is expected that statements are factual and possibly backed by some recorded or witnessed evidence. In the case of religious discourse, the requirement for evidence takes on a modified or different meaning from that of historical discourse. Hence, modes of verification such as an appeal to divine revelation or reference to scripture may be accepted in the 'language game' of religious discourse.

Through the language-game analogy, Wittgenstein thus draws our attention both to the multidimensionality of language and to its dynamic state of change and development. However, while the game analogy works well in drawing our attention to the fluidity, open-endedness and complexity of language, it may also give the impression that, like conventional games, language-games serve merely for entertainment or playful purposes. To counter this impression, Wittgenstein emphasizes that the game analogy holds for all discourses equally, and it is not intended to draw distinctions between serious or authentic discourses and less serious or playful discourses. At the level of language, the distinction between 'the real world' and the 'play world' does not apply. Each of these discourses has its specialized function and should be regarded as one of multiple layers or different facets, each contributing to the complexity and wealth of what Wittgenstein calls a 'form of life'. In other words, it is the multiplicity of such discourses, the way they engage, overlap and interact that makes a 'form of life' possible.

This complexity and complementarity of the different discourses is further highlighted in Wittgenstein's analogy of the locomotive's instruments:

> It is like looking into the cabin of a locomotive. We see handles all looking more or less alike. (Naturally, since they are all supposed to be handled.) But one is the handle of a crank which can be moved continuously (it regulates the opening of a valve); another is the handle of a switch, which has only two effective positions, it is either off or on; a third is the handle of a brake-lever, the harder one pulls on it, the harder it brakes; a fourth, the handle of a pump: it has an effect only so long as it is moved to and fro. (2001, p. 6e)

For the locomotive to run efficiently and safely, it requires that these different specialized mechanisms, cranks, switches, pumps, etc., function well and are handled and used appropriately. Similarly, the success and efficiency of our use of language depends on our ability to operate and employ the different subgames, or discourses that make it up. Each specific discourse adds to the overall efficiency, range and functions of language, in the same way that each of the mechanisms in the locomotive – brakes, accelerators, gears, whistles, etc. – adds to its range and function.

A key point of Wittgenstein's analogy is that the levers by which the locomotive driver handles these mechanisms all look very similar, even though the internal mechanisms that they operate may be very different. Similarly, in language, different discourses though 'looking more or less alike' may also hide different constitutive features and functions. A lack of awareness of such differences in language users may be as problematic and possibly as dangerous as a lack of familiarity regarding the different uses and functions of locomotive levers in its driver. Thus, by putting the focus on the differences in the internal (hidden) mechanisms of discourses, the locomotive metaphor highlights the importance of awareness in language users of the functions and requirements of the discourses they may be engaged in. It also hints at the dangers of a lack of such awareness.

Wittgenstein's analysis and the insightful analogies to the diversity and complexities of the discourses that make human language possible, as well as the dangers that may result from conflating one type of discourse with another, will now be employed to carry out a structural analysis of the two discourses: the discourse of History and the discourse of Myth. Following this analysis, I will turn to Barthes' semiological analysis of the structure of first-order and second-order signs, to investigate the hybridization of these two discourses and to further investigate the consequences of such a hybridization.

Structure and content analysis of the discourse of Myth and the discourse of History

The aim of this section is to uncover the distinguishing structural features and rules of engagement that are specific to the discourses of myth and history. In his treatment of classical Greek mythology, Roberto Calasso (1994) starts each telling of the different mythological episodes of abductions of women between Asia and Europe with the question: 'But how did it all begin?'

Herodotus' (historical) claim that the everlasting war between Europe and Asia is the consequence of the childish reaction of the Hellenes who 'set the first example of war' in response to the abduction of Helen, is clear evidence that his histories draw their nourishment from Mythology. Conversely, the discovery and excavations of the archaeological site of Troy show that the taproots of myth are intertwined with those of history. It is thus clear that we find no clear-cut distinction between the discourses of Mythology and History at the point where it all begins.

The discourses of myth and history are not, never were, and will probably never be completely distinct from one another. Like two intertwining spirals, they continually merge, overlap and separate, drawing nourishment both from their common traits and from the differences in their structures and content. Yet, we have to be aware of the different nature of the two discourses. The hybridization of Myth and History discussed in this chapter is not meant to suggest that this is a one-off event that took place at a particular point in time. Rather, what is suggested here is that although the cross-fertilization of the two discourses is an ongoing perpetual dynamic, nevertheless, a closer analysis of the ways such cross-fertilization does occur, can help us understand our own contemporary myths (including those related to peace and war) and therefore enable us to respond more reflectively when we are called to action by events that are projected through, and shaded by these hybridized discourses. Critical Education cannot ignore these two types of discourse and contemporary myths, and ought to enable reflective responses to these phenomena.

Analysis of the discourse of myth

What is myth? Much has been written about the uses and the functions of mythology. Early nineteenth-century theories of myth mostly regard mythologies as primitive attempts at proto-science, proto-cosmology or proto-religion (Ackerman 2002; Dowden 1992; Segal 1996), which were eventually superseded by the more mature and competent forms of these discourses. By contrast, twentieth-century theories tend to view mythology as a type of discourse that has its own distinctive functions, which remain relevant irrespective of the level of development of other discourses. In this view, mythology enriches the diversity and potential of language, by adding another layer to the various other possible ways of engaging with our lifeworld (Segal 1996; Stiegler 1994; Vernant 1988). Furthermore, while acknowledging that contemporary myths differ from classical myths in that they are shaped by our contemporary reality and reflect our own world view (Vernant 1988), more recent theorists (Dowden 1992; Segal 1996) regard the main functions of Mythological discourse, namely its explanatory and social cohesion functions, to have remained unchanged from those of classical mythology.

For the purpose of this chapter, Mythology is regarded as one discourse among others that together constitute our linguistic toolbox, which we then employ in the construction of our culture or form of life. This enables our understanding of reality and guides our relations with it. The view of mythology on which this argument is based is that while the gods and heroes that populate contemporary myths may be very different from those of Greek mythology, the concerns, themes and structures of our own myths remain very much the same.

The structure of myth – Thematic necessity

Mythological discourse, whether classical or contemporary, is characterized by the retelling of narratives drawn from an interconnected collection of tales, most of the contents of which are already familiar to the audience. Because the narrative content of mythology does not claim strict factual correspondence to known or evidenced historical events, each retelling of these tales allows space for changes and modifications to be introduced to the narrative. These content modifications, in turn, allow for different interpretations so that the same themes, or reworked familiar narratives, will 'reveal' truths, meanings or explanations that are in tune with the particular context and contextual requirements of each particular occasion of its retelling (Calasso 1994; Stiegler 1994; Vernant 1988). While the content may vary, the theme around which it is woven remains unchanged, thus giving the retelling a familiarity that allows both recognition and acceptance of the tale, as well as the possibility of new interpretations and meaning.

The theme of the abduction of prize women would be an example of one such thematic structure, which functions as a narrative scaffold that can be assembled and dismantled repeatedly to be reused in different occasions and locations and to serve different purposes. Using the familiarity of the theme as a supporting scaffold, the mythologist or storyteller can work around the tale, reshaping its contours and carefully reconstructing its details, even giving it new reach and new meanings without weakening or compromising its foundational structure.

The themes of the survival and return of the abandoned child, or that of the gift which turns out to be a curse, are other examples that emerge repeatedly not only in classical mythology, but also in our own popular narratives. The iteration of these identifiable themes allows the audience or readers to follow them more securely, and gives them the confidence to accept and engage with the newly introduced twists and adaptations. The familiarity of themes also creates a bond or a resonance between the teller, the audience and the tale. It provides the footholds or the rhythm that entices that entices the audience to be drawn into the narrative space with enough confidence to engage with and embrace novel developments. The continued relevance and development of mythological retellings, therefore, depends on both the *thematic necessity* and the changes in narrative content that this structure allows. This possibility of introducing changes and modulations in the narrative content and meanings within the fixed thematic structures of known myths will be called the *interpretative possibility* of myth.

The content of myth – Interpretative possibility

While the structure of mythological discourse is characterized by *thematic necessity*, its narrative content allows for *interpretative possibility*. Thus the structure and content of mythological discourse work together to produce that minimal difference required for the continued emergence of meaning in different contexts. Interpretative possibility gives myth its tenacity even in the face of the emergence of the seemingly competitive and more accomplished discourses such as those of philosophy, science or history: 'But Zeus chose the copy; he wanted that minimal difference which is enough to overturn order and generate the new, generate meaning. ... All Zeus' other adventures, all Hera's other vendettas, would be nothing more than further heaves on the same wheel of necessity which Hera set rolling to punish the woman most like herself' (Calasso, p. 24).

One example of interpretative possibility is provided by the well-known classical myth of Pandora and her box. It is common knowledge that Pandora let all the curses fly out of her jar, but Hope (*Elpis*) remains trapped inside. This is part of the rigid thematic necessity of the myth, which draws on the familiar thematic structure of gift exchange running through this myth. This was initiated by Prometheus's disguised gift of bones to Zeus (Hesiod 1988; Vernant 1988). In contrast to the strict thematic necessity, the narrative content related to hope, allows for the myth's wealth of interpretative possibility (Verdenius 1971). Why does hope remain in the jar? Is it locked away from the reach of humans, or is it kept in store for them? Is hope to be considered as another curse like strife and death? Is it left in the jar to make human life possible despite its futility? Or is it trapped out of humanity's reach, thus adding to the misery of the human condition? 'In fact, the story of Pandora is best known for its presentation of Hope (Elpis), the precise meaning of which has puzzled commentators from antiquity' (Bartlett 2006).

Examples of the *interpretative possibility* of mythological discourse abound. Was Helen seduced or abducted? Was Prometheus the saviour of mankind, or was he its curse? Would mankind have been better off had the lover of man not meddled with Zeus to give them the gift of fire? The *structure* and *content* of mythological discourse can thus be said to be characterized by *thematic necessity* and *interpretative possibility,* respectively.

The discourse of history – The parting of the ways

For the Western tradition, History and Mythology part ways around the fifth century BC with the writings of Herodotus of Halicarnassus. Less than two centuries before Herodotus, Hesiod (c. 700 BC) would start his myths by invoking the muses, the daughters of memory, praising them for their gifts of 'glorious song' and 'good judgment worthy of noble princes' (Theogony, c. 700 BC).

In direct contrast, Herodotus launches a new genre of discourse by proclaiming his authority on his accounts and insists on the factual nature of their contents:

This is the Showing forth of the Inquiry of Herodotus of Halicarnassos, to the end that neither the deeds of men may be forgotten by lapse of time, nor the works great and marvelous, which have been produced some by Hellenes and some by Barbarians, may lose their renown; and especially that the causes may be remembered for which these waged war with one another. (Herodotus 1954, p. 1)

Hesiod and Herodotus inhabit different regions of an era in which the world view shifted from the mythological to the philosophical (Vernant 1988). Hesiod seeks inspiration, placing himself within the flow of a dance whose source is beyond his own self and his memory. His song is the song of the Muses for whom he is the instrument through which they bestow wisdom and harmony. He is the singer of myths whose source lies beyond the knowledge and memory of mortals.

In stark contrast, Herodotus' opening declaration stamps his authority. The sources of his narrative are his own searches and efforts, and his stated objective is the conquest of memory over forgetfulness. The sources of these narratives will no longer be lost in myth, nor will they be sought in the inspirations granted by the muses of forgetfulness. History starts by identifying and proclaiming its sources and explicitly cutting itself from the source of myth.

Modelled on Herodotus' proclamation, historical discourse consists in the recording of historically significant events with the aim that these events become part of cultural memory. This discourse adds another tool to the linguistic toolbox, with its aim being to supplement living memory and create a recorded narrative of the past that is based on evidence-based records of historically significant events.[2] This requirement for recorded evidence is what gives the discourse of history its distinctive structure. *Evidence-based facts* form the underlying structure of historical discourse.

While the requirement for evidence gives structure to this discourse, the content that fills this structure and completes the narrative is made up of *contingent events* of historical significance. The contingence of these events, the possibility that things could also have happened otherwise, is essential for their historical significance.

What may be of historical significance is not the fact that this or that particular monarch or leader died. That humans, no matter how important they may be, must die, is a necessary fact. What may give this necessity its historical significance may be the contingent circumstances of that particular death. The fact that the king died, sad as it may be, has no historical significance in itself. All humans die, kings included. The king's death teaches us nothing. It reveals nothing. It is the contingent facts surrounding this particular. What is historically significant may be whether the king lived to a ripe old age and died peacefully, or that he died in battle, or was poisoned by a treacherous rival. It is this contingency of the events of history that we draw on when we regard history, or use it, as a source of indication of how events may possibly play out. History is about important events that happened, which may not have happened, or may have happened otherwise.

The condition or requirement of *evidence-based facts* distinguishes history from mythological discourse. This rule constitutes the *formal structure* of historical discourse. The *narrative content* that fills this structure and completes historical discourse is made up of *contingent historical events*.

The structures and content of the two discourses of Mythology and History can thus be presented in a comparative grid as follows:

	Formal structure	Material narrative content
Mythology	Thematic necessity	Interpretative possibility
History	Evidence-based facts	Contingent historical events

The transformation of discourse

Having analysed the discourses of Myth and History, and presented them as two related language-games (Wittgenstein 2001) with distinct formal structures and narrative contents, we can now show how elements of the two discourses can merge to form a hybridized discourse. The following presentation of this process of hybridization draws heavily on Barthes' analysis of the semiological process by which linguistic signs, such as words or pictures, are 'hijacked' and put through a transformation process from which they re-emerge with newly acquired persuasive powers of 'myth'. By focusing on Barthes' seminal essay *Myth Today* (1973), and by juxtaposing the process of hybridization with that of Barthes' second-order signification process (the emergence of myth), I will argue that the proposed hybridization of the discourses of myth and history runs parallel to the semiological process described by Barthes.[3] This will also highlight the continued relevance that Barthes' analysis for our understanding of the power that myths such as that of the inevitability of war bear on our own cognitive processes and the resulting modes of our engagements with reality.[4]

In *Myth Today*, Barthes describes myth as 'a mode of signification', a way in which language and its use refer to our reality or lifeworld. Myth is a special type of speech with its own features, which distinguish it from other types of speech. Myth is a second-order signification, which emerges through a parasitic hijacking of first-order linguistic signs. A first-order sign may be anything that can be endowed with meaning: 'language itself, photography, painting, posters, rituals, objects, etc.' (1973, p. 123). At the first-order level, signs associate a signifier with a signified concept. For example, the signifier DOG, which may be the spoken word or a picture or even the sound of a dog barking, is associated with a signified concept that is formed through the interaction of a number of features such as 'pet', 'domestication', 'protection', 'friend', 'fear', 'growl', etc. The association of the signifier with the signified results in the emergence of the sign with its multilayered meanings. This association and the emergent meanings of the sign are, therefore, also dependent on the context and the contingent factualities within which it is made.

The process of myth formation (in the Barthian sense) takes hold of first-order signs, empties them of all contingent references, and then uses them to build new associations between them and ahistorical (timeless) concepts. In this way, myths both construct and present a new reality in which these contingent facts are endowed with unquestionable necessity. Since there is no outward change in the sign itself, the transformation in its level of signification (from one of contingent associations to one of necessary impositions) is subtle and unobserved:

> In passing from history to nature myth acts economically: it abolishes the complexity of human acts, it gives them the simplicity of essences, it does away with all the dialectics, with any going back beyond what is immediately visible, it establishes a world without contradictions because it is without depth, a world wide open and wallowing in the evident, it establishes a blissful clarity. (1973, p. 156)

Consider an example Barthes gives. An object, say a red rose, can act as a signifier that, when associated with the concept 'passion', can take on the function of a linguistic sign, one which in this case Barthes calls 'passionified roses'. At the start of this process of first-order signification, the signifier, the rose, is empty of meaning. The rose itself is arbitrary in its significance; it could mean anything or nothing. By its association with a signified concept (passion or love), the sign emerges as filled with meaning. Meaning (the content of a sign), therefore, emerges from the association of an arbitrary (empty) signifier and a concept. But this emergence of meaning, as well as the success of its use or conveyance is also dependent on the particular context in which it is embedded: 'The meaning (of the first order language sign: the word or picture) is already complete, it postulates a kind of knowledge, a past, a memory, a comparative order of facts, ideas, decisions' (1973, p. 127).

The success of the 'passionification' of the roses depends on contingent facts such as, to take just one example, the way they are presented or offered (say in literature or movies). It is not difficult to envisage how different shades or nuances of any of the contingencies of the same event of an offer of roses, could easily change the sign from one of passion into one of ridicule, insult or cruelty. Even when the context and the build-up is right, there can still be room for multiple shades and levels of interpretation of the same linguistic sign.

By contrast, in the second order of signification (involving the process of shifting the sign to the force of myth), this openness or possibility is drained out and the sign is associated with an ahistorical concept. This robs the myth of any space for interpretation or nuance: 'When it becomes form, the meaning leaves its contingency behind; it empties itself, it becomes impoverished, history evaporates' (1973, p. 127).

At this level, roses, irrespective of context or history, must *necessarily* signify passion. Passion is no longer *signified by the roses*, an association requiring history and context. Passion becomes *the very nature of roses*. Within the construction of the myth, the association between the signifier and the signified loses the arbitrariness of a linguistic sign, and becomes a naturalized connection: 'We reach here the very principle of myth: it transforms history into nature' (1973, p. 140).

Myth, therefore, does not signify a possible association; rather, it notifies a nature, proclaiming that the nature of roses is necessarily passion. In contrast to the arbitrariness and openness of first-order signification, myth: 'makes us understand something and it imposes it on us' (1957, p. 126). It not only points out a fact, but also makes that fact a necessary fact. All gifted red roses are naturally, and must necessarily be, 'passionified'.

The hybridization of myth and history

The insights on the effects and consequences of the shift from first-order to second-order semiological levels drawn from Barthes' analysis can now be used as a model to analyse the parallel process at the discourse level, whereby the first-order discourses of history and myth merge into the suggested second-order mytho-historic hybrid discourse. This analysis will throw light on the changes that take place in the internal mechanisms of the two discourses and show how these changes give the second-order mytho-historic discourse its power to announce and impose reality.

In his famous analysis of the picture of 'the negro saluting the French flag', Barthes (1973) holds that the shift to the second level of signification drains the picture of its historical content and transforms or refills the emptied sign with a natural and universal connection between the signifier (the image content of the picture) and the signified concept (loyalty to the French flag). If we shift the same analysis from the semiological to the discourse level, we find that the picture would pertain to historical discourse since it portrays an evidence-based fact of a (potentially) historically significant event, namely that of the official raising of the French flag at a particular ceremony in which at least one French military man was black. It therefore fulfils both the structural requirement (factual evidence) and the content requirement (historically significant *contingent* event) that together make up historical discourse.

It is clear from Barthes' analysis that it is the *historic contingency* of the event (the content of historical discourse) that is being drained out of this picture. As a result of this draining of its historical contingency, the 'historical' picture acquires its mythical power by taking on aspects of mythological discourse – an appeal to thematic universality – while holding on to the force attributed to it by its evidence base. To be precise, the *contingent nature* of historical content is now associated with the *thematic necessity*, that is, the structure that defines myth.

As a result of this exchange, the evidenced fact of this historical picture is no longer merely the fact that at least one black military member was pictured saluting the French flag, but becomes evidence for a newly established necessary fact, seemingly backed by solid historical evidence; all French subjects, irrespective of their ethnicity or background, universally salute the French flag. The result of this shift from a first-order (historical) discourse to the second-order mytho-historical hybrid discourse can be portrayed schematically as follows:

From the two first-order discourses:

The resultant hybrid discourse emerges from a selective cross-fertilization of formal structures and material narrative contents:

1st order discourse	Formal structure	Material narrative content
Mythology	Thematic necessity	Interpretative possibility
History	Evidence-based facts	Contingent historical events
2nd order hybrid	Formal structure	Material narrative content
Mytho-historic hybrid discourse	Thematic necessity (from mythology)	Contingent historical events (from history)

This discourse analysis shows that at this level, the shift from history to myth is only partial, that the resulting discourse is not a full-blooded myth, but a hybrid discourse that maintains genetic elements of both parent first-order discourses. While the *structural* constitution of the hybrid discourse remains that of myth (*thematic necessity*), the nature of its *content* is taken from history (*contingent historical events*).

It is also essential that through this process of hybridization, some fundamental elements of the first-order discourses are not carried forward but discarded. The formal structural constitution of historical discourse – the requirement for evidence-based fact – does not pass on into the genetic structure of the hybrid as there is, in fact, no evidence that all black military personnel do salute the French flag. The narrative content of myth, that is, the interpretative possibility, is also discarded.

As a result of the discarding of the requirement of evidence-based facts and the possibility of interpretation, the picture thus takes on the mythic power of establishing thematic necessity. Drawing on its new power, the picture now states categorically that all black French soldiers salute the French flag, that this is a natural fact not a historical one, and that it will always be like that. Furthermore, this myth now takes on the further strength that its content is backed by the photographed contingent event which it now endows with necessity. The thematic necessity drawn from the structural form of myth replaces the contingent nature of the event that it shows and gives this event its universal and unquestionable quality.

The constitutive ambiguity of the myth arises from a two-step process whereby 1) it establishes a factual sign: 'Look, this is the French empire' and 2) it establishes this fact as a self-evident, necessary fact, as though it could not have been otherwise: 'Here is undeniable evidence that all subjects respect, and are loyal to, the empire.'

Conclusion

How does this discourse function in the case of the emergence of the myth of the impossibility of peace? At the discourse level, the myth of the inevitability of war is established through the following parallel steps:

> Step 1: It takes hold of a first-order sign, for example, a picture of the shelling of the city of Kobani, or a convoy of armed vehicles advancing through the desert. At this level, the sign says: 'Look, this is an explosion that took place during the shelling of Kobani on the 18th of October 2014.' This sign is emptied of the

contingent contents of the event, thus preparing it to be used as raw material for a new association.

Step 2: The emptied sign is filled with a new signified concept, in this case not a particular explosion, but the fact of war itself. Through this new association, the sign says and shows more than just a contingent event of an explosion during a shelling campaign. By taking on the thematic necessity of myth, the sign now says: 'Look, this is war, here is factual evidence of war, it is a necessary fact that cannot be denied.'

Step 3: The emergence of the myth, through sustained production of signs of war takes on the force of a self-evident necessary fact. It not only indicates that this is war, but 'it also imposes this fact' on nature (Barthes 1973). 'Can you not see it? How can you deny that war is a permanent necessary condition? Here is undeniable evidence of this fact.'

The hybrid constitution of the mytho-historic discourse gives it the constituent qualities required for it to be able to force one to acknowledge the logical necessity of this evidenced fact: '*Look, peace is shattered. It is impossible to establish, and furthermore, to believe in peace is to invite the terrors that may result from naive complacency. Do you still want to maintain that there is a hope for peace? Is this what you want to invite upon us?*' Forced by the weight of such myths and the constant bombardment of images and signs which re-enforce them, educational and opinion forming institutions, feel obliged to endorse them rather than exposing their nature or challenging them.

In one of his recent articles in *The Guardian* newspaper, George Mason (2014) raises some very pertinent questions about the goals and objectives of publishing pictures of war. He highlights the urgency of these questions by pointing out the fact that despite the horrific content of the visual imagery of war that bombards us daily, people still see war as an option and will sanction it even when it is put up to the test of democracy. While I agree with Mason's sharp, informed and compelling analysis of the ethical dilemmas raised by the reporting of war, especially in the light of the dangers that war journalists and their crews face on a daily basis, in this chapter I have been arguing for another reason why war journalism will not stop war. The argument presented here is that the signs used in war journalism, rather than showing the horrific unnecessary absurdity of war, become themselves the second-order signifiers that support the mytho-historic hybridized discourse described above. The language and pictures of war journalism thus act as the signifiers in the construction of the myth of the inevitability of war and the impossibility of peace.

My argument is not a blanket indictment of war photography or war journalism. I think that the signifier does not act alone. It operates within a complex realm of signifiers that act together to form a cultural mindset which projects and nourishes the myth. But awareness of how these myths are constituted and how they operate may allow us to be better equipped to understand them and to expose them. Education, both formal and informal, has an important role in this regard. Critical Education should enable us to unearth the true process of such signifiers and how they came about. We must strive to provide the necessary critical tools, even at the earliest stages of teaching. While remaining informed of unfolding significant events, we will be able to see through their mythic force, and thus loosen the grip of a myth that keeps us enslaved to a constructed reality in which the hope of peace has come to be regarded as not only futile, but also dangerous.

Finally, this analysis should also act as a further reminder of the importance and urgency of continuous efforts to ensure that, in a world where we are continually and relentlessly bombarded by the ubiquitous and ever more insidious media, we are also armed with the intellectual tools required to engage critically and meaningfully with its products.

Notes

1   Athanassakis (1983) argues that in the *Theogony*, Hesiod indicates that the shift from chaos to order, which was the essential foundation required for the possibility of the establishment of human civilization, was brought about largely by the birth of these three sisters, that is, that civilized human life is founded on the birth of Peace, Good Law and Justice.

2   Discussions regarding the possibility of objectivity in recording history (historical epistemology) and the nature of the factuality of events themselves (historical ontology), though interesting and relevant, are beyond the scope of this chapter. The relevant points being highlighted here are how history is generally understood and the accepted rules with which we engage in this discourse.

3   Clarification on the use of the term 'myth' may be required at this point. This term is being used in two senses. In a conventional sense, 'myth' refers to mythological discourse, which would have a narrative constituted of the structure (thematic necessity) and content (interpretative possibility) as analysed in the previous part of this chapter. As used by Barthes, however, this term refers to any linguistic sign, a word, a phrase, a picture, an object, which was altered by the process of second-order signification, as described in *Myth Today*.

4   The structural analysis being presented here, suggesting that language is composed of compartmentalized discourses constituted of content and form, may easily be read and criticized as succumbing to a type of structuralism. While I acknowledge the limits of structuralism and remain wary of its underlying presuppositions regarding ontological features of structures, I would also acknowledge that such structural analyses can also be useful, especially if one heeds Derrida's suggestion that one could conserve 'the old concepts within the domain of empirical discovery while here and there denouncing their limits, treating them as tools which can still be used'. (1993, p. 359).

References

Barthes, R. (1973). *Mythologies*. Translated by A. Lavers. London: Paladin. (Original work published 1957).

Bartlett, R. C. (2006). 'An Introduction to Hesiod's Works and Days'. *The Review of Politics*, 68 (2): 177–205.

Calasso, R. (1994). *The Marriage of Cadmus and Harmony*. Translated by T. Parks. London: Vintage. (Original work published 1988).

Dowden, K. (1992). *The Uses of Greek Mythology*. London: Routledge.

Eliade, M. (1959). *The Sacred and the Profane: The Nature of Religion*. Australia: Harcourt Brace.

Herodotus. (1954). *The Histories*. Translated by A. De Selincourt. London: Penguin.

Hesiod. (1988). *Theogony and Works and Days*. Translated by M. L. West. Oxford: Oxford University Press.

Mason, P. (2014). 'Horrific Pictures Of Dead Bodies Won't Stop Wars'. *The Guardian*. Retrieved from http://www.theguardian.com/commentisfree/2014/nov/23/horrific-pictures-of-dead-bodies-wont-stop-wars.

Stiegler, B. (1994). *Technics and Time, 1: The Fault of Epimetheus*. Translated by R. Beardsworth and G. Collins. Stanford: Stanford University Press.

Verdenius, W. J. (1971). 'Hesiod, "Theogony" 507-216: Some Comments on a Commentary'. *Mnemosyne*, 24 (1): 1–10.

Vernant, J. P. and Vidal-Naquet, P. (1988). *Myth and Tragedy in Ancient Greece*. Translated by J. Lloyd. New York: Zone Books.

Wittgenstein, L. (2001). *Philosophical Investigations*. 3rd Ed. Translated by G. E. M. Anscombe. Oxford, UK: Blackwell Publishing. (Original work published in 1953).

Zammit, C. (2014). 'Responding to the Call of Peace: In Memory of a Future That Might Have Been'. In C. Borg and M. Grech (Eds), *Lorenzo Milani's Culture of Peace; Essays on Religion, Education, and Democratic Life*, pp. 77–90. 1st ed. New York: Palgrave Macmillan.

8

Liberal Peace and Media Debates around the Cases of *Jyllands-Posten* and *Charlie Hebdo*

Carmen Sammut

Introduction

At the turn of the millennium, media reports fixed their attention on terrorist threats to Western centres of power. In the context of post- or neo-colonial relationships, media texts often linked these threats to conflicts in failed or weak states. While the end of the Cold War supposedly ushered in a period of Liberal Peace, Islam and the anti-terror ideology quickly replaced Communism as the new enemy; with 'anti-terrorism' and the 'war on terror' constructing the new Face of Evil. Although the media have a strong potential to nurture dialogue among civilizations, mediated texts often popularized the thesis of a clash of civilizations expounded by Huntington (1996). Clashes among seemingly incompatible cultures became matter of fact in a world of intense global political, economic and social interactions.

This chapter discusses the controversies around the Danish newspaper *Jyllands-Posten* and the French magazine *Charlie Hebdo*. These debates include old issues and emerging dilemmas related to media representations of the Face of Evil. The chapter begins with a historical perspective that explores ways in which states in the past employed the media to advance their ambitions. The two cases will then be considered in relation to this theme and to two different approaches to the exercise of freedom of expression. The libertarian view of freedom of communication will be discussed in relation to waves of anti-Islam hysteria that virtually swept Europe. This approach will be contrasted to the social responsibility approach to communication. The chapter will argue that a return to social responsibility theories of communication may open opportunities for more dialogue and less confrontation, and so enhance peace on national, regional and global levels.

Selling war: The rise of propaganda and political communication strategies

While the realist tradition of International Relations dictated that foreign policy should be based on rational decisions, not on 'the support of a public opinion whose preferences are emotional' (Morgenthau 1978, p. 558), in liberal democracies the state needs to legitimize its decisions with 'the people'. The First World War was considered as the first public relations war. In war, truth became the first casualty, as aptly experienced by George Orwell (1938) during his coverage of the Spanish Civil War. In the twentieth century, the word 'propaganda' turned into a derogatory term to the extent that the United Nations General Assembly of 1947 passed a resolution that acknowledged that propaganda undermines peace and provokes acts of aggression (Resolution 110/11).

Nonetheless, as soon as the Allies fell out with the Soviet Union, some of the fiercest battles of the Cold War were fought by propagandists. Thussu (2000) describes the 'battle of the airwaves' when radio and even television broadcasts were used by both superpowers to advance their agenda in their respective spheres of influence. As the battle-lines of the ideological war were drawn, the Cold War spread to the Third World where Western prevalence over the information flow was frequently resented, particularly when the developmental efforts and interests of newly independent states were misrepresented or ignored.

By the 1970s, politicians in many liberal democracies had become more media savvy and employed impression-management consultants to help them deliver their messages. In the United States, the political class needed to react to the defeat in Vietnam, a defeat that was blamed by some on the media. This was the first televised war, and distressing news reports helped galvanize the pacifist movement. During this war, it transpired that the media had the power to set the agenda and influence political outcomes whenever there were severe cracks within the military and political elite (Hallin 1986).

Similarly, in the 1980s, the Soviet Union employed media strategists to rebut years of demonization of the Soviet leadership; constructing a charismatic and appealing image of Mikhail Gorbachev. Together with substantive reforms, Gorbachev's new packaging rendered the 'Soviet threat' anachronistic and American rhetoric irrelevant (McNair 1995). Superpower summitry brought together leaders at the highest level and media exposure encouraged both sides to break some diplomatic deadlocks. Positive media hype may have helped to raise expectations and mobilize support for peacemaking processes. The fall of the Berlin Wall and the collapse of the Soviet bloc became what Dayan and Katz (1992) termed as 'media events' that were broadcast live to a wide global audience.

The end of the Cold War coincided with the rise of CNN, which facilitated the live coverage of history just as the world appeared to be momentarily unipolar. New conflicts emerged and in 1991, CNN became the eyes and ears of the world during *Operation Desert Storm* in Iraq. It was soon followed by global television channels like BBC World. Both later served as models for the Qatari station *Al Jazeera*. These channels are significant sources of 'soft power', having 'the ability to affect others to obtain the outcomes one wants through attraction rather than coercion or payment' (Nye 2008, p. 94).

Leading international figures retrospectively acknowledged that they were influenced by CNN (Gilboa 2005). Media scholars started toying with the 'CNN Effect theory', which holds that in the post-Cold War era, global television had become a dominating actor. This suggested that real-time television accelerates the momentum of international events and exerts pressure on both policymakers and diplomats, but not vice versa. Such assertions were however, empirically challenged by Livingston and Eachus (1995) who found that diplomatic and bureaucratic efforts preceded news coverage, that the international agenda was still state-centric rather than media-centric. In spite of professional considerations and technological advancements that have rendered old-style censorship obsolete in war and peace, the political elites still exert ample subtle power to manage information and construct powerful images that influence people's behaviour and thought – images like those of the Face of Evil. International journalists are still susceptible to news-management and cueing. As Robinson (2000) confirmed, it is only when policy is ambiguous and communicated ineffectively that the media are more likely to determine (rather than merely influence) the public agenda and take an immensely powerful role. Thus, in general, there is mutual influence between media and the political establishment. This mutual influence between media and politics is not always conducive to peace.

The media in the era of liberal peace

It is often assumed that the world has entered the era of Liberal Peace. In international relations, this approach holds that democracy and human rights may secure long-term peace and security. In the era of Liberal Peace, the establishment of democratic institutions is prioritized, together with the setting up of market economies, even when old tensions and polarization continue to be a cause of conflict and to undermine peace processes in many parts of the world. Coercion and military force are still employed when major Western powers feel the need to resort to their use. Yet, Western media often contribute to the construction of consensus around the idea that democracies have a lesser propensity to violence than other political set-ups.

Some suggest that Liberal Peace is a tool for extending the reach of neo-liberal economic policies (Salih 2009). In the era of Liberal Peace, developing countries are frequently forced to embrace free trade and foreign investment, in line with the 'trade-not-aid' mantra of Reaganism and Thatcherism. This occurs in a context of 'a major commitment to a new geopolitical order, swelling military expenditure, "hard power" and the construction of a ring of bases, client states and dictators and ... if necessary, direct military intervention in humanitarian disguise. On the "soft" side, it involv[es] the promotion of "the American dream" and way of life as a universal global commodity' (Hall 2010, p. 716).

Global media businesses have flourished in this context. A small number of Western-based media oligarchies gained control of media structures across borders and nurtured a rather monopolistic media market that reinforced the notion of liberal peace and the new geopolitical order that ensued. Critics like Tahranian (2002) and McChesney (2008) lament that while media pluralism is deemed to be a significant factor in democratization processes, oligopolies have, in fact, come into being, undermining media diversity. As a result, the mediatic world is largely ruled either by state-sponsored media or by commercial media oligopolies. Challenges to Western prevalence came, to varying degrees of success, from stations like MBC (Saudi Arabia), Al Jazeera (Qatari), Telesur (Venezuelan), Russia Today (Russian) and CCTV (Chinese) – all financed by powerful states eager to win the hearts and minds of international audiences, while hoping to set or influence the international agenda.

Western media organizations continue to advocate the liberal peace-building narrative, even though dozens of new wars are being fought and intra-state wars are increasingly being internationalized. Mainstream media frequently legitimize international intervention in these conflicts. Concomitantly, inexpensive warfare and access to new media technologies permits warlords to spread their ideologies and to mobilize support. Demonizing some party or other may play a role in such legitimization.

Media and the anti-terror ideology

As Manoff (1997) suggested, media practitioners must identify ways in which they can become instruments of dialogue, promoting human rights, publicizing violations of these and facilitating public censure of hate groups. Satire can be a powerful instrument in such regard. The media, however, frequently adopts a different attitude – legitimizing and sustaining war. In the current scenario, mainstream Western media frequently do this through implicitly or explicitly demonizing Islam.

The attacks on the Twin Towers in New York in September 2001 led to the 'war on terror', which was packaged by the media as a 'just war' and led to unilateral military interventions by the United States in Afghanistan and Iraq. The latter was backed by a public campaign that falsely put Saddam Hussein, a secular dictator, in the same basket with Al-Qaeda jihadists. In the United States and Europe, there was already a context that was susceptible to Islamophobia. This had been built up over many years, the storming of the American embassy in Tehran (1979), the First Gulf War (1991) and the bombing of the World Trade Centre (1993) being important milestones. By 2001, American news media were already prone to portray Islam as a monolithic entity,[1] synonymous with terrorism and religious hysteria (Said 1996). Islamophobia reached new heights after the attacks of September 2001 with approximately one billion Muslims being depicted as potential terrorists, a label that soon groomed a broader and deeper anti-Western sentiment as a reaction (Thussu 2006).

Mainstream media repeatedly failed to explain to global audiences phenomena like Islamic revivalism. Radical Islam garnered support from underprivileged classes in some countries where urban secular regimes had failed to provide the basic needs of their nations, nations that were themselves on the brink of failures of different sorts. Whereas the Clausewitzian wars of the past advanced state-building, recent privatized intra-state wars are often linked to processes of state disintegration and regional destabilization. Warlords sometimes cater for basic needs like food, shelter and medical assistance, and this earns them support.[2] Apart from economic failures, unemployment, the population explosion and massive rural – urban migration, long-standing historical resentments such as the failure of pan-Arabism became the causes of Muslim revivalism. Already, after the First World War, pan-Arab aspirations faded because of the secret Sykes-Picot Agreement between the British and the French, which segmented the Arab Middle East into two spheres of colonial influence. After the Second World War,

Arab nationalism fuelled some of the aspirations of newly independent states in the Middle East and North Africa. Some of the secular nationalist regimes that took hold of these countries retained power until the revolutions of the so-called 'Arab Spring'. In a media landscape that was under the clutches of these authoritarian regimes, the social media and global media networks encouraged mass mobilization on the streets in favour of reform. The social media helped shape the international media narrative and, in turn, exerted pressures on the international community.

Western media expected Arab states to immediately embrace the liberal democratic model when, in fact, some of the groups involved in the uprisings had a different agenda. Islamist groups challenged the objectives of secular parties, believing that sovereignty resides in God, rejecting individual freedoms and aspiring to a perfect society that resembled the early years of Islam. Mandaville (2014) noted that although there are stark differences among Islamist movements like the Muslim Brotherhood, En-Nahda, Hamas, the Taliban, Al-Qaeda and Boko Haram, there are also common traits between them, which include (a) provision of services that states failed to deliver; (b) leading popular resistance against foreign influence; (c) 'offer[ing] the conflation of Islamism with a variety of sub-national identity formations' (pp. 323–4) and hence providing alternative identities when national identities are increasingly seen to be superseded.

Awareness of these complexities is limited in the West. Instead, a proliferation of stereotyped images infuse media representations of Islam and Muslims. Already in the 1960s, Galtung and Ruge (1965) had empirically established that media texts were frequently influenced by propaganda and public relations that dehumanize the enemy and render rapprochement difficult. Media workers often internalize the 'us' against 'them' distinctions, which become matter-of-fact assumptions that impact the everyday practices of professionals and their output. In our day, mainstream Western media frequently trigger hysteria by implicitly portraying all Muslims in the category of 'folk devils' (Cohen 1972) and as a threat to Western society's values and interests. When society panics, apprehensive governments are more prone to deploy drastic measures against particular groups. Ironically, violent fundamentalists themselves thrive on these caricatures.

In Europe, reductionist perspectives of Islam culminated when ISIS combatants took control of Mosul in Iraq and, later, of extensive territory in Syria. As the Islamic State spread its wings, journalist Graeme Wood (2015) described it as a caliphate bigger in size than the United Kingdom. Mass hysteria gripped Europeans when the hidden face of ISIS combatants eclipsed the elusive Al-Qaeda as they appeared on the social media committing acts of carefully choreographed brutality to effectively terrorize societies that had long abandoned public executions.

The *Charlie Hebdo* attacks of January 2015 occurred in the context of fears of ISIS, and should be evaluated in light of this background, even if the attackers were linked to Al-Qaeda rather than the IS. The attackers' goal was more far-reaching and long term than is often presumed; they were aware their violent attacks would foment public hysteria and anti-Muslim prejudice in France and in Europe. Their aim was to further polarize European public opinion as this suited their ambition to further disenchant and radicalize disillusioned members of different Muslim communities in France, Europe and elsewhere. Freedman (2015) observed that it is unlikely these operatives were motivated by the images in the magazine per se: 'They did not shoot down an idea but targets they perceived to be representative of the forces with whom they are in conflict' (n.p.). This was clearly a call for resistance against Western policies and values.

Clashes over *Jyllands-Posten* and *Charlie Hebdo*

Jyllands-Posten and *Charlie Hebdo* hail from European contexts, where the integration of immigrant communities, including Muslims, remains highly problematic. In spite of the stark ideological differences between them, both publications rallied for freedom of the press, which they believe should include the option to offend Muslims by equating Islam with terrorism. The question that will be tackled in what follows is not whether there should be legal limits to satire, particularly with regard to religious representation, but whether in exercising their 'right to offend', they reinforced prevalent conceptions of Islam as the contemporary Face of Evil, and were directly or indirectly supporting the prevalent Western narrative of the post-Cold War period.

The Muhammad cartoons and the clashes that ensued immediately invoked symbolic significance where interpreters read them in ways that reinforced their convictions and perspectives. Hervik (2012) claimed that the newspaper *Jyllands-Posten* had long published anti-Islamic articles in relation to the preservation of Danish identities. In the aftermath of the Twin Tower attacks in New York, these articles mirrored the concerns of leading political figures.

Prime Minister Anders Fogh Rasmussen had launched a 'cultural war' that led to debates on the preservation of Danish values and eventually to strident anti-immigrant discourse.[3] To large segments of the Danish public, the Muslim community started to invoke a type of globalization that for various reasons had to be resisted (Linde-Laursen 2007). In turn, this fomented a type of identity politics that centred on religion.

Religious identity politics is often rejected or mistrusted in those European states that value a secular paradigm in relation to the complex nexus between civil society and democracy. In France, for instance, home of the largest Muslim community in Europe, the political activism of religious groups is seen as a threat to republicanism, which is deemed to be a mainstay of French identity. Republicanism claims that sovereign citizens enjoy a direct relationship with the state, and the notion of *laïcité* is central. Politics that revolves around religious identification is rejected in many circles, including the mainstream media. Religion is sometimes deemed to obstruct Muslims from full integration and is accused of keeping individuals from becoming 'fully French' (Fredette 2014). In spite of their diverse ethnic backgrounds and religious practices, European Muslims are frequently branded by their religion, ignoring or downplaying the other multiple variables that impinge on an individual's identity. This further reinforces the perceived 'clash of civilizations'.

Controversy in Europe first erupted in November 2004 when a Muslim fanatic murdered the Dutch film-maker Theo Van Gogh in protest against *Submission*, a film series that was discontinued. The European press and art world felt under additional pressure to self-censor when an artist who produced a children's book on the life of Muhammad claimed that she was unable to find an illustrator. The clashes on the Muhammad cartoons spiralled against this heated backdrop. The Danish cartoons provoked a war of words after they depicted the prophet Muhammad as a terrorist wearing a Sikh turban that appeared to be nesting a bomb. Apart from considering them as being offensive, many Muslims also considered them provocatively blasphemous since their religion is essentially iconoclastic and the portrayal of the figure of the Prophet is prohibited.

As soon as *Jylland Posten* published the cartoons in September 2005, death threats were made to the Danish cartoonists and there were a few small demonstrations by Danish Muslims that were brushed aside by the government. Prime Minister Rasmussen initially cited freedom of the press when he refused to meet the ambassadors of Islamic nations who were pressing for the prosecution of the newspaper. An escalation immediately scarred Denmark's bilateral relations. By late October 2005, the story of the cartoons, accompanied by allegations of persecution, appeared in Islamic media across the world and on many websites. In January 2006, Saudi Arabia boycotted Danish goods and recalled its ambassador to Copenhagen. At this time, *Jyllands-Posten* published regrets for any offence caused, and Prime Minister Rasmussen met the Muslim ambassadors to try to beseech them to be calm. By then, however, outrage had spilled into the streets of the Muslim world.

Sensing that the Danes were regretting Muslim pressure and the anti-Danish rage, some European newspapers, like *France-Soir* and *Die Welt*, flagged libertarian values and claimed that calls by political and media exponents for social responsibility[4] constituted censorship and/or self-censorship. In response, they republished the provocative cartoons and were followed by other newspapers in Norway, Spain, Italy and Ireland. The internet was widely used to add fuel to the fire: '[The] Danes suddenly found themselves apparently at the centre of Samuel Huntington's harrowing prophecy of a "clash of civilizations"' (Dalgaarda and Dalgaarda 2006, p. 28). As the dispute spiralled out of control, the target of Muslim anger eventually became Europe itself. Iran's supreme leader Ayatollah Ali Khamenei went as far as to allege that the Muhammad drawings were linked to an Israeli conspiracy against Hamas in their bid to win the Palestinian elections in Gaza in early 2006.

It was support for the Danish cartoonists that led to the first attack on the *Charlie Hebdo* Paris offices in 2011. Rallying behind the battle cry of freedom of expression, *Charlie Hebdo* reprinted the Muhammad cartoons. Born in 1970 (and reborn in 1991), this French non-mainstream satirical magazine with a flair for religious irreverence, brought together cartoonists that hailed from the left of the political spectrum, ranging from the far left to anarchism. By branding itself as '*journal irresponsable*', it was always clearly disconnected from the social responsibility model, and had no intention to stop provoking strong reactions from the Muslim community. In March 2006, *Charlie Hebdo* published a declaration (*Manifeste des douze*) by twelve intellectuals wherein these intellectuals, while rejecting Huntington's thesis of a civilizational clash, clamoured for Western liberal and secular perspectives.[5] They claimed that their statement should be considered in the light of a global struggle that pits democrats against theocrats. *Charlie Hebdo*, hence, considered itself a bulwark of secular thought.

As opposed to *Jyllands-Posten*, *Charlie Hebdo* was not manifestly anti-immigrant. Eighteen years earlier, two of the victims of the 7th January 2015 attacks, François Cavanna and Stéphane Charbonnier, had led an initiative to ban Jean Marie Le Pen's anti-immigrant Popular Front Party. The magazine fought anti-immigrant sentiment and populist movements. In spite of its history of resolute resistance to conformism and xenophobia, the magazine still got entangled in reductionist perspectives on Islam; partly attributable to the tendency of political cartoons themselves to resort to commonly accepted assumptions and mainstream symbols to deliver their messages with ease (Pace Nilsen and Nilsen 2008).

The satirical magazine recycled images of the Face of Evil that we often see in mainstream media. By doing so, it reinforced stereotypes of Islam, Muslims and non-Muslims in France and globally. Implicitly, it sustained the clash of civilizations rhetoric it explicitly rejected. It also indirectly sustained uneven relations of power. When the media denigrate less powerful communities (as many Muslim communities in Europe are), they may become complicit in 'structural violence' (Galtung 1975). Following the attacks on *Charlie Hebdo*, Valenta (2015) wrote that 'their spoofs on all that is sacred to Muslims … constitute[ed] neither a cheeky snub of the powers that be nor a courageous stance for freedom of speech, but simply an insulting denigration. It is not the sign of a free society but of an unequal society' (n.p.). Valenta's claim is consistent with the gist of earlier work by the cultural theorist Stuart Hall (1997), who argued that perceptions of cultural differences often lead to oversimplified representations where distinctions within groups evaporate. This engenders 'othering' whereby cultural differences are reified to construct 'us' and 'them' distinctions (binary opposites). Hall claims that such binary opposites are hardly ever neutral because one pole is usually dominant over the other, having the power to exclude, ridicule or belittle the other. Hence the *Charlie Hebdo* episode involves broader concerns that relate to ways in which freedom of speech is exercised in contexts where a more powerful (and privileged) group exerts greater influence on the way that less powerful social groups are portrayed. Because of various types of inequality (including cultural inequality), less powerful groups may still feel the need of some safeguards, not necessarily legal safeguards, against abuse by more powerful groups. The media-establishment itself may provide or fail to provide such safeguards.

During the Cold War, Seibert et al. (1956) provided an analytical framework to assess journalistic professional ideology. They proposed four theories of the press that are now often deemed to be rather simplistic and obsolete, even though their influence has not completely faded.[6] In fact, references to the libertarian and social responsibility perspectives resurfaced in the protracted controversy raised by the Danish Muhammad cartoons in 2005 and peaked in the aftermath of the attacks on the Paris offices of *Charlie Hebdo* in 2015.

Different models

From the Libertarian standpoint, freedom of expression is seen as a pillar of Western democracy and it is deemed to be 'as sacred, in its own way, as Muhammad is to pious Muslims' (*The Economist* 2006). In media theory, this supports the notion of complete media freedom even when it is merely a normative ideal rather than an actual state of affairs. Empirical evidence suggests that complete media freedom is a myth, since there are ample implicit and explicit influences by owners, advertisers, sources and even audiences (Herman and Chomsky 1988). As suggested in the previous section, there is also a rather incestuous relationship between the media and the political and economic establishments.

The social responsibility approach, on the other hand, proposes greater sensibility towards different groups in society; in our case, it would enjoin sensibility towards followers of Islam. While the social responsibility perspective does not accept censorship by the state, it acknowledges that freedom of expression inherently offers us the right to decide when to use it and that the grounds for our decision *ought to* include common sense and prudence. Social responsibility implies adherence to a code of conduct supervised and enforced by self-regulatory professional structures, such as a media ethics commissions that are appointed by the media industry itself. This perspective is closely related to the notion of 'peace journalism'. There were many Western media organizations that adhered to the social responsibility model and rejected the or re-publication of the Muhammed cartoons, even if this led to criticism by segments of the press that accused them of self-censorship.

The case of the *Jyllands-Posten* cartoons and the attacks on *Charlie Hebdo* revived debates on the 'right to offend', and on the limits and possibilities of the exercise of such rights. The debates concerned the effects of the exercise of such rights in relation to social peace as well as to possible reactions by groups who feel that their identity is being attacked by virtue of the exercise of such rights. For many years, identity politics was employed by socially marginalized and vilified groups who organized to improve their status. Their self-affirmative action often sought political correctness in media discourse and public policy. Political correctness has, however, come under attack by libertarian public intellectuals, including some media exponents. Salman Rushdie, for instance, downplays the dangers of provocation in increasingly complex multicultural societies: 'The idea that any kind of free society can be constructed in which people will never be offended or insulted is absurd. … In democracies people … argue vehemently against each other's positions. But they don't shoot' (2005). Yet, even in democratic and multicultural societies people feel deeply insulted when faith, religious convictions or some other aspect of the identity of a group is denigrated. Resentment may occur, which may trigger irrational responses. The social responsibility model is sensitive to the sensibilities of different groups, while being aware that this ought not to imply the erosion of media-related freedoms. Having said that, although the social responsibility approach is more conducive to peace and dialogue, this approach has become much harder to follow or implement.

In the modern-day democratic agora, the internet is a technology that challenges the *status quo*, one where multiple actors articulate their positions with ease via the social media. Sometimes this plays a positive function. For instance, the *Charlie Hebdo* attack inspired millions of people to identify with the victims through the *Je Suis Charlie* slogan that first appeared on Twitter and then spread online via other social media like Facebook. Hence, social media provided a platform for grass-roots responses. Soon, another Twitter hashtag, *Je Suis Ahmed*, called public attention to the fact that a Muslim policeman had lost his life in defence of the values of freedom and tolerance. Ahmed became the good face of Islam in moments of intense mistrust between communities, and may have helped soften some of the prevalent hostility towards Islam and Muslims.[7] Also, whereas the traditional media tend to rely on official voices, the social media offer an opportunity for a plethora of diverse opinions. They offer people the opportunity to interact and engage in debates. Yet, online engagement has its downside. Social media provide significant sites for unbounded hate speech and racial incitement. Many radicalized groups migrated online to promote, recruit and reinforce divisions. It is next to impossible to enforce codes of conduct and social responsibility on all virtual communities, but such practices should be retained as valid traits of professional practice. Education on how to responsibly participate in virtual interactive groups may contribute towards a dialogue between different groups that enjoy unequal access to different forms of power (economic, political, cultural, etc.), even if virtual communities are frequently trapped in an echo-chamber where individuals are likely to hear their own opinion resonate within their community of like-minded participants.

Conclusion: Challenges for the media

The Western media tend to uncritically employ the liberal peace narrative where democracy in tandem with the free market is deemed to be the formula for conflict resolution and peace building. Such perceptions had raised expectations that a range of countries (from Afghanistan, to Iraq, Tunisia, Egypt and Libya) would rapidly embrace the liberal democratic model, hopes that soon proved illusory. After the collapse of autocratic regimes (most of which were secular), Western media organizations broadly underestimated the influence of adherents to strands of Islam that reject individual freedoms. They frequently struggled, and failed, to explain to their audiences the rise of radicalism and the implications of this for global, national and regional security.

The global response to the cartoon crisis, then, demonstrates the extent to which mainstream media have adopted the notion of incompatible cultures as a matter of fact in a world where intense global, political, economic and social interactions are juxtaposed against a context of fear, mistrust and civilizational clashes. The two case studies of *Jyllands-Posten* and *Charlie Hebdo* illustrate how the media may, on the one hand, facilitate dialogue but, on the other, may also poison the information stream with their emphasis on extreme and sensational viewpoints and their fascination with conflict. Both cases have now become icons of press freedom as they revived debates on the 'right to offend' as an extension to 'freedom of expression'.

The 'right to offend' has superseded political correctness and the social responsibility approach as the main mainstream tendency, with political correctness and the social responsibility approach coming under attack by libertarian public intellectuals. They frequently disregard issues of power and control, and access to the media, ignoring or downplaying the fact that media texts (including visuals) may reflect and reinforce inequalities, hate, stereotypes and the oversimplification of 'others'. Critical Education ought to be aware of this, and not be easily swayed by libertarian banners. The links between power, politics and the media should be highlighted even in those cases where these associations are implicit rather than explicit.

Jyllands-Posten and *Charlie Hebdo* both rallied for freedom of the press, which includes the option to offend Muslims by equating Islam with terrorism. In exercising their 'right to offend', they reinforced prevalent conceptions of Islam as the contemporary Face of Evil. In both instances, the cartoons invoked symbolic connotations where Islam appeared as a homogeneous religion and all Muslims were demonized and presented as threats to Western security. These negative images were consistent with the underlying messages that were often employed by Western states in their effort to demonize enemies. With each violent attack by Muslim radicals against Western centres of power, some of these negative outlooks become self-fulfilling prophecies.

This chapter argues that the social responsibility approach to communication is more conducive to peace because it respects different communities and provides opportunities for more dialogue and less confrontation. At a normative level, the social responsibility model blends freedom of expression with common sense and prudence in relation to the sensibilities of specific groups. This entails adherence to a code of conduct and the existence of self-regulatory professional bodies. We must acknowledge, though, that in the age of the social media, it is increasingly difficult to chart the route towards the social responsibility approach. Individuals and multiple actors may now influence issues and events but the social responsibility approach can continue to serve as a mark of professional distinction. While society explores new facets of cultural rights, the media may advance the integration of minorities rather than their exclusion.

Notes

1　Islam has as many as 72 different divisions or variations.
2　It has been documented that the Muslim Brotherhood, Hamas and the Islamic State provide basic social services (Wood 2015).
3　Rasmussen launched his *kulturkampf* on 1 January 2002, when he initially focused his critical attention on the cultural elite and experts, whom he described as 'judges of taste' (*smagsdommere*). He fired some committees and boards whom he accused of elitism because they advocated political correctness as opposed to his appeal for a return to 'Danish values' (Lykkeberg cited by Hervik 2012, p. 27).
4　In normative theories of mass communication, the social responsibility perspective supports a free press and rejects censorship. Yet, it asserts that the media must necessarily shoulder its obligations even by means of professional self-regulatory structures. This approach will be considered in greater detail later in the chapter.

5　These included Salman Rushdie, the French philosopher Bernard Henri-Levy, the Bangladeshi writer Taslima Nasreen, Mehdi Mozaffari who is an Iranian academic exiled in Denmark and Ayaan Hirsi Ali, the Dutch-Somali who was living in fear of her own life because she had collaborated in Theo Van Gogh's film project on Islam.

6　Seibert et al. distinguish between the authoritarian and the Soviet communist models where the media are under total state control, and the libertarian and the social responsibility models.

7　At this stage, one must note, however, that online 'activism' is rather illusive because it hardly ever leads to actual deliberative and substantive action. People often tend to stop at a virtual 'like', a 'share' or signing their name to an online petition, actions that are not necessarily empowering. As a result, '*Je Suis Charlie*' and *Je Suis Ahmed* did not create significant and long-term 'movements'.

References

Chelini-Pont, B. (2013). *Freedom of Religion and Freedom of Expression*. International Consortium for Law and Religion Studies. Milan: Universita' degli Studi. Available from: http://www.iclars.org/media/pdf/abstract/Abstract_workshopsabato_mattina.pdf

Cohen, S. (1972). *Folk Devils and Moral Panics*. London: MacGibbon and Lee.

Dalgaarda, S. and Dalgaard, K. (2006). 'The Right to Offend: The Causes and Consequences of the "Danish Cartoon affair"'. *The RUSI Journal*, 151 (2): 28–33.

Dayan, D. and Katz, E. (1992). *The Live Broadcasting of History*. USA: Harvard University Press.

Freedman, D. (2015). *Charlie Hebdo Tragedy: Free Speech and its Broader Contexts*. [Online] 9 January 2015. Available from: https://www.opendemocracy.net/des-freedman/charlie-hebdo-tragedy-free-speech-and-its-broader-contexts.

Fredette, J. (2014). *Constructing Muslims in France: Discourse, Public Identity, and the Politics of Citizenship*. Philadelphia: Temple University Press.

Galtung, J. and Ruge, M. H. (1965). 'The Structure of Foreign News: The Presentation of the Congo, Cuba and Cyprus Crises in Four Norwegian Newspapers'. *Journal of Peace Research*, 2 (1): 64–91.

Galtung, J. (1975). *Essays in Peace Research*. Vol. 1. Copenhagen: Christian Ejlers.

Hall, S. (1997). *Representation: Cultural Representations and Signifying Practices*. London Thousand Oaks, CA: Sage in association with the Open University.

Hall, S. (2010). 'The Neo-Liberal Revolution'. *Cultural Studies*, 25 (6): 705–28.

Hallin, D. (1986). *The Uncensored War: The Media and Vietnam*. Oxford: Oxford University.

Herman, E. and Chomsky, N. (1988). *Manufacturing Consent*. New York: Pantheon.

Hervik, P. (2012). 'The Danish Muhammad Cartoon Conflict'. *Current Themes in IMER Research*. No. 13. Sweden: Malmö Institute for Studies of Migration, Diversity and Welfare (MIM), Available from http://www.mah.se/upload/Forskningscentrum/ MIM/CT/CT%2013.pdf.

Huntington, S. P. (1996). *The Clash of Civilisations and the Remaking of the World Order*. US: Simon and Shuster.

Linde-Laursen, A. (2007). 'Is Something Rotten in the State of Denmark? The Muhammad Cartoons and Danish Political Culture'. *Contemporary Islam*, 1 (3): 265–74.

Livingston, S. and Eachus, T. (1995). 'Humanitarian Crises and U.S. Foreign Policy: Somalia and the CNN Effect Reconsidered'. *Political Communication*, 12 (4): 413–29.

Livingston, S. and Lance Bennett, W. (2003). 'Gatekeeping, Indexing, and Live-Event News: Is Technology Altering the Construction of News?' *Political Communication*, 20 (4): 363–80.

Manoff, R. K. (1997). 'The Media's Role in Preventing and Moderating Conflict', Available from http://www.globalissues.org/article/534/the-peace-journalism-option #THENEWSVALUESofPEACEJOURNALISM.

Mc Chesney, R. (2008). *The Political Economy of the Media*. New York: Monthly Review Foundation.

Mc Nair, B. (1995). *An Introduction to Political Communication*. London: Routledge.

Salih, M. (2009). 'A Critique of the Political Economy of Liberal Peace: Elements of an African Experience'. In E. Newman, R. Paris and O. P. Richmond (Eds), *New Perspective on Liberal Peacebuilding*, pp. 133–58. Tokyo, New York and Paris: United Nations University Press.

Morgenthau, H. J. (1978). *Politics Among Nations: The Struggle for Power and Peace*. 5th Ed. New York: Knopf.

Nye, J. (2008). 'Public Diplomacy and Soft Power'. *The Annals of the American Academy of Political and Social Science*, 616 (1): 94–109.

Orwell, G. (1938). *Homage to Catalonia*. London: Secker and Warburg.

Pace Nilsen, A. and Nilsen, D. L. F. (2008). 'Political Cartoons: Zeitgeists and the Creation and Recycling of Satirical symbols'. In J. C. Baumgartner and J. S. Morris (Eds), *Laughing Matters*, pp. 67–80. New York and London: Routledge.

Robinson, P. (2000). 'The Policy-Media Interaction Model: Measuring Media Power during Humanitarian Crisis'. *Journal of Peace Research*, 37 (5): 613–33.

Rushdie, S. (2005). Defend the Right to be Offended. [Online] 7 February 2005. Available from: https://www.opendemocracy.ne t/faith-europe_islam/article_2331. jsp.

Said, E. (1996). *Covering Islam: How the Media and the Experts Determine How We See the Rest of the World*. US: Vintage.

Siebert, F. S., Peterson, T. and Schramm, W. (1956). *Four Theories of the Press: The Authoritarian, Libertarian, Social Responsibility and Soviet Communist Concepts of What the Press Should Be and Do*. Urbana: University of Illinois Press.

Tahranian, M. (2002). 'Peace Journalism: Negotiating Global Media Ethics'. *International Journal of Press/Politics*, 8 (2): 58–83.

Thussu, D. K. (2000). *International Communication*. London: Arnold.

Thussu, D. K. (2006). 'Televising the "War on Terrorism": The Myths of Morality'. In I. A. P. Kavoori and T. Fraley (Eds), *Media, Terrorism and Theory*, pp. 3–18. London: Rowman and Littlefield.

Valenta, M. (2015). *Charlie Hebdo – One week later*. [Online] 16 January 2015. Available from: https://www.opendemocracy.net/markha-valenta/charlie-hebdo-%E2%80%93-one-week-later

Wood, G. (2015). 'What ISIS Really Wants'. *The Atlantic*. [Online] March 2015. Available from: http://www.theatlantic.com/features/archive/2015/02/what-isis-really-wants/384980/?fb_ref=Default.

Part Three

Pedagogy of Peace

9

Some Reflections on Critical Peace Education

Michalinos Zembylas and Zvi Bekerman

Introduction

It has recently been argued that peace education as a field, a philosophy and a movement has to reclaim its *criticality* (Bajaj 2008, 2015; Brantmeier 2010; Diaz-Soto 2005; Bekerman 2007; Trifonas and Wright 2013; Zembylas 2008, 2015), to become more critical about theoretical assumptions concerning issues of power relations, social justice, as well as the terms of 'peace' and 'conflict' themselves. Clarifying the theoretical assumptions involved in these issues is valuable, because theoretical assumptions have important implications in terms of our (in)ability to envision and enact particular pedagogical responses to conflict.

Surveying the scholarly work on peace education over the past three decades, one encounters a set of fundamental assumptions that seem to be taken for granted (Bekerman and Zembylas 2012; Ben Porath 2003; Gur-Ze'ev 2001; Page 2004, 2008). One such assumption is that 'peace' is the opposite of 'conflict', and that peace is 'good' and conflict is 'bad'. If a strict dichotomy is drawn and any conflict is viewed as evil or destructive, then there will be consequences in terms of whether individuals are able to distinguish between productive and destructive forms of conflict in their lives. A similar assumption is made about peace or peace education as a general deontological 'thing' to which humanity ought to be committed (Page 2008). This 'fideistic' approach, as Page points out, takes for granted that one ought to believe in peace and peace education, assuming the 'goodness' of peace rather than exploring the contextual meanings and implications of the term (Gur-Ze'ev 2001). We, on the other hand, believe that when education sets peace as a self-evident universal utopia, peace loses much of its positive potentiality.

In this chapter, we want to question some fundamental assumptions of peace education in the present, especially those that are grounded in Western paradigms. We discuss the consequences they have for educational reforms and schooling. The chapter will attempt to figure out how these assumptions operate to normalize particular meanings of 'peace', 'conflict', 'education' and other related concepts. We will argue that if theoretical work is not used to interrogate assumptions about peace and peace education, peace education may become part of the problem it tries to solve. Peace education needs to grapple with foundational educational issues which, if left unaccounted for, risk consolidating the same reality peace education intends to overcome. We will then produce a general characterization of *critical peace education*, built on distinctive premises concerning peace, educational reform and schooling.

Lack of criticality in peace education

Peace education is now officially accepted as a distinct field of study in education. Yet, it is misleading to refer to 'peace education' as though it were a monolithic entity (Bajaj 2008; Gur-Ze'ev 2001). There is a variety of (often unrelated) subjects that are amalgamated under the headline 'peace education' (Ben Porath 2003), including human rights, women's rights, environmental education, international and development education, and conflict resolution (e.g. see Harris 2004). All these areas are promoted 'with a similar sense of urgency and good will' (Ben Porath 2003, p. 527). One intriguing gap has been the failure to develop and expound systematically the philosophical premises of peace education: the assumptions and rationale on which peace education, meanings and practices are grounded (Page 2008).

In a provocative article published more than a decade ago, Gur-Ze'ev argued that 'many of the difficulties and shortcomings peace education practitioners face are because of this lack of conceptual work and reflection' (2001, p. 315). He went on to state that this lack of theoretical coherence or philosophical elaboration is not always considered as a bad thing for peace education since 'at times philosophical work is understood as unnecessary, artificial, or even dangerous for this educational cause' (ibid.). Gur-Ze'ev disagreed, and criticized much of mainstream peace education as being a justification of the status quo: 'Many versions of peace education work within the framework of modernist technical reason, manifested through various positivist, pragmatic, and functionalist views of knowledge, which pay scant attention to the social and cultural context' (ibid., p. 316). Although in recent years there has been important new work showing how peace education programs differ in regions of relative tranquillity compared to regions of conflict (Bar-Tal and Rosen 2009), arguing for the need to develop peace education as 'critical' (Bajaj 2008; Brantmeier 2010) or suggesting a solid educational philosophy (Synott 2005), we believe that Gur-Ze'ev's fundamental claims still hold. There is an important necessity for peace educators to address the direct political, sociological and historical consequences of their theoretical premises in their work.

An example of the lack of this criticality is evident in the fact that many peace education programs often set 'peace' as a universal goal. Peace is usually defined as the absence of any conflict (Hayden 2002). Conflict is presumed to be something that needs to be 'resolved' through appropriate knowledge and skills. Otherwise, there is no peace. This duality of peace–conflict bears remarkable similarities to paradigmatic dichotomies set by Western epistemology (male/female; good/evil; us/them), and, as such, seems only to be able to replicate a similar epistemology in peace education.

More importantly, issues are frequently set in the realm of meaning – finding the correct meaning of the term and its proper extension – not in the realm of *power relations.* Power inequalities and social injustices are thus often ignored. Such an essentialist understanding of peace (and peace education) not only rejects the multiple representations of peace, justice and other ideals but, most importantly, also disregards the social arrangements that institutionalize inequality and injustice. It ends up promoting 'one version of "normalizing" peace education' (Gur-Ze'ev 2001, p. 329).

Many peace education versions – especially conflict-resolution ones, psychologized interventions and political documents such as UNESCO's declarations (see Bekerman and Zembylas 2012; Ben Porath 2003; Gur-Ze'ev 2001, for detailed critiques) – are founded on fundamentally modern characterizations of Natural Law and of the *nation state.* As a product of modernity, the nation state has produced a distinct social form, characterized by very specific forms of territoriality and surveillance capabilities that monopolize effective control over social relations across different contexts (Foucault 1983a, b, 1984). The nation state can be viewed as a political phenomenon that seeks to exercise control over populations by establishing a culture that is at once homogeneous, anonymous (all the members of the polity, irrespective of their personal subgroup affiliations, are called upon to uphold this culture) and 'universally literate' (all members share the culture the state has canonized). The modern nation state seeks to create a direct and unobstructed relationship between itself and all its 'individual' citizens (Rose 1990, 1998, 1999). No tribe, ethnic group, family or church is allowed to stand between the citizen and the state (Mendus 1989). This institution, that is, the nation state and its characterizations, are frequently taken for granted in many educational processes that have peace as their ideal.

In our own previous work (e.g. Bekerman 2007; Bekerman and Zembylas 2010, 2012; Zembylas 2008; Zembylas and Bekerman 2008), we have pointed at the Enlightenment's moralistic and monologic philosophical grounding of many versions of peace education, including some psychologized perspectives. In particular, we have emphasized the need to acknowledge the complex historical processes that have brought the West and the colonial powers of old to successfully replace the force of arms with the force of homogenization and surveillance. These processes nowadays take place not only by the coercion of currency and consumerism but also, especially, by the chronic social proneness to create or construct the 'other' through rhetoric and deed in a way that inevitably leads to the demonization of those who are not like 'us', and who do not comply to the hegemonic standards of Western white males. Peace education that does not take this into consideration may end up abetting such processes rather than challenging them.

Critiquing psychologized assumptions

A fundamental assumption behind many educational reforms in and of peace education projects that needs to be seriously reconsidered is the assumption that lack of peace, tolerance, justice, equality and recognition is primarily a product of 'ignorance' rather than bad will. Educational reforms, then, would aim at transferring knowledge and skills to students and teachers. Two important implications follow from this assumption. The first is that peace, tolerance, justice, equality and recognition can be achieved through reforms in the educational system that focus on instilling the 'appropriate' knowledge in students. Second, the implication is that with proper training, teachers can foster the implementation of peace, tolerance, justice, equality, and recognition for all. Both implications, however, fail to investigate and cultivate critical praxis and transformative agency in ways that are relevant to economic, political, historical and social contexts (Bajaj 2008).

The above assumption and its implications, in turn, rest on a second set of cultural assumptions that are equally important in terms of defining the aims and consequences of peace education initiatives. These assumptions refer to how values of peace, tolerance, justice, equality and recognition are culturally perceived in a particular setting. For example, in the case of the countries that we hail from (i.e. the Republic of Cyprus and the State of Israel), this second set of assumptions presupposes that the very basic values of the Hellenic or Jewish civilizations deny racist perspectives and emphasize respect for and recognition of 'otherness' (The same could be argued for the foundational values of the Western civilization.). It is also assumed that these civilizations can only produce peace, tolerance, justice, equality and recognition, unless unexpected obstacles turn up. Given these assumptions, it is often considered that reform efforts need simply to achieve technical changes such as restructuring the curriculum, reorganizing the time devoted to old and new school subjects and training of teachers to achieve the above aims. The assumptions in question are taken for granted and are never interrogated. Yet, it is vital that these assumptions are questions and their consequences to peace education, educational reforms and schooling are exposed.

Undoubtedly, education as a discipline has moved forward, at least within some constructivist traditions. Debates about normativity and ideals have been left behind and the activities and practices of education no longer occupy centre-stage. Contents might be still in focus but not as isolated subject-matter, waiting for the right opportunity or the right conductor (i.e. a wonderful teacher and/or a perfect teacher-proof curriculum) to inject them into the innocent heads/brains of young individuals. Instead, activity and practice have become the centrepiece of serious research. The path towards this still-new approach to education has not been easy and the politics of education – the elite's ongoing attempt to use education as a homogenizing tool for the creation of passive and obedient citizens – are always lurking. Yet, progress has been made. Peace education, though, as a specific field, is still lagging behind (Brantmeier 2010).

We question mainstream perspectives/paradigms in peace education because we want to instil doubt into the usual rhetoric that puts the responsibility to find solutions to the problems of society on schools and education. Peace is rhetorically constructed by nation states as a necessary and worthy goal, achievable through education and schooling. It is exactly this rhetorical construction, so consequential for the achievement of peace, that worries us. For just as social equality has not been achieved through schooling and education,

so peace can or will be achieved through schooling alone. Our attitude in this regard is not pessimistic, but pragmatic and critical.

In the rest of this chapter we present our own suggestion of how to reclaim criticality in peace education.

Our proposition

Our point of departure is that we should expect little and be modest, knowing very well that the struggle to change pedagogical practices and strategies might have very little influence. Educators cannot do it all. They cannot change the world, but should do the most they can to change their immediate contexts a little. The explicit acknowledgement of this important premise is valuable as a starting point for a reclaimed critical peace education, and a pragmatic call to prevent one-size-fits-all approaches. We need to take into account the historical and political context where peace education efforts occur. The acknowledgement of the multiplicity, contingency and complexity of these efforts should be enough to prevent us from expecting a straightforward picture of the whats and hows of 'doing' peace education. We are not after recipes but after interrogating present understandings, which, if not subjected to analysis, will lead to self-deception and to problematic claims about universality and objectivity.

What follows is an outline of the possible philosophical foundations of our understanding of critical peace education, consisting of four elements (as shown below in Figure 9.1), namely, reinstating the materiality of 'things' and practices, reontologizing research and practice in peace education, becoming 'critical experts of design' and engaging in critical cultural analysis.

All four elements emphasize that our access to the world is socially and conceptually mediated – hence the emphasis on recognizing the materiality of things and the need to reontologize research, both of which highlight the importance of situating things in the world rather than abstracting ideas and generalizing them. Such a perspective, then, recognizes that even if we accept the existence of an objective world, our 'realities' are constructed, these constructs actively reproducing the social world. For instance, goods and resources are distributed according to identity labels, be they ethnic, national, religious and so on (these labels being constructs rather than natural categories). In this manner, we avoid the dualism between the real and the non-real, and focus on *how* we should *act* to change underlying structures and mechanisms that determine social

Figure 9.1 The four elements of our understanding of critical peace education.

arrangements and understandings. Such a theoretical foundation mitigates the detrimental influences of versions of constructivism that assume the world to be purely a human construct, while avoiding the narrowly calculative rationality of positivism that treats knowledge as simply the accumulation of data we gather from outside. The four elements of our understanding of critical peace education are explained in what follows.

1 Reinstating the materiality of things and practices

Western epistemological dualism divides meanings from contexts, and hence is unable to cope with meaning in its totality. We do not consider words and their meanings as pre-packed discrete units readily available for implementation in social life. Rather, words and their meanings are authored in-process and in-context by reflecting users. These users are both constituted by and constituting of the environments in which words and sentences make sense. Meaning is hence bound to the materiality of 'things' and to practices in relation to which concepts are *performed*, contextually and historically.

This characterization of meaning goes against psychologized and idealistic perspectives in peace education, which frequently entail essentialized conceptions and characterizations of individuals, peace and conflict. Critical peace education, on the other hand, requires a different understanding. Words such as 'education', 'peace' and 'conflict' should not be taken as homogeneous units bridging referents and proper meanings. Rather, we take these words to be tricky constructs whose meaning is negotiated by active participants and put to work in the network of complex social relations. In a sense, we believe that these words are akin to active *verbs,* always making and in-the-making. This takes place constantly and can be perceived when properly attending to human (in our case educational) activity.

We are, then, critical of approaches in peace education that ignore contextual and historical factors such as power inequalities and social injustices: 'fix' the 'sick' (e.g. nationalist, racist) mind of troubled individuals, and you overcome conflict. The theoretical basis on which such approaches rest are limiting; grounded in abstractions about the internal minds of individuals and about the external (and essentialized) characteristics of cultures. Instead, we want to highlight the materiality of things and practices, suggesting that more attention be paid to ontology.

2 Reontologizing research and practice in peace education

Even though we cannot but use abstract concepts, we should not consider them as though existing in some realm of their own, but should conceive them in their concrete settings of use. We argue for the need to *reontologize* what has been epistemologized. We need to materialize abstractions and ask about their consequences in everyday life. We need to get researchers, teachers, policymakers, and students (to convince teachers to do this with their students in terms of pedagogy) to read the details of the world as they are, to try and understand how the world is built/constructed, instead of trying to find what stands 'inside' or 'behind' things. The details, the materiality of things and concrete practices, rather than the abstract ideas and the policy decisions, constitute the focus of our interest. Consider a child belonging to a conflicting group approaching a teacher and asking about the 'other': for instance, what is a Jew or a Palestinian? Given current peace education curricula, the teacher committed to peace may be inclined to provide some abstract, culturally descriptive and benevolent characteristics of the group in question (see Bekerman, Zembylas and McGlynn 2009; Zembylas and Bekerman 2008). Though this response might seem appropriate for accommodating perspectives expected from a cross-cultural initiative, we believe that in the long run, it sustains the basis on which the conflict initially developed. A more appropriate answer might be that Palestinians or Jews are not a (an essentialized/natural) 'what', but a 'when' and/ or a 'how' (a becoming) of these particular and diverse realities. The teacher should encourage the student himself or herself to look for these whens and hows, rather than for some abstract and essential characterization of what a Jew or Palestinian is.

3 Becoming critical experts of design

Related to our call for reontologizing research and pedagogical practice, we argue that peace education and its main categories – identity, culture and so on – will be stripped of their overly psychologized baggage, if we were trained as *critical experts of design* (Bekerman and Zembylas 2012). By 'critical experts of design' we mean people who are able to recognize and criticize how the world is designed and how it can be redesigned if it is reimagined, rather than trying to simply picture this 'as it is' in passive fashion. For example, we might realize that nationalism and patriotism are not inside people's heads, but are produced in the minds of people through popular culture, social practices, school ceremonies and so on (Anderson 1983; Billig 1995; Gillis 1994). The same might be said regarding other notions that the issue of peace considers. People would become aware that everything which is thought to be 'internal' (or personal) hides and refers to strategies and practices that inter-actionally and dialogically create it.

Reclaiming criticality in peace education and encouraging students and teachers to become critical experts of design implies confronting the whole spectrum of activities that go under the category of education. Peace education cannot be treated as a special educational track, but has to be considered within its macro-level *context* and how this is in continuous transaction with micro-level *practices*. If students and teachers are to become critical experts of design, they need to engage in an in-depth interrogation of these two elements – that is, 'context' and 'practice' – and their consequences for peace education efforts.

As critical experts of design, teachers and students need to become able to view the wider political and social context and engage those contextual elements that are important in deconstructing and reconstructing their efforts.

4 Engaging in critical cultural analysis

Our philosophical approach is aligned with what has come to be called 'cultural therapy' (Spindler and Spindler 1994; Trueba 1993). This involves the process of becoming aware of one's own cultural and ideological predispositions and framework, thus perceiving one's potential bias in social interaction, learning and knowledge (Varenne and McDermott 1998). The process starts by restoring the concept of identity/culture to its historical sources, thus de-essentializing it. It follows by developing this restored meaning into a methodology or cultural analysis. This involves gaining skills on how to read/describe the world through careful observation and recording of practical activity, which, in turn, permits a shift from the individual or the socializing group as the crucial analytic unit for (educational) analysis, to the processes and mechanisms of *producing* cultural contexts through social interaction. Finally, the process leads to a new articulation of major policy issues related no longer to identity/culture and its components (individual, texts, etc.), but to the analysis of particular identities/cultures and to how these are produced/constructed in the particular context of particular societies. Looking at the world in this way, seriously and critically, means being open to finding new criteria through which to categorize phenomena.

But how can this be concretely achieved? Engaging in critical cultural analysis in peace education can take the following forms. First, teachers need to base programs for developing community relations around an exploration of the roles that 'identity' and 'culture' play in real life. Second, teachers need to challenge the idea that notions of identity and culture are neutral categories that objectively describe aspects of the world. Teachers and children need also to develop the skills of cultural analysis rather than 'knowledge' of the characteristics of the 'other'. They should not start with the 'other' as a given but engage in a collaborative process that dismantles rather than assembles existing categories. Finally, efforts need to be redirected from a focus on the 'other' towards collaborative efforts for change.

What we are suggesting is to direct efforts to the sphere of daily localized and contextualized interactions in their historical trajectories, trying to identify the specific practices (discursive and material) that enable these to exist. We should be aware that the ways through which teachers ask questions, give feedback, speak the 'correct language' and decide on the criteria for identifying students are not neutral. These include practices that are skilfully enacted daily, so as to allow for the identities/cultures of individuals to be organized and identified. The struggle for nation-building in our schools, the discourse of individuality in our media, the unequal distribution of resources in our society, and many other deeply entrenched perceptions and their consequent practices have first to be identified and described and then offered to all of the interactants as tools through which change, if so desired, might be achieved. The issue is not the use of categories, like ethnic categories, but the interrogation of how and why these labels are (still widely) used and the consequences they have.

Conclusion

This chapter started by identifying a set of fundamental assumptions that are frequently taken for granted in peace education, which operate to normalize particular meanings for peace, conflict, education and other related concepts. In response, we put forward an approach consisting of four elements, aiming to reclaim criticality in peace education. This involves reinstating the materiality of things and practices, reontologizing research and practice in peace education, becoming critical experts of design and engaging in critical cultural analysis. Our suggestion is theoretically grounded in post-positivist realism and critical realism, emphasizing that the world is socially and conceptually mediated. Our constructions, however, have consequences that play an important part in how we act to educate children and ourselves for a peaceful world.

At times, the tone of our writing has been polemic, especially when we have criticized the assumption that peace and peace education are by definition 'good' and that conflict is necessarily 'bad'. We have also criticized the Western-centric and psychological foundations of some peace education versions and the assumptions on which they are based, assumptions that are ultimately counter-productive in that they perpetuate problematic conceptions of theory and practice.

The main points that run contrary to the widespread assumptions in peace education that we put forward are the following. First, the (at times) perceived failure of peace education has little to do with the quality of individual teachers or students and much to do with the quality of the systems we (all) cooperatively construct. Failing to understand this means confusing failure with what are adaptive moves to local and global systemic circumstances. Second, Western positivist paradigmatic perspectives in the social sciences are largely responsible for the present educational perspectives that guide peace educational theory and practice, although recent work in peace education has begun to distance itself from this paradigm. Change will be available after Western positivist paradigmatic perspectives are seriously criticized and there is more systematic engagement with post-foundational paradigmatic ideas. Part of this process means realizing that everything is interactional, contextualized and historicized rather than isolated inside (individual), static and well defined outside (culture), and specific-task-oriented and measurable transmission (education). Lastly, peace education would do well to look for educational solutions in the organization of present Western world politics rather than in the limited parameters of school settings or of individual teachers or students. When looking inside schools, we should be looking at contexts and practices and not at abstract individual minds and values.

This is why we have called on teachers and students to engage in this critical awareness as 'critical experts of design'. For teachers, cultural therapy can facilitate an awareness of the cultural assumptions that they bring into the classroom and which affect their behaviour and their interactions with students. For students, cultural therapy is essentially a means of critical consciousness-raising, which helps them identify and critique unequal power relationships in school, the classroom and society. In general, cultural therapy encourages everyone involved in educational activity to appreciate the relevance of culture to educational activity as well as to be able to identify the contextual obstacles that stand in their way when trying to engage in a peace culture.

In conclusion, it goes without saying that our approach has limitations; some of these limitations have been identified and discussed in this chapter. Although we have provided examples, we have generally avoided exploring their direct relevance to practical approaches for peace education research and pedagogy, on the grounds that this was outside the scope of this initial analysis. Future research may focus explicitly in making these connections between the theoretical premises of our proposition and specific pedagogical implications. The elements outlined, however, constitute an important point of departure for reconstructing some fundamental theoretical premises in peace education and articulating further how different versions of critical peace education may have a pragmatic impact on the world.

References

Anderson, B. (1983). *Imagined Communities*. London: Verso.
Bajaj, M. (2008). "'Critical' Peace Education'. In M. Bajaj (Ed.), *The Encyclopedia of Peace Education*, pp. 135–46. Greenwich, CT: Information Age Publishing.

Bajaj, M. (2015) 'Pedagogies of resistance' and critical peace education praxis, Journal of Peace Education, 12:2, 154–166

Bar-Tal, D. and Rosen, Y. (2009). 'Peace Education in Societies Involved in Intractable Conflicts: Direct and Indirect Models'. *Review of Educational Research*, 79 (2): 557–75.

Bekerman, Z. (2007). 'Rethinking Intergroup Encounters: Rescuing Praxis from Theory, Activity from Education, and Peace/Co-Existence from Identity and Culture'. *Journal of Peace Education*, 4 (1): 29–41.

Bekerman, Z. and Zembylas, M. (2010). 'Victims and Perpetrators, Memory and Forgetting: In Search of Pedagogical Openings to the Paralyzing Effects of Victim-Perpetrator Narratives'. *Journal of Curriculum Studies*, 42 (5): 573–96.

Bekerman, Z. and Zembylas, M. (2012). *Teaching Contested Narratives: Identity, Memory and Reconciliation in Peace Education and Beyond*. Cambridge: Cambridge University Press.

Bekerman, Z., Zembylas, M. and McGlynn, C. (2009). 'Working Towards the De-Essentialization of Identity Categories in Conflict and Post-Conflict Societies: Israel, Cyprus, and Northern Ireland'. *Comparative Education Review*, 53 (2): 213–34.

Ben-Porath, S. (2003). 'War and Peace Education'. *Journal of Philosophy of Education*, 37 (3): 525–33.

Bhaskar, R. (1989). *Reclaiming Reality: A Critical Introduction to Contemporary Philosophy*. London: Verso.

Bhaskar, R. (2002). *Reflections on Meta-Reality*. London: Sage.

Billig, M. (1995). *Banal Nationalism*. London: Sage.

Brantmeier, E. J. (2010). 'Toward Mainstreaming Critical Peace Education in U.S. Teacher Education'. In C. S. Malott and B. Porfilio (Eds), *Critical Pedagogy in the 21st Century: A New Generation of Scholars*, pp. 349–75. Greenwish, CT: Information Age Publishing.

Diaz-Soto, L. (2005). 'How Can We Teach Peace When We Are So Outraged? A Call for Critical Peace Education'. *Taboo: The Journal of Culture and Education*, 9 (2): 91–6.

Foucault, M. (1983a). 'The Subject and Power: Afterword'. In H. Dreyfus and P. Rabinow (Eds), *Michel Foucault: Beyond Structuralism and Hermeneutics*, pp. 208–27. Chicago: University of Chicago Press.

Foucault, M. (1983b). 'On the Genealogy of Ethics: An Overview of Work in Progress'. In H. Dreyfus and P. Rabinow (Eds), *Michel Foucault: Beyond Structuralism and Hermeneutics*, pp. 229–52. Chicago: University of Chicago Press.

Foucault, M. (1984). 'Space, Knowledge and Power'. In P. Rabinow (Ed.), *The Foucault Reader*, pp. 239–56. London: Penguin.

Gillis, J. R. (Ed.) (1994). *Commemorations: The Politics of National Identity*. Princeton: Princeton University Press.

Gur-Ze'ev, I. (2001). 'Philosophy of Peace Education in a Postmodern Era'. *Educational Theory*, 51 (3): 315–36.

Harris, I. (2004). 'Peace Education Theory'. *Journal of Peace Education*, 1 (1): 5–20.

Hayden, R. M. (2002). 'Antagonistic Tolerance: Competitive Sharing of Religious Sites in South Asia and the Balkans'. *Current Anthropology*, 43 (2): 205–19.

Latour, B. (2002). *War of the Worlds: What About Peace?* Translated by C. Bigg. Chicago: Prickly Paradigm.

McDermott, R. (1980). *Profile: R. L. Birdwhistell. Kinesis Report* 2, 1: 1–16.

McGlynn, C., Zembylas, M., Bekerman, Z. and Gallagher, T. (Eds) (2009). *Peace Education in Conflict and Post-Conflict Societies: Comparative Perspectives.* New York: Palgrave, MacMillan.

Mendus, S. (1989). *Toleration and the Limits of Liberalism.* New York: Macmillan.

Moya, P. and Hames-Garcia, M. (Eds) (2000). *Reclaiming Identity: Realist Theory and the Predicament of Postmodernism.* Berkeley: University of California Press.

Opotow, S. and Luke, T. J. (2012). 'Complexities and Challenges of Peace'. *Peace and Conflict: Journal of Peace Psychology*, 18 (4): 351–3.

Page, J. (2004). 'Peace Education: Exploring Some Philosophical Foundations'. *International Review of Education*, 50 (1): 3–15.

Page, J. (2008). *Peace Education: Exploring Ethical and Philosophical Foundations.* Charlotte, NC: Information Age Publishing.

Rose, N. (1990). *Governing the Soul: The Shaping of the Private Self.* London and New York: Routledge.

Rose, N. (1998). *Inventing Our Selves: Psychology, Power and Personhood.* Cambridge: Cambridge University Press.

Rose, N. (1999). *Powers of Freedom: Reframing Political Thought.* Cambridge, UK: Cambridge University Press.

Spindler, G. and Spindler, L. (1994). *Pathways to Cultural Awareness: Cultural Therapy with Teachers and Students.* Thousand Oaks, CA: Corwin Press Inc.

Synott, J. (2005). 'Peace Education as an Educational Paradigm: Review of a Changing Field Using an Old Measure'. *Journal of Peace Education*, 2 (1): 3–16.

Trifonas, P. and Wright, B. (Eds) (2013). *Critical Peace Education: Difficult Dialogues.* Dordrecht/, The Netherlands: Springer.

Trueba, H. (1993). 'Cultural Therapy in Action'. In H. Trueba, C. Rodriguez, Y. Zou and J. Cintron (Eds), *Healing Multicultural America: Mexican Immigrants Rise to Power in Rural California*, pp. 155–68. London: Falmer.

Varenne, H. and McDermott, R. (1998). *Successful Failure: The Schools America Builds.* Colorado: Westview Press.

Zembylas, M. (2008). *The Politics of Trauma in Education.* New York: Palgrave, MacMillan.

Zembylas, M. (2015). *Emotion and traumatic conflict: Re-claiming healing in education.* Oxford: Oxford University Press.

Zembylas, M. and Bekerman, Z. (2008). 'Dilemmas of Justice in Peace/Coexistence Education: Affect and the Politics of Identity'. *The Review of Education, Pedagogy and Cultural Studies*, 30 (4): 399–419.

10

School Textbooks and Entanglements of the 'Colonial Present' in Israel and Palestine[1]

André Elias Mazawi

Introduction

How should textbooks be conceived of when being designed and used in contexts of 'intractable conflicts' associated with military occupation, colonization, or struggle for national self-determination? In this chapter, I discuss the controversies over school textbooks in Israel and Palestine by situating them over the backdrop of Israeli colonialism, Palestinian statelessness, and intra-social political struggles within each group, respectively.

Positioning

My interaction with school textbooks is marked by an ambivalent relationship. As a Palestinian Arab, born and raised in Israel, I was schooled in a Catholic institution that follows the official *Baccalauréat* program in effect in France. Yet, it was not until a couple of months following my high school graduation that I visited Paris for the first time. How powerful was my astonishment when, on one September afternoon stroll to the *Arc de Triomphe*, I 'discovered' the name of my hometown, *JAFFA*, carved in capital letters on one of the pillars. Upon scrutiny, it turned out that in March of 1799, Napoleon had invaded Ottoman cities along Palestine's coast, among which was Jaffa, which he besieged and occupied. The surrendered Ottoman soldiers were executed despite their status as prisoners of war. The French soldiers did not spare Jaffa's civilian population neither.[2] Étienne

Louis Malus (1775–1812), a mathematician and member of the French force, who witnessed the massacres, reported:

> the soldiers spread in all parts butchered men, women, old folk, children, Christians, Turks; all that had a human face fell victim to their fury.
>
> The tumult of the carnage, the broken doors, the houses shaken by the noise of shooting and arms, the screaming of women, the father and the child thrown down one over the other, the daughter raped over the dead body of her mother, the smoke of the dead singed by their clothes, the smell of the blood, the moaning of the wounded, the shouts of the victors quarrelling over the spoils of an expiring victim, the infuriated soldiers replying to the cries of despair by shouts of rage and by redoubled blows, lastly men satiated with blood and gold falling, exhausted, over heaps of dead bodies, such was the sight which this unfortunate city offered until the night had come.
>
> (Malus 1892, pp. 135–6; author's translation)

With the sacking of Jaffa, 'a rhetoric specific to the Revolutionary and Napoleonic Wars was invented, secular in nature, to justify mass killings' (Dwyer 2009, p. 390). Jaffa thus encountered the French revolution – not through its idealistic and liberatory slogans – but through the decimating effects of mass killings and military occupation. How have I missed such a conjuncture, between the French revolution and its colonial legacies? Why and how did French history school textbooks remain silent on these events, preferring instead to emphasize the scientific contributions brought by a military 'expedition' [*sic*] in terms of bringing the Arab east into a European project of modernity?

On hindsight, I now realize that that silence of history school textbooks reflects potent speech acts undergirded by layouts, erudite texts, explanations, analyses, multicoloured pictures and paintings, and a teacher's classroom performance. It determined what I could or could not know about France and its revolution, as a student living in a region that continues to experience Western imperial designs. Indicatively, my 'discovery' at the *Arc de Triomphe* emphasized the incommensurability that separates school textbooks – as semiotic spaces of a particular kind – and cities, as semiotic spaces where imaginaries of self, nation and Other are also purposefully and intently choreographed.

Whither textbooks?

The representation or misrepresentation of Napoleon's (and other colonial) endeavours raises wider questions regarding the roles played by school textbooks in relation to conflicts, colonial histories, injustice and violence. While some decision-makers omit conflict-loaded representations purposefully, others have called for the rewriting of school textbooks in an effort to mitigate the negative effects of violent colonial and nationalistic legacies. The aim often revolves around offering younger generations an opportunity to 'learn to live together' within an inclusive and humanizing framework (Pingel 2010; Soysal, Bertilotti and Mannitz 2005, pp. 30–1).

Efforts to revise school textbooks in this direction continue to be invested in the Israel–Palestine context too. The underlying assumption of those advocating this line of action is that, on both sides of the conflict, school textbook narratives 'stand as a major obstacle to any peacemaking process and later processes of reconciliation' (Israeli-Palestinian School Book Project 2013, p. 2). It is claimed that school textbook 'narratives may need to be modified in order to facilitate building a new reality of peace' and 'serve as one agent among others in socializing new generations' (p. 2).

Notwithstanding, one wonders what it means for school textbooks to be revised independently of the protracted conflict in which Palestinians and Israelis continue to be engulfed – as individuals and national communities. What are the implications of revising school textbooks regardless of the imbalances in power relations prevailing between Israel and Palestinians, as colonizer and colonized, respectively? Certainly, one can productively negotiate school textbook reforms agreed upon by equally positioned parties, such as two sovereign entities (states), whose territorial integrity is not at stake. But, what does it mean to apply the same premise and set of expectations to a context in which one of the parties – in this case, Palestinians – is still subject to an ongoing and deeply entrenched Israeli domination in all spheres of life, with no control over its land, economy, politics and natural resources, curtailed in its inalienable right to struggle for self-determination and national liberation? In such a context, how equitable and ethical is it to place the colonized in an epistemic position under which they cannot name, let alone represent in their school textbooks, their colonizer *as* colonizer, and their colonization *as such,* with all its brutality and inhumanity?

In his book *The Colonial Present*, Derek Gregory (2004) observes in relation to the challenges that face reforms in colonized societies:

> We forget the exactions, suppressions, and complicities that colonialism forced upon the peoples it subjugated, and the way it withdrew from them the right to make their own history, ensuring that they did so emphatically not under conditions of their own choosing. … We forget that it is often ordinary people who do such awful, extraordinary things. … To acknowledge this is … to recall

the part we are called to play – and continue to play – in the performance of the colonial present. (p. 10)

Gregory's observation helps capture the challenges associated with the design of school textbooks in contexts of protracted national conflict and colonialism, such as in the context of Israel and Palestine. Gregory's observation also points to the subtle ways in which colonialism persists in its effects in the guise of projects of modernity, progress and – as I argue more particularly in this chapter – in the guise of notions of 'peace education' that do not address the colonizing effects of power inequities that operate both within and between societies trapped in protracted conflicts. Paradoxically and irremediably, the result is the perpetuation of a 'colonial present,' in and through school textbooks.

Textbooks, signatures and the field of power

A school textbook is more than just a text used in school and more than just a book, in the narrow sense of these words. It has much more to it. For Stray (1994), a school textbook represents 'a book designed to provide an authoritative pedagogic version of an area of knowledge' (p. 2). It represents a claimed 'authority' to mobilize diverse forms of social and political capital, including narratives, counter-narratives and visual layouts to construct 'image realities' (Crawford and Foster 2007, p. 7) of the political. 'Image realities' objectify history and ritualize remembrance. They translate conceptions of self, nation, state and territorial space into particular 'reading paths'. These 'image realities' are endorsed as objectified forms of knowledge, differentially relayed across the field of power to members of different social groups.

The political aesthetics within which the writing and design of school textbooks is undertaken is underpinned by complex semiotic work. By its writing, a school textbook 'organizes and concludes a mode of intelligibility' (de Certeau 1988, p. 21). Its designers do so by deploying a wide array of stylistic, literary, disciplinary and cultural strategies. This deployment forges the contours of narrative landscapes that transform a disparate set of resources into imaginary tales choreographed along a plot, with finite representations of a hegemonic political order. One could argue that choreographies operate as 'pan-semiotic categories of language' (van Leeuwen 1996) that mediate what can be known, remembered and enunciated within school textbooks, and what cannot. They also weld differential systems of signs, into what Giorgio Agamben (2009) calls 'signatures' – multimodal pan-semiotic assemblages, which enact relationships among systems of representation to reference a particular interpretation of an object. As 'multimodal' media, textbooks weave visual and textual layouts along a 'reading path' that seeks to shape students' imaginaries in particular ways (Peled-Elhanan 2009, p. 95; 2012; Weiner 2016).

The discussion so far has a number of implications for school textbooks in the context of Israel and Palestine. First, school textbooks are situated and positional political objects; they not only construct world orders; they also serve as resources in seeking and mobilizing support for particular political projects and agendas. If so, what are the differential trajectories attached to school textbooks within the wider context of the conflict that pervades relations between Palestinians and Israel is? Second, political struggles shape the epistemic signatures around which textbooks are organized. How does the imbalance of power between colonizer and colonized in the Israel–Palestine context impact the capacity of designers to ensure the coherence and integrity of epistemic signatures of their school textbooks? Third, school textbooks establish political aesthetics and 'visual orders' that offer to sense-perception spectacled performances of the 'national' body politic. If so, within the Israel–Palestine conflict, what are the political aesthetic and visual landscapes through which each side delineates the boundaries of its body politic?

War zones, curricular fields, textbook sites

School textbooks (and curricula more generally) are intricately interwoven into the context of the conflict opposing the Zionist movement and Palestinians. From its inception to the period leading to the establishment of the State of Israel in 1948, the Zionist movement's settlement of Ottoman, later British-ruled Palestine, established autonomous Hebrew curricula and school textbooks. These diverged significantly from those enacted by the ruler of the day, in both contents and emphases. Hebrew school textbooks served as political tools in the consolidation of the institutional completeness and in the forging of a sense of collective identity and political will among Palestine's Jewish society composed largely of migrants. In contradistinction, school curricula and textbooks imposed on Palestinian Arab communities, particularly under British (1917–48), and subsequently Israeli, Egyptian and Jordanian rules, have been associated with their national subjugation and territorial fragmentation, over which Palestinians exerted virtually no control.

Between 1948 and 1967, Palestinian students in the West Bank and Gaza Strip used an assortment of school textbooks, Egyptian in the Gaza Strip and Jordanian in the West Bank. Between 1967 and 1993, following Israel's military occupation of these territories, the Israeli military excised from school textbooks references to Palestinian national history and identity, and geographic terms that referred to Palestine were also removed (Moughrabi 2001a). One United Nations report noted a 'constant Israeli interference in the functioning of schools and other educational institutions in the [occupied] territories'. School textbooks were 'closely censored and revised by the occupying authorities', leading to the 'distortion of facts' and to the implementation of 'punitive measures' against teachers who tried 'to remedy these shortcomings' (United Nations 1985, pp. 37–8).

Under *The Declaration of Principles on Interim Self-Government Arrangements* (popularly known as the 'Oslo accords'), signed in 1993, Israel committed to grant the Palestine Liberation Organisation (PLO), in its locally visible manifestation as a 'Palestinian Authority' (PA), some powers over the design of curricula and school textbooks in the West Bank and Gaza Strip. At the same time, despite these accords, Palestinian statelessness and Israeli colonization persisted, trickling into the most mundane daily aspects of Palestinian life. At this juncture of contradictions, what does it mean for Palestinians to claim jurisdiction over, and 're-inhabit', a decolonized field of education, within the wider context of persisting colonization? Similarly, how do Israeli school textbooks engage the architecture of power Israel exerts over the lives of Palestinians, both those Palestinians who hold Israeli citizenship and those who, since 1967, continue to be subject to Israeli military occupation in the West Bank and Gaza Strip?

Following the PA's establishment in 1994, new school textbooks were gradually introduced from 2000 onward as part of wider efforts to design a Palestinian curriculum supported by international agencies, such as UNESCO and the World Bank. A Curriculum Development Center (CDC) team, led by the late Professor Ibrahim Abu-Lughod (1929–2001), undertook the work between October 1995 and September 1996, as a 'semi-independent operation'. According to Hovsepian (2008), Abu-Lughod kept the PA and its Ministry of Education at bay by emphasizing that 'his mandate was actually conferred upon him by UNESCO' (p. 166). Abu-Lughod's team adopted a participative approach, holding town hall meetings and engaging teachers and civil society actors. They produced 'a damning indictment on virtually every aspect of the existing educational system' (Murray 2008, p. 44), laying the foundations for 'a radical plan for the construction of the first Palestinian curriculum' (p. 158), taking 'into account the Palestinian aspiration to reconstitute its social fabric and prepare the skilled personnel for the process of state-building' (p. 167).

The Plan envisioned a school system organized along three 'stages' – 'preparatory' (four years, starting at age five), 'empowerment' (five years), and 'take off' (three years, ending at age seventeen). It recommended that in the last stage, a distinction between vocational and academic 'streams' of study be avoided, and that the elimination of the secondary school matriculation exam be considered. The Plan contemplated the teaching of a third language, in addition to Arabic and English, 'such as French or the teaching of Hebrew as a functional language of the region' (Abu-Lughod 1996, p. 8).

Work on the first Palestinian curriculum generated considerable tensions between civil society organizations (and their local and diasporic articulations) and PLO cadres administering the PA's apparatuses. It also fuelled tensions between Palestinian academics and intellectuals who were initially based in the United States, and the nascent structures of the PA. The CDC's head, Abu-Lughod, who returned from the United States to the West Bank in 1992, was involved in institution-building, together with Edward Said in relation to the PLO, the Palestinian National Council and with US-based Professor Fouad Moughrabi, founding director of the Qattan Centre for Educational Research and Development (Ramallah). Abu-Lughod maintained 'vast connections with the Palestinian intellectuals in the diaspora'. But he 'had not participated directly with the educational reform movement that flourished [in the West Bank and Gaza Strip] during the intifada' (p. 163).[3] This movement witnessed an unprecedented Palestinian grass-roots participation in developing transformative pedagogies of emancipation, creating and publishing pedagogic materials and textbooks (Fasheh 1995).

Once Abu-Lughod's mandate at the CDC reached its term, the PA's Ministry of Education appropriated the Plan, signalling greater PA centralism. The CDC was eventually incorporated into the Ministry of Education, and the Abu-Lughod plan was reissued in 1997 as an amended 'draft plan' (Hovsepian 2008, p. 171). Helen Murray's (2008) study of the 'curriculum wars' that ensued suggests a blurring of the distinctions between 'civic' and 'national' representations within textbooks, as the PA moved in, to assert its authority (p. 44).

'Ali Al-Jarbawi's question

A member of the CDC team, 'Ali Al-Jarbawi (1996), emphasized the need to devise a new and unified Palestinian social science and civic education curriculum as 'one of the most important means, if not the most important, to ensure the integration' of the West Bank and Gaza Strip, as 'a major Palestinian aim' (p. 445; author's translation). In relation to the general framework of the new curriculum, Al-Jarbawi (1996) wrote:

> The most important and sensitive question regarding the design of such a curriculum is … *which Palestine should we teach*? Is it historical Palestine with its comprehensive geography, or is it Palestine that would result from the accords signed with Israel? And how should Israel be treated, is it just a neighbour or is it a state built on the ruins of most of Palestine? (pp. 454–5; emphasis in the original; author's translation)

Al-Jarbawi acknowledges that the corporeality of a political community is mediated by its literary production. Yet, for him, to ensure a coherent and viable literary representation of the nation, its underpinning epistemic signature should be translatable into classroom-performed practices. Here, a core challenge facing Palestinian education policymakers is to craft a 'standpoint of what is common to the community' (Rancière 2004, p. 13), in relation to which Palestinians can recognize themselves, as a body politic, both internally and in relation to the Israeli state and the wider world community.

'Visual orders' and constructions of the body politic

A cursory review of PA school textbooks shows that the literary production of the nation, and its underpinning epistemic signature, have significantly shifted since the initial introduction of these textbooks. Brown (2007) observes that the initial CDC approach emphasized a national identity 'that was designed to foster appreciation of pluralism and variety while simultaneously developing a spirit of mutual accommodation and belonging' (p. 127) among social class, religious and regional groups within Palestinian society. This was judged 'too radical' by the PA Ministry of Education, and greater visibility was subsequently granted to 'authoritative structures,' such as the family and the 'Islamic dimension' of identity (p. 128). Brown (2007) further points out that, 'despite the attempt to depict Palestinian society as a seamless fabric of family, nation, and religion, the textbooks obliquely acknowledge possible tensions' (p. 134). He adds that the composition and value orientations of individual textbook team members play a role in the way Palestinians as a group are portrayed. Civic Education textbooks were 'the most daring and provocative in adopting a critical pedagogy'

(p. 136), while 'those responsible for teaching students Islam show few signs of enthusiasm for individuality and creativity among elementary and intermediate school students' (p. 136). In contrast, representing family and gender roles remains challenging, 'though the textbooks have shown growing boldness in this regard' (Brown 2007, p. 134). Differences prevail across textbooks. W. Reiss (2004) points out that in Islamic Education textbooks (Grades 1–3 and 6–8), all women and almost all girls 'are depicted with veils and clothes which cover them from head to toe, even in a home setting' (p. 6). In contrast, National Education textbooks for elementary grades and Civic Education textbooks (Grades 1–9) portray men and women and occasionally children 'as equal parties' (Nordbruch 2002, p. 5).

Visualizing the body (politic)

An analysis of the PA's National Education textbooks (published in 2001–5) illustrates how the contours of the Palestinian body politic were represented. It highlights several conflict-loaded sociopolitical cleavages operating within Palestinian society in the post-Oslo period.[4]

For instance, Lesson 5 in the NE textbook for Grade 1 (Part 2), 'The People of My Country' (*sha'b biladi*), aims to acquaint students with Palestinian society. In this lesson, people work in commerce, agriculture or industry (p. 60). Next, Palestinians are presented according to the sites they inhabit: city, village, refugee camp and desert/pasture-grounds (*al-badiya*) (pp. 61–2). 'Towns' are added in the NE textbook for Grade 2 (Part 1, Lessons 6–11, pp. 22–41). The taxonomy is taken up for a third time in the NE textbook for Grade 5 (Unit 2, Lesson 3, pp. 34–7). On p. 34, drawings of a city, an agricultural area, a village and a refugee camp are shown. Students are asked to name each category and identify where they live: *al-badiya* and towns are absent. On p. 35, the text describes 'cities', 'villages', 'Bedouin encampments' and 'camps'. Here, towns are absent but 'Palestinians of the diaspora' are added. Finally, on p. 37, as student activity, the categories are abstracted into a schematic figure of three distinct circles – the city, the village and *al-badiya* – each maintaining an economic exchange of specific goods, named and marked by arrows, with the other two. Students are asked: 'In what do the city and *al-badiya* depend on the village?' and 'Would any of the [three] inhabited concentrations give up on the other two? Why?'

Throughout, the exercise reifies the groups constitutive of the nation into fixed spatial attributes of affiliation. A functional economic exchange of goods between spatial categories stands for social solidarity as an act of consumerism.

There are few interactions between categories. For instance, it is not mentioned that teachers living in one category can work in any other category (though they do hold government positions). When a sense of community is invoked, it is internal to the category (village).

Cities and villages are constructed as immutable categories. In contrast, it is implied that refugee camps will dissipate once their residents return to their places of origin, a nod to the right of return. They are absent in the figure depicting economic transactions, suggesting that they make no contribution to the economic cohesion between the various groups. Bedouins in *al-badiya* are portrayed as exiting their category, part of a naturalized process of modernization. In the NE textbook for Grade 6 (pp. 79–82), two pictures are presented side by side: (A) a stick-holding Bedouin crouching on the ground next to a camel, and (B) a flying jet plane (p. 80). One of the questions is: 'What is necessary to move a person from using the camel to using the airplane as a mode of transportation?' (p. 81). In a stroke, the lifestyle of Bedouins is emptied of creativity, depicted as incompatible with modernization and progress. Bedouins are cast as pathologized outliers within a semiotic hierarchical rendition of Palestinian society.

When the nation is visualized engaging political action, questions arise about the extent of diversity involved. One drawing, 'Procession of the Palestinian People' (NE, Grade 4, Part 1, p. 42), shows two boys, three women and six men (no girls) raising four Palestinian flags and two banners. Participants wear clothes that reference urbanized upper-middle/middle-class backgrounds. A second drawing depicts an 'Independence Day' celebration, under the title 'Palestinian Society' (NE, Grade 5, p. 25). There are two national flags and an audience of twenty-three individuals (five in silhouette form) clapping hands while seated on lined-up chairs. A man, with a black and white *hatta* (headdress cloth) on his shoulders, addresses the audience through a microphone. This time, no Palestinian from *al-badiya* or from agricultural localities is present; neither are children, adolescents, workers or people from working-class backgrounds shown. In both drawings, the women's clothing suggests some lifestyle variations in relation to religion and culture (more in the second drawing). However, men are portrayed within a very narrow range of clothing: they may have a moustache, but all men are shaven. No men are depicted with a beard or a garb, which could be interpreted as signs of conservatism. The second drawing portrays society as a 'passivated' (van Leeuwen 1996) audience lined up in a chair formation, being talked to, and reacting by clapping (audience members do not communicate with each other, all are focused on the speaker). The drawing portrays a sense of disciplined ritualized normalcy.

NE textbooks construct a 'visual order' that invokes sectorial spatial representations of the body politic, muting social class distinctions among Palestinians by reifying groups as spatially situated consumers. When the body politic is invoked, it reflects world views of able-bodied men and women from urbanized classes, of particular ideological backgrounds. The 'reading path' is saturated with discourses on progress, and by an Orientalist 'epistemic signature' of the nation, the 'visual order' enacts a 'colonial present' from within.

Power geometries and inter-textualities

PA textbooks have not remained subject to intra-social Palestinian debates exclusively. Israeli groups, comprising right-wing activists, settlers (Hovsepian 2008, pp. 216–17) and former members of the Israeli military, launched what Murray (2008) describes as 'a political campaign against the newly emerging Palestinian curriculum' (p. 42). 'The battle of the books in Palestine' (Moughrabi 2001b) raged in media outlets, political international circles and institutions, leading to congressional hearings, and 'prompting threats from the US Congress and President to cut off international assistance to the PA' (Hovsepian 2008, p. 159. See also, Naser-Najjab and Pappé 2016).

Despite strong arguments to the contrary (Brown 2003, p. 99; Israeli-Palestinian School Book Project 2013), mediatized accusations continued to be made against PA school textbooks. It was claimed that they 'incite violence' against Israel and Jews because they deploy statements built around notions of 'martyrdom', 'jihad' or 'sacrifice' for one's homeland and its liberation (see Pina's 2005 summary tables of reports). At the same time, those same critics and mediatized reports disregarded the persisting colonization of Palestinian lands, and the displacement of entire Palestinian communities, particularly cave-dwelling and farming communities in rural areas, still under Israeli control. These contradictory dynamics introduced a chasm between a sanitized representation of occupation Palestinians continue to be pressured to represent in their textbooks and the effective material conditions created by Israeli military and colonial policies in the Palestinian territories. Mediatized political discourses could thus inscribe the colonized victim as the promoter of senseless and aimless violence, disconnected from national struggle for liberation.

A second critique against PA textbooks focuses on constructions of Palestinian memories of place (Nordbruch 2003, p. 97). Here again, the case of the city of Jaffa serves to illustrate some of the issues involved. Up to 1948, Jaffa evolved to become a major Palestinian Arab port city and an intellectual and political hub, which was entirely destroyed as part of the war and subsequent annexation to the city of Tel-Aviv. Representations of Jaffa – now a southern suburb integrated into the municipal territory of Tel-Aviv – in PA textbooks have been vehemently contested: How Jaffa is narrated, what pictures depict it, how they are or should be subtitled, how the city figures on a textbook map in relation to the Palestinian territories, all these have been interpreted as 'evidence' that Palestinians still entertain a dream to reclaim Jaffa, and hence 'destroy' the State of Israel. Critics thus deny Palestinians their capacity to forge imagined narrative horizons of their past on which any community rests, while the imaginary narratives associated with the founding of the State of Israel and its construction as a Jewish state remain largely unchallenged.

A third critique levelled against PA textbooks pertains to how political borders are represented on school textbook maps. A most recent study, published by Adwan, Bar-Tal and Wexler (2016) found that the cartographic representations of the land that lies between the Mediterranean and the Dead Sea, and its current political borders, remain a contested aspect of school textbooks (pp. 213–14). Challenged on this point, the PA stated that borders 'will be decided on by representatives of both countries and peoples through negotiations and agreements. Once these decisions are made, and are ratified by the international community through the UN, then they will be included in the future Palestinian textbooks' (PA, Ministry of Education 2001, p. 116). Palestinian decision-makers argue that, as 'politicians have not reached an agreement about the final status' (Khouri 2003, p. 72), tracing the 'borders' of the PA would determine those of Israel and vice versa. Similarly, a study by Ruth Firer and Sami Adwan (2004, p. 154) shows that maps included in Israeli textbooks tend to disregard the 1949 ceasefire lines (see also Adwan et al. 2016). Israeli textbooks further refer to cities and locations within the Palestinian areas as an integral part of *Eretz Yisrael* (Land of Israel, in Hebrew) and its geography. Thus, within the wider political stalemate over borders and their delimitations, textbooks have turned into contested sites yet to be colonized by treaties and their outcomes.

Vanishing inter-textualities

Despite the multilayered monitoring of PA textbooks, Palestinians – whether those who hold Israeli citizenship (within Israel) or those who live in a stateless condition under the PA's jurisdiction – exert very little political leverage, if any, on the contents of Israeli school textbooks and their representation of

Palestinians or of Israeli history and geography that references Palestinian rights, lands and history. It is not that Israeli textbooks do not raise concerns. Israeli textbooks stereotype Arabs negatively, while positive stereotyping is marginal (Bar-Tal 2006, p. 145). Moreover, Israeli secondary school history and geography textbooks were found to deny the national and territorial identity of Palestinians. For instance, Peled-Elhanan (2010, 2012) argues that Israeli history textbooks legitimize, on utilitarian grounds (p. 399), massacres perpetuated against Palestinians. Israeli textbooks are underpinned by epistemic signatures of the land as a Jewish national space, in which the 'architecture' of military occupation and colonization is complemented by an elaborate semiotic textbook architecture that preserves the hegemonic dominance of nationalist perspectives and reading plots in the education of Jewish youngsters.

Some researchers who examined Israeli textbooks take exception with these analyses. They argue that significant changes did occur in the representation of the Palestinian and the Arab 'Others' in civic education and history textbooks. Ichilov, Salomon and Inbar (2005) claim that 'important strides were made over the years to promote citizenship and democratic education', recognizing that 'it is naive to expect that citizenship education in its present form, and under current circumstances, could foster the emergence of a shared civic identity that would bridge the national, cultural, ethnic and social divides within Israeli society' (p. 320). Adopting a nuanced position, Elie Podeh (2000) points out that history textbooks shifted from an ideologically oriented genre, which aligned historical truth with a hegemonic Zionist/Israeli position, to a 'textbook generation' that offers a relatively multiperspectival narrative.

Critics disagree over the meaning of these changes, as reviewed in the previous paragraph. Mikhal Barak (2005) counterargues that a new civic education textbook introduced in 2001 still reflects 'an ethnocentric program focusing on Israel as a Jewish and democratic state; it does not challenge students to think critically or discuss the inherently problematic character of a Jewish and democratic state. This situation stems from the conception that civic education is a political field competing with education in Zionist and national values' (p. 4; see also Jamal 2009, p. 499). Aryeh Kizel (2008) argues that, despite claims to the contrary, Israeli general history textbooks are still subordinate to narratives serving political ends associated with the nation state. He adds that, despite their innovative textual overlays and multicoloured layouts, their narratives scaffold a pre-determined Zionist vision and ethos (see also Raz-Karkotzkin 2002, on the limits of national remembrance in Israeli history textbooks). Following the 2013 and the 2015 parliamentary elections, which saw right and far-right parties associated with Israeli settler movements represented forcefully in government, school textbooks and curricula judged to exhibit 'leftist' leanings have been particularly targeted. For instance, 'citizenship education' textbooks have been revamped and ideologically aligned with the broad lines underpinning the notion of Israel as an ethnic (Jewish) and Zionist state, at the expense of marginalizing its democratic bearings (Kashti 2015). Israel's Ministry of Education compiled lists of banned or unrecommended books or novels for public schools (Kashti 2016). Some of these policy trends are not new. Yet, the latest policies considerably narrow the bases of a shared experience of the Israeli body politic, with less and less space left for Palestinian Arabs and Jews in Israel to articulate a shared construction of citizenship in and through school textbooks. Furthermore, the mediatized controversies surrounding the excising of textbooks suspected of exhibiting 'leftist' or 'post-Zionist' world views are indicative of the deepening chasms *within* the Jewish society, among groups defined along socio-economic, ethnic, religious and ideological lines of demarcation. The power politics that surrounds school textbook reforms in Israel thus reflects an increasing fragmentation of the Israeli body politic, and the emergence of distinctive forms of identity politics among ethnic, cultural and racialized communities. In these controversies, some endorse the position that Israel's history and civic education can inculcate a 'shared' political culture without interrogating the political philosophy that underpins the State of Israel as an ethnic (Jewish) and a democratic state. Others, often dubbed as 'post-Zionists', argue that Israel's ethnocultural pluralism must be reflected 'in a historical and multicultural civic narrative that would replace the national historical narrative, in order to prepare the children of Israel for a democratic life in a conflict-loaded multisectorial society' (Naveh and Yogev 2002, p. 146). Distinct imagined horizons separate these two conceptions of Israel, as state and political community; and radically different perceptions of school textbooks as social media. These competing positions have become aligned along the fault lines of parliamentary right – left politics within Israel, highly politicized and, therefore, highly controversial.

With regard to public schools that serve Palestinian students living in Israel, Israel's Ministry of Education pursues a policy line that marginalizes in school textbooks the historical and experiential realities relevant for the Palestinian community in Israel. For instance, a ban was instituted on the use of the Arabic term '*nakba*' (catastrophe) or its commemoration in school textbooks and schools (Haaretz 2010). Quite differently, an experimental school textbook, *Learning Each Other's Historical Narrative*, developed jointly by a team of academics and teachers from Israel and the Palestinian West Bank was also disqualified (Kashti 2010). Sami Adwan and Dan Bar-On (2004), involved in the textbook's drafting, point out that it adopts a constructivist and participative narrative approach to history. Israeli and Palestinian narratives are presented side by side for students to engage in an attempt to break the 'culture of enmity' (p. 515) between both sides. In this instance, the State asserts its role as an arbiter of narratives that frame the construction of a sense of place and a sense of self within public education and the public sphere at large. One could also consider such policies as part of wider efforts to enact what Uri Ram (2009) refers to as a 'narrated' (p. 370) 'regime of forgetting' (p. 390), which constructs history to fit a given ideological mould.

School textbooks as performed spectacles

School textbooks in the Israel–Palestine context manifest themselves in a wide range of forms and shapes. Researchers increasingly realize the need to revisit their notions regarding what stands for a 'school textbook' within the Israel–Palestine context, given the different structures and expansion patterns of each society's schooling systems. For instance, school textbooks used in the autonomous Ultra-Orthodox Jewish schools 'focus almost entirely on the study of holy books and offer very little in terms of secular subjects,' presenting 'a relatively closed, undisputable religious dogma' (Adwan et al. 2016, p. 203). Similarly, in the semi-autonomous state religious schools within Israel, or still, in schools and equivalent educational settings located within Israeli settler colonies across the occupied West Bank, very little research – if any – has been undertaken into the panoply of textual and visual materials to which students are exposed, particularly with regard to the representation of Palestinians. To understand the implications of this state of affairs, it is useful to observe here that, for instance, in 2014–15, almost half of all Jewish primary students and over 40 per cent of all upper division high school Jewish students studied in Ultra-Orthodox and religious public schools (Addi-Raccah et al. 2015, pp. 26–7). Thus, while PA schools and those Israeli public and church (community) schools that serve Palestinians within Israel use mainly conventional state-mandated school textbooks, this is much less the case in schools that serve Israeli Jewish children. In the latter, there is a greater reliance on religious sources that fall outside the conventional conception of a school textbook, and a higher exposure to a range of subsidized 'para-curricular' activities that target the strengthening of 'Jewish identity'. Moreover, these schools also draw on textbook materials produced and supplied, beyond the formal curriculum, by semi-funded and non-governmental organizations active in the strengthening of Jewish identity among students. This state of affairs raises considerable conceptual and methodological challenges. To understand how these curricular materials operate within the school space, it becomes necessary to devise sensitive methodologies that capture which hermeneutic traditions these programs and schools draw on and how they are situated in relation to state-mandated school textbooks and related curricula.

The emphases placed by international observers, pundits and scholars on the way Palestinian and Israeli textbooks 'represent the Other,' heightens the visibility of national aspects of each group's representation. Such a focus, however, leaves entirely unproblematized how school textbooks engage questions of social justice, poverty, exclusion, racism, social and economic inequities and social diversity *within* each society. Emphases placed on the national (and to some extent on the gendered) dimensions of school textbook narratives – most of them associated with the protracted political conflict – thus actively render invisible the powerful forms of *internal* colonization, exclusion and marginalization taking place within each society, and ultimately entrenching the wider conflict.

In conclusion, state-mandated school textbooks in the Israel–Palestine contexts – and particularly the Palestinian ones – have become highly sanitized constructions, very much along the lines of those French history textbooks that remained silent on Napoleon's massacres in Jaffa, as they did on other aspects of French colonialism. Notwithstanding, while strolling through the landscaped spaces of school textbooks can be engineered, to some extent, disregarding those silences inevitably leaves open, if not deepens, the festering wounds of alienation, injustice and exactions of colonialism – both national and internal. This comes at the cost of mimicking life as a play reminiscent of Samuel Beckett's *Waiting for Godot*, whose actors seem to have lost their plot, unable to utter a meaningful aim or direction.

Notes

1 The present chapter is based, in part, on a paper entitled '"Which Palestine Should We Teach?" Signatures, palimpsests, and struggles over school textbooks,' published in *Studies in Philosophy and Education*, 30 (2011), pp. 169–83.

2 The French conquest of Jaffa was romanticized by Antoine-Jean Gros (1771–1835) in his 1804 imposing yet propaganda-motivated painting, displayed in the Louvre museum, in Paris, France (Grigsby 1995).

3 The (first) *intifada* (uprising) erupted in December 1987 in the Gaza Strip and spread to the West Bank.

4 State of Palestine, Ministry of Education (2001, 2002a, 2002b, 2004a, 2004b, 2005). Textbooks are available at http://www.pcdc.edu.ps. Translations by the author.

References

Addi-Raccah, A., Greenstein and Bahak, H. (2015). Trends in differentiation and integration in the locality of residence on the basis of the students' socio-economic status in the school. Paper presented at the Initiative for Applied Education Research. *The Israel Academy of Sciences and Humanities*, December. [Hebrew]

Adwan, S. and Bar-On, D. (2004). 'Shared History Project: A PRIME Example of Peace-Building Under Fire'. *International Journal of Politics, Culture and Society*, 17 (3): 513–21.

Adwan, S., Bar-Tal, D. and Wexler, B. E. (2016). 'Portrayal of the Other in Palestinian and Israeli Schoolbooks: A Comparative Study'. *Political Psychology*, 37 (2): 201–17.

Agamben, G. (2009). *The Signature of All Things: On Method*. Translated by L. D'Isanto and K. Attell. New York: Zone Books.

'Alayan, S. (2010). 'Evaluating History School Curricula and Textbooks in Palestine: Towards the Building of a National Identity and Quality Education'. In S. 'Alayan, S. Zweib and A. Rhode (Eds), *Educational Reform in the Middle East: Self and Other in School Curricula*, pp. 149–82. 'Amman, Jordan: Dar Al-Shuruq. [Arabic]

Al-Jarbawi, 'A (1996). 'Evaluating the Social Sciences Curricula in the West Bank and Gaza Strip'. In I. Abu-Lughod (Ed.), *The First Palestinian Curriculum for General Education: The Comprehensive Plan*, pp. 403–81. Ramallah, Palestine: The Palestinian Curriculum Development Center. [Arabic]

Apple, M. W. and Christian-Smith, L. K. (Eds) (1991). *The Politics of the Textbook*. New York and London: Routledge, pp. 1–21.

Barak, M. (September 2005). 'Civic Education in Israel'. *Adalah's Newsletter*, 18: 1–5.

Bar-Tal, D. (2006). 'The Arab Image in Hebrew School Textbooks'. In H. Schenker and Z. Abu-Zayyad (Eds), *Islamophobia and Anti-Semitism,* pp. 135–51. Princeton, NJ: Markus Wiener.

Bar-Tal, D., Sharvit, K., Halperin, E. and Zafran, A. (2012). 'Ethos of Conflict: The Concept and its Measurement'. *Peace and Conflict: Journal of Peace Psychology*, 18 (1): 40–61.

Brown, N. (2003). 'Democracy, History, and the Contest Over the Palestinian Curriculum'. In F. Pingel (Ed.), *Contested Past, Disputed Present: Curricula and Teaching in Israeli and Palestinian Schools*, pp. 99–125. Hannover, Germany: Verlag Hansche Buchhandlung.

Brown, N. (2007). 'Genesis of a New Curriculum'. In E. A. Doumato and G. Starrett (Eds), *Teaching Islam: Textbooks and Religion in the Middle East,* pp. 125–38. Boulder, CO: Lynne Rienner.

Crawford, K. A. and Foster, S. J. (2007). *War, Nation, Memory: International Perspectives on World War II in School History Textbooks*. Charlotte, NC: Information Age.

de Certeau, M. (1988). *The Writing of History*. Translated by T. Conley. New York: Columbia University Press.

Dwyer, P. (2009). 'War Stories: French Veteran Narratives and the "Experience of War" in the Nineteenth Century'. *European History Quarterly*, 41 (4): 561–85.

Fasheh, M. J. (1995). 'The Reading Campaign Experience Within Palestinian Society: Innovative Strategies for Learning and Building Community'. *Harvard Educational Review*, 65 (1): 66–92.

Firer, R. and Adwan, S. (2004). *The Israeli-Palestinian Conflict in History and Civics Education Textbooks of Both Nations*. Hannover, Germany: Verlag Hansche Buchhandlung.

Gregory, D. (2004). *The Colonial Present*. Oxford: Blackwell.

Grigsby, D. G. (1995). 'Rumor, Contagion, and Colonization in Gros's Plague-Stricken of Jaffa (1804)'. *Representations*, 51: 1–46 (Summer).

Haaretz (14 July 2010). Editorial (haaretz.co.il) [Hebrew]

Israeli-Palestinian School Book Project (2013). Victims of Our Own Narratives? Portrayal of the 'Other' in Israeli and Palestinian School Books. Available at http://israelipalestinianschoolbooks.blogspot.com.es/.

Kashti, O. (27 September 2010). 'The Ministry of Education Instructed High School to Stop Teaching the Arab Version of the Conflict Next to the Zionist Version'. *Haaretz* (haaretz.co.il) [Hebrew].

Kashti, O. (18 December 2015). 'The New Citizenship: Much More Jewish'. *Haaretz* (haaretz.co.il) [Hebrew].

Kashti, O. (21 January 2016). 'The Ministry of Education to Compile a List of Creative Works Not to be Shown to Students'. *Haaretz* (haaretz.co.il) [Hebrew].

Hovsepian, N. (2008). *Palestinian State Formation: Education and the Construction of National Identity*. Newcastle: Cambridge Scholars.

Ichilov, O., Salomon, G. and Inbar, D. (2005). 'Citizenship Education in Israel – A Jewish-Democratic State'. *Israel Affairs*, 11 (2): 303–23.

Jamal, A. (2009). 'The Contradictions of State-Minority Relations in Israel: The Search for Clarifications'. *Constellations*, 16 (3): 493–508.

Khouri, M. (2003). 'On the Road to Self-Determination: The Development of the First Palestinian School Curriculum'. In F. Pingel (Ed.), *Contested Past, Disputed Present: Curricula and Teaching in Israeli and Palestinian Schools*, pp. 59–81. Hannover, Germany: Verlag Hansche Buchhandlung.

Khoury, N. (2016). 'National Narratives and the Oslo Peace Process: How Peacebuilding Paradigms Address Conflicts Over History'. *Nations and Nationalism* (published first, March).

Kizel, A. (2008). *Enslaved History: A Critical Analysis of General History Curricula and Textbooks, 1948–2006*. Tel-Aviv: Mofet Institute [Hebrew].

Naser-Najjab, N. and Pappé, I. (2016). 'Palestine: Reframing Palestine in the Post-Oslo Period'. In R. Guyver (Ed.), *Teaching History and the Changing Nation State: Transnational and Intranational Perspectives*, pp. 9–29. New York: Bloomsbury.

Malus, L.-E. (1892). *L'agenda de Malus: Souvenirs de l'expédition d'Égypte 1798-1801.* Publié et annoté par le Général Thoumas. Paris: Honoré Champion, Libraire. Accessible through France's National Library. http://gallica.bnf.fr/ark:/12148/bpt6k64983628.

Moughrabi, F. (2001a). 'The Politics of Palestinian Textbooks'. *Journal of Palestine Studies*, 31 (1): 5–19.

Moughrabi, F. (October 2001b). 'The Battle of the Books in Palestine'. *The Nation*. Available at http://www.thenation.com/article/battle-books-palestine.

Murray, H. (2008). 'Curriculum Wars: National Identity in Education'. *London Review of Education*, 6 (1): 39–45.

Naveh, E. and Yogev, E. (2002). *Histories: Towards a Dialogue with the Israeli Past*. Tel-Aviv: Bavel [Hebrew].

Nordbruch, G. (2002). *Civic Education in the Palestinian Curriculum: A Review of the New Textbooks*. Braunschweig, Germany: Georg Eckert Institute for International Textbook Research.

Nordbruch, G. (2003). 'Forming Palestinian Society: The Narration of the Nation in the New Palestinian Textbooks'. In F. Pingel (Ed.), *Contested Past, Disputed Present: Curricula and Teaching in Israeli and Palestinian Schools*, pp. 83–98. Hannover, Germany: Verlag Hansche Buchhandlung.

Palestinian Authority, Ministry of Education (2001). 'The Palestinian Curriculum and Textbooks: Clarification from the Ministry of Education – Palestine'. *Palestine-Israel Journal*, 8 (2): 115–18.

Peled-Elhanan, N. (2008). 'The Denial of Palestinian National and Territorial Identity in Israeli Schoolbooks of History and Geography, 1996-2003'. In R. Dolón and J. Todolí (Eds), *Analysing Identity in Discourse*, pp. 77–107. Amsterdam, The Netherlands: John Benjamins.

Peled-Elhanan, N. (2009). 'Layout as Punctuation of Semiosis: Some Examples from Israeli Schoolbooks'. *Visual Communication*, 8 (1): 91–116.

Peled-Elhanan, N. (2010). 'Legitimation of Massacres in Israeli School History Textbooks'. *Discourse and Society*, 21 (4): 377–404.

Peled-Elhanan, N. (2012). *Palestine in Israeli School Textbooks: Ideology and Propaganda in Education*. London: I.B. Tauris.

Pina, A. D. (27 April 2005). *Palestinian Education and the Debate Over Textbooks*. Washington, DC: Congressional Report Service.

Pingel, F. (2010). *UNESCO Guidebook on Textbook Research and Textbook Revision*. 2nd revised and updated edition. Paris and Braunschweig: UNESCO and the Georg Eckert Institute for International Textbook Research.

Pingel, F. (Ed.) (2003). *Contested Past, Disputed Present: Curricula and Teaching in Israeli and Palestinian Schools*. Hannover, Germany: Verlag Hansche Buchhandlung.

Podeh, E. (2000). 'History and Memory in the Israeli Education System: The Portrayal of the Arab-Israeli Conflict in History Textbooks (1948-2000)'. *History and Memory*, 12 (1): 65–100.

Ram, U. (2009). 'Ways of Forgetting: Israel and the Obliterated Memory of the Palestinian Nakba'. *Journal of Historical Sociology*, 22 (3): 366–95.

Rancière, J. (2004). *The Politics of Aesthetics*. London: Continuum.

Raz-Karkotzkin, A. (2002). 'History Curricula and the Limits of Israeli Consciousness'. In A. Ben-Amos (Ed.), *History, Identity and Memory: Images of the Past in Israeli Education*, pp. 47–67. Tel-Aviv University: Ramot [Hebrew].

Reiss, W. (2004). 'Palestinian Textbooks on the Subject of Islamic Religion'. In Georg Eckert Institute, *Reviews of current Israeli and Palestinian textbooks*. Braunschweig, Germany: Georg Eckert Institute for International Textbook Research.

Soysal, Y. N., Bertilotti, T. and Mannitz, S. (2005). 'Projections of Identity in French and German History and Civics Textbooks'. In H. Schissler and Y. N. Soysal (Eds), *The Nation, Europe, and the World: Textbooks and Curricula in Transition*, pp. 13–34. New York and Oxford: Berghahn Books.

State of Palestine, Ministry of Education and Higher Education (2001). *National Education for Grade 1* (Part 1). Al Bireh - Ramallah: Curriculum Center [Arabic].

State of Palestine, Ministry of Education and Higher Education (2002a). *National Education for Grade 1* (Part 2). Al Bireh - Ramallah: Curriculum Center [Arabic].

State of Palestine, Ministry of Education and Higher Education (2002b). *National Education for Grade 2* (Part 1). Al Bireh - Ramallah: Curriculum Center [Arabic].

State of Palestine, Ministry of Education and Higher Education (2004a). *National Education for Grade 4* (Part 2). Al Bireh - Ramallah: Curriculum Center [Arabic].

State of Palestine, Ministry of Education and Higher Education (2004b). *National Education for Grade 5*. Al Bireh - Ramallah: Curriculum Center [Arabic].

State of Palestine, Ministry of Education and Higher Education (2005). *National Education for Grade 6*. Al Bireh - Ramallah: Curriculum Center [Arabic].

Stray, C. (1994). 'Paradigms Regained: Towards a Historical Sociology of the Textbook'. *Journal of Curriculum Studies*, 26 (1): 1–29.

Sultana, R. G. (2006). 'Education in Conflict Situations: Palestinian Children and Distance Education in Hebron'. *Mediterranean Journal of Educational Studies*, 11 (1): 49–81.

United Nations Committee on the Exercise of the Inalienable Rights of the Palestinian People (1985). *Living Conditions of the Palestinians in the Occupied Territories*. New York: United Nations.

van Leeuwen, Th. (1996). 'The Representation of Social Actors'. In C. R. Caldas-Coulthard and M. Coulthard (Eds), *Texts and Practices: Readings in Critical Discourse Analysis*, pp. 32–70. London: Routledge.

Weiner, M. F. (2016). 'Colonized Curriculum: Racializing Discourses of Africa and Africans in Dutch Primary School History Textbooks'. *Sociology of Race and Ethnicity* (published online before print, 8 February).

Weizman, E. (2007). *Hollow Land: Israel's Architecture of Occupation*. New York: Verso.

11

The Long Shadow Thrown over the Actions of Men

Michael Zammit

Introduction

This chapter reflects on how different ways of doing philosophy may bring about or fail to bring about peace. It begins with Levinas' distinction between *totalizers* and *infinitizers* – his thoughts about how these different philosophies may influence life beyond philosophy. It then considers Shankara's interpretation of some passages of *the Bhagavad Gītā*, and his *Advaita* (Non-Dual) philosophy culled from the Upanishads in relation to the issues raised in the first part. *Advaita* entails both a participation in, and a renunciation of, actions. What he means by this and its effects are discussed in the final sections.

The shadow

The state of war suspends morality. … In advance its shadow falls over the actions of men. The art of foreseeing war and of winning it by every means – politics – is henceforth enjoined as the very exercise of reason. Politics is opposed to morality, as philosophy to naïveté.

(Levinas 1998, p. 21)

In today's situation, the priority for humanity is still, as Heidegger might have put it, *to keep our mastery in check*, that is, keeping hold of what we are, who we are and how we are, without conceiving a chasm between our thought and our being. This feature has unfortunately characterized Western philosophy, particularly since the birth of modernity. So philosophers have concocted pictures and theories of the term 'good' and what constitutes a good life, without bothering with the practical means of making people better. Likewise in ontology, many were/are abstractly preoccupied with what is the ultimate and fundamental reality, not caring as to how individuals experience reality themselves. Indeed, the latter is frequently conceived as inferior to the former. Heidegger was alluding to these fragmentary distinctions when referring to this mastery and to the terrible effects that follow when it is lost. He himself did not manage to keep his mastery in check, and this perhaps explains why he embraced Nazism – the misguided belief that humanity was ill-equipped to face the challenge of cultivating such expert skill.

Even Levinas wants to avoid this chasm. He refers to the struggle between what he calls the *totalizers* and the *infinitizers*. The consequences of this struggle stretch beyond the merely philosophical and academic. *Totalizers* are those who promote a uniform characterization of reason and truth; insisting, and possibly imposing, that reason is one and the same, and that truth is one and monolithic. Reality to them is a totality (hence, *totalizers*). Reason, if properly exercised, can grasp this totality in its entirety. Hence, there is a limit to totality and to our thoughts about it; there are definite and objective truths. Anything that strays outside these thoughts and these boundaries is by definition mistaken and misguided. To give an example, a totalizing person discussing God believes that there are well-defined concepts and ideas about God, some kind of 'orthodoxy' (correct beliefs). He or she would think he or she can grasp these beliefs and would reject anything that differs from them, being much preoccupied by what to him or her are 'errors' rather than different ideas that suggest other interpretations of the divine. *Totalizers* adamantly refuse to acknowledge that life *itself* shows that truth is diverse. A totalizing approach to reality in general may be adopted in relation to many fields, for example, science and morality and, quite frequently, in philosophy too. Regarding the latter, *totalizers* frequently hold the universal and the objective to lie outside space and time; the particular, the diverse, the heterogeneous and the vigorous are believed to occur in history and hence are inferior to the former. Since the foundations of *objective* thought are frequently believed to lie outside the ordinary and mundane, this philosophy is thus fundamentally dualistic, splitting reality into the eternal and the temporal, the objective and the subjective, the scientific and the folkloristic. Acts like thinking, sensing and existing are discounted as subjective, private and unstable; priority is given to objective thought.

This *totalitarian* point of view has dominated the course of human history, especially in the Western tradition, where it is often presented as neutral and impersonal. Totalizing thought tends to favour the group-cum-class over the individual, with the multiple identities both may have. It is conducive to such an approach because just as a *totalizer* has a propensity to believe that there should be limits to clear definitions and classifications to reality, so there should be clear limits and boundaries in relation to human beings and their alignments. Groups (national, social or otherwise) particularly when these are perceived in essentialist ways, tend to put definite limits and boundaries between humans, and hence reproduce totalizing tendencies in human relations. To be free is to merge with and to become lost in the rationally grounded characterization or group where one belongs, which is clearly delineated and distinct from other groupings.

Infinitizers reject this totalitarian approach, deeming it partial and biased, a doctrinaire attitude that rejects philosophy as a way of life. *Infinitizers* follow philosophers like Husserl who refute all forms of absolute knowledge and rigid definitions. Rather than seeking limits and boundaries to reality and thought, *infinitizers* believe in an ever-receding *horizon of awareness;* that is, they are aware that their thoughts and ideas have limits, yet these limits are ever-receding and hence cannot disclose a totality with fixed and definite boundaries. Hence, the term *infinitizers,* since the limits of thought and reality are seen as infinitely complex, receding and redefined/able. Consider once again someone thinking about God. *Infinitizers* would focus on the limitlessness of God, rather than on the 'correct' characterization of the divine, stressing what one cannot say about God, rather than what beliefs are orthodox. They are aware that anything said is tentative, and subject to fecund reinterpretations.

Infinitizers consider reality and life to be unfathomable, in the sense that one can never ever succeed in providing anything that amounts to a definite and final explanation of life, reality or any other category that characterizes being. One cannot arrive at some ultimate characterization concocted in terms of some set of categories (be they religious, scientific or metaphysical) rather than others. Reality, then, is something that constantly escapes and eludes us. *Infinitizers* creatively engage with boundaries and limits, believing that any claim of presence ineffably supposes absence; any immanence presupposes transcendence. Since one can never succeed in holding on to anything as final, *infinitizers* deem philosophy to be a way of life rather than a doctrine or some absolute method. Hence, they reject the distinctions between thought and action, 'being in itself' and how we act and live in our mundane existence. Systematic thinking is important to support those structures that satisfy necessary needs. When it is made absolute, though, these same structures can become violent and oppressive – a constraint and a burden imposing tyrannical power structures that free men ought simply to resist. Regarding the aggregation of human beings, for *infinitizers,* the individual gains freedom and carries responsibilities not by vanishing into a totality, but rather by confronting it (not necessarily in a negative manner) and seeing beyond the limits and boundaries that this imposes.

Levinas claims that the tension between these two approaches has consequences that go well beyond academic circles and universities. In particular, he notes how the intellectual situation in Germany, dominated by totalizing philosophy, failed to prevent, if not actually abetted, the dramatic events that occurred in the 1930s and 1940s. Hitler's rise to power fed on the fact that Germany had little democratic history. Since its unification in 1870, politics had been dominated by the military and by the Junker class, despite the existence of a parliament. Even after its defeat in the First World War, the military played an overbearing part in the Weimar Republic. The educational set-up in the Weimar Republic did not help the situation. While Weimar's education curricula were imbued with democratic ideas, those who were assigned with implementing them retained an anti-democratic, ultra-nationalistic and autocratic approach to education, being themselves the products of an academic set-up that inculcated these features.[1] Education was anything but critical.

Following the First World War, the country splintered into factions, each blaming the others for all that was wrong. Where prior to the republic there had been the *Kaiser* to stand for law and order, there were now only petty politicians. It was as though their babbling summoned a strange evil genius out of the marred national psyche. In the light of this, the *Führer* (literally 'The Leader') appeared as no mere mortal. He was terrible, authoritarian, totalitarian, self-centred and self-justifying, a god unto himself that dazzled even some of the finest minds aspiring to fathom the truths of being and existence. Thus, on that eventful 30th of January, the German people democratically elected the same man who had sworn to trounce the democratic government which many had grown to hate so vehemently, voting to destroy the very same office to which they had elected him.

The popular concept *der Führer* had been around for decades, coming from the German Youth Movement of the early twentieth century. Hitler and *der Führer* were originally distinct. Quickly, of course, Hitler rode the concept of this *Führer* principle right into the Chancellorship until, eventually, he came to embody the concept. The authority of the *Führer* was to be subjected to no one. It carried fully the mark of the time, not merely in Germany but all across Europe – a messianic slant that was self-derived and autocratic. As Bonhoeffer rightly noted: 'Whereas earlier leadership was expressed in the form of the teacher, the statesman, the father … now the Leader has become an independent figure. The Leader is completely divorced from any office; he is essentially and only *the Leader* (der Führer)' (Bonhoeffer 1965, p. 195).[2]

The *Führer* filled the vacuum left by the death of God and, politically speaking, carried humanity into a dark, tenebrous spiral. But how is this related to the failure of keeping our mastery under check?

For Levinas, the causes of Hitler's rise to power were not simply political or economic. In his prefatory note to the republication of one of his earlier papers, *Reflections on the Philosophy of Hitlerism*, Levinas claims that

> the source of the bloody barbarism of National Socialism … stems from the essential possibility of elemental Evil (du mal elemental) into which we can be led by logic and against which Western philosophy has not sufficiently insured itself. This possibility is inscribed within the ontology of a being … de l'être soucieux d'être … a being concerned and anxious with being. (Levinas 1990, p. 63)

Hitlerism, therefore, is more than a mere spate of madness. It represents an awakening of elementary feelings that covertly call for a violent way of life; one that questions the very principles of civilization and throws the foundations for much that is awry with our contemporary political set-up and behaviour. The totalizing philosophy that dominated Europe in general and Germany in particular since modernity did not provide tools and antidotes to contrast this. Much of the philosophical and political thought of modernity tended to open up a chasm between the human being and the world, one where the so-called *human spirit* is placed on a plane that is superior even to reality:

> This makes it impossible to apply the categories of the physical world to the spirituality of reason, and so locates the ultimate foundation of the spirit outside the brutal world and in the implacable history of concrete existence. It replaces the blind world of common sense with the world rebuilt by idealist philosophy, one that is steeped in reason and subject to reason. In place of liberation through grace there is autonomy, but the Judeo-Christian leitmotif of freedom pervades this autonomy. (Levinas 1990, p. 66)

In due course, the *Führer* came to embody the human spirit. The *Führer* seems to echo Heidegger's '*being of beings*' (a phrase Heidegger actually used to define Hitler) – a phrase in the possessive case, used to mean something that is more than a being, a reality above reality, reminiscent of Plato's good beyond being. According to Levinas, what was needed, on the other hand, was *l'être soucieux*, by which he means something that involves both concern and anxiety (reminiscent of the Existentialist *angst*). Had philosophers, intellectuals and others displayed this *être soucieux*, Nazism would not have had a field day. It might have displaced Heidegger's authoritarian possessive case, dragging in its wake a profound change of attitude that, in turn, would have signified radically new priorities for humanity. A gauntlet would have been thrown in the name of ethics and of the alterity of any human being.

Alterity refers to the unlimited obligation anyone owes to his or her neighbour. It entails being for 'the other' without indent. What Levinas means here is at best enigmatic, especially when later he insists that one is responsible for the *other*, even for what took place before one's birth. What his thoughts entail is that to speak to and with the *other* involves the *other*'s absolute difference, which inevitably marks *his* or *her* (i.e. the *other*'s) inviolability; that in acknowledging the *other*'s separateness, I admit my responsibility not to transgress or violate him or her. The possibility of dialogue *subtends discourse* (Levinas 1998, p. 195).

This involves transcendence; moving through and beyond what one believes one is and the possibilities concomitant with one's assumed identity. Such transcendence can be potentially infinite. But what does this involve? The infinity of transcendence is a consequence of *re(an)nunciation*, a letting go and, concurrently, a renaming. The latter requires the human ability to both participate in and respond immediately to events, while concurrently being distant from the same event one is performing. Humans may act and/or be something, while at the same time be *thinking* about what they are (doing). I may be singing a song, yet concomitantly, I may be *thinking* about what I am singing. Hence, I can be a subject, while at the same time, strangely, be the object of my thoughts. I may consider myself objectively and this may be highly important in a lot of respects. One may be German, Christian, European, liberal and male and have other identities, and act and behave in relation to these identities. Yet, concomitantly, one may stand back and think about being German, being Christian, being liberal, being European, being male and so on. This would enable one to be aware of the limits as well as of the possibilities of being German, etc. Rather than immersing oneself in a group and losing one's identity in this *totalizing* fashion, one would be both a part of the group, while being able to think objectively on this, and not be limited by the boundaries it sets. One would be both involved in something, and not curtailed rigidly by it in dogmatic fashion: 'This infinity *(i.e. relating to the infinitizer tendencies and not be bound by limits)* stronger than murder, already resists us in [the *other*'s] face, is his face, is the primordial "expression", is the first word; "you shall not commit murder". … The epiphany of the face is ethical' (Levinas 1998, p. 199).

This requires the cultivation of a philosophy that allows for renunciation (of identity) while at the same time for participating fully (in events, i.e. history) a philosophy of Non-Duality. In Sanskrit, this is called *Advaita Mimamsa* (i.e. the Non-Dual Investigation).

Advaita

This section will consider the revelation, the *epiphany* (a word derived from the Sanskrit seminal sound, *bhā,* literally meaning *shining* and carrying a sense of transcendence) of the *other* in relation to the ancient Sanskrit epic *Mahabharata* (put to writing in c. 500 BCE). Arjuna, the protagonist, is struck by the *other*'s inviolability. This recognition is what causes his profound neurosis, his nervous breakdown on the battlefield just prior to the eruption of war. Krishna, his charioteer, uncle and divine incarnation, in addressing the event, responds with the famous 700-verse poem *the Bhagavad Gītā* (*the Lord's Incantation*). In turn, the Non-Dualist (*Advaitin*) Shankara's philosophical commentary (c. 800 CE) on this epic sheds light on a possible manner of addressing what becomes Levinas' and contemporary philosophy's struggle with this phenomenon. The *epiphanies*, the shining or what strikes one when coming across some *other* is for Levinas 'the face', which he considers a conundrum, a mystery of infinite depth.

A superficial reading of the epic would make it seem paradoxical to set *the Bhagavad Gītā* enunciation right at the commencement of a terrible war, on the battlefield of *Kurukshetra* where thousands are imminently destined to lose their lives. But then life itself *is* a battlefield. While reading these very words, thousands of lives are being withdrawn, even in violent circumstances.

The blind king (Dhritarashtra, he who upholds *national* identity) poses a question in the opening words of the *Gītā*, invoking karma (action) and dharma (convention): 'What did my army and that of the sons of Pandu [my brother] do' (Sargeant 2009, p. 39)?

Even though Dhritarashtra is present at the events about to unfold or, rather, erupt, the question is set in the imperfect tense: '*what did [they] do?*' In this manner, the events and conversation forming the narrative are presented in a *contingent*, perhaps even *virtual*, relationship to the *actual* historical battle that occurred in Northern India around 5000 years or so ago. This is the magic moment of the epic, when the message of the *Gītā* gets entrenched in the eternal, meandering between the changing and the changeless. The discourse stops referring to someone's historical conflict and invokes the cosmic (cosmetic) strife between opposites, between good and evil. Vivacity comes to be seen as a series of scuffles between spirit and matter, soul and body, life and death, knowledge and ignorance, health and disease, the changeless and the transitory, self-control and indiscipline, discrimination and the sightless sense-mind (*manas*).[3] Is bloodshed therefore inevitable? Ought humanity to resign itself fatalistically to war and destruction? What philosophy could address this dichotomy 5000 years or so ago, in the 1930s or, indeed, today?

Shankara's *Advaita* commentary on *the Bhagavad Gītā* certainly does not advocate fatalism. The epic, he claims, promotes the philosophy of the 'field of action' (*Kurukshetra*) that the blind king Dhritarashtra enunciates by the following locative declaration in the very opening words: 'Dharmakshetre kurukshetre. When in the field of virtue, in the field [of action]' (Sargeant 2009, p. 39).

Kshetre, a neuter singular term in the locative case, indicates position, placement, namely the field where the battle-lines have been drawn. The word means *in the field* or *on the field* – of dharma in the first instance (*dharmakshetre*) and of *kuru* (*kurukshetre*) in the second. *Kuru* from the seminal form *kri*, is karma, action; that is, the *most desired* for any agency, where the subject (*karta*, agent) assumes responsibility for whatever is done or not done (i.e. *kriya*, the verb). The field of action where the human stance is set is also the field of virtue (dharma, excellence). In relation to the eternal cosmic struggle, Dhritarashtra enunciates a principle that relates *kuru* (action) to *dharmakshetre* (the field of excellence) thus positioning and placing oneself in relation to what is occurring and assuming responsibility for whatever is done and/or not done.[4] But what does this concretely entail?

In the introduction to his *Advaita* commentary (*bhashya*) on *the Bhagavad Gītā*, Shankara refers to the transcendent, which he calls *nivritti* (re[an]nunciation) and to the immanent, which he calls *pravritti* (participation) in terms that relate to human affairs and to action (karma). These aspects are very pertinent to the achievement of peace: 'It is the twofold Vedic [Tradition] of Works [pravritti] and Renunciation [nivritti] that maintains order in the universe. This [Tradition] which directly leads to liberation and worldly prosperity has long been practised by all ... who sought welfare' (Sastri 1981, p. 2).

The aspect of renunciation here might seem to superficially suggest the opposite of a philosophy that means to confront fatalism and exorcise evil presences when these leap out of their lamp. This impression, however, is imprecise. In effect, these two *vritti* denote two sorts of reflection on Shankara's Non-Dual advice to the contemporary human condition, and on the state of emergency it has brought itself into. How to renounce while at the same time participating in the affairs of the life and the world becomes the object of this philosophy.

The term *vritti* is rich in meanings and includes 'moral conduct', 'mode of being', 'profession' and 'livelihood'. The seminal form (*dhatu*) *vrit* identifies the activity of 'turning round', 'revolving' and 'rolling' as the central notions suggested. The prefix *pra* provides this term with the sense of 'happening in such a way as to proceed forward', while the prefix *ni* fills the term with 'an overwhelming sense of restraint'. The principle, then, allows for *love* (i.e. growth and creativity) in the event of *re(an)nunciation*, and for *discipline* (viz. knowledge and measure) that indicates direction and defines the limits describing the expression of life and, so, one's participation therein. Love promotes growth and discipline forms it. Shankara's proposal in this regard, *nivritti through pravritti*, is a philosophy suggesting renunciation *through* participation rather than exclusively one or the other. In Pierre Hadot's terms, Shankara's primary objective is to expose and make public this philosophy as *a way of life* (Hadot 1995) through a manual whereby Krishna is said to have taught Arjuna and shown him this path of the Non-Dualist life. The intent is to help the common individual (the one who cannot become a monk or an ascetic) who finds himself *deeply plunged in the ocean of grief and delusion* (Sastri 1981, p. 4). One needs to be educated into this path. Philosophy, as well as education, cannot turn into mere intellectual exercises, but must strive to teach to renounce through participation. This is one way to keep one's mastery in check and to engage with the epiphany of the *other*. What this entails is called *Adhyātma Yoga*, the method that always starts from the most subtle, the *Ātman*, and is briefly described in what follows.

Re(an)nunciation

The *holding of awareness* is *pravritti* (participation). For Shankara, this also necessarily includes *nivritti*, renunciation, which should, however, be understood not as 'repudiation' but as a *re(an)nunciation,* and, so, also a 'renaming'. But what does this renaming entail? Suppose one comes across someone else. On meeting 'the other', one already 'names' him or her, not necessarily in the sense of attaching a proper name, but of forming (even implicitly) an opinion or picture of 'the other', an opinion or picture that will influence how one relates to it, him or her.

Suppose Peter comes across John who hails from Nigeria. Peter will automatically 'name' John in this sense of drawing a characterization of John – John's identity, what one may or may not expect of him, how to relate to John, etc. Yet, Peter may rename John, in the sense that his first characterization of John is not etched in stone. Peter is free to reannounce John. Though Peter's experience may have influenced the original naming as a result of his upbringing, his culture, his formal education and/or other variants, he will always have the freedom to redefine his relationship with this *other*, this John. *Renaming*, therefore, is a skill that has to be cultivated for it to operate from the deep, calmest recesses of one's being (Sanskrit, *as*, is-ness). Re(an)nouncing causes a paradigmatic shift not merely in viewing others (in the example of Peter's characterization of John) but also in the appreciation of who or what the observer himself is (i.e. Peter himself). In fact, in renaming 'the other', one not only changes the relationship one has with whomever or whatever has been renamed, but one also re-names [hence re(an)nounces] himself. This re(an)nouncing of oneself, in turn, does not entail throwing away one's identity, beliefs, one's material goods, as one may at first presume. It entails, rather, one's re(an)nouncing one's relationship with all these, to regard them as belongings. The skill this requires is the subject of *Gītā Shāstra* (The Science of *Gītā* study), and will ultimately lead to *param nihshreyasa*, that is, optimal bliss, consisting of 'a steady devotion to the knowledge of the Self, preceded by the re[*an*]nunciation of all works' (Sastri 1981, p. 4).

This involves different stages. The first should lead to the cessation of *samsāra*, the common, empirically dominated, existence. What exactly is *samsāra*? Peter is German, a carpenter, a Christian, *etc.* All these identities are related to the observable. Now suppose he defines himself primarily as German; Peter may still renounce this, his first identity, not by ceasing to be German, but by re(an) nouncing himself as being *not merely* German, but also Christian, a carpenter and other such titles. In turn, each of these other names may be re(an)nounced.

That one can rename oneself and others, therefore, is something that opens up limitless opportunities for being creative (although, unfortunately, also for being destructive). These limitless opportunities are both a blessing and a curse and hence the pressing need for both discipline and vision. One could rename oneself and others in a manner that sharpens divisions and creates conflict lines. Peter can rename John as fundamentally non-European and intrinsically inimical to him. Yet, the ability to rename can also help open up oneself to 'the other'. Peter can both re(an)nounce himself and rename John in ways that enhance peace and dialogue, or do the opposite.

Further still, the human ability to re(an)nounce also makes possible going beyond all these names. One may re(an)nounce oneself as human, without ceasing to be German, Christian, a carpenter, etc. The difference between being *or* knowing and being *and* knowing oneself as merely human is profound and similar to the distinction we make between being human and being other than human. Rather than identifying oneself with one's doing, something that provides one with certain particular identities (member of a social class, profession, nation, etc.) one realizes that first and foremost one is simply human. In Sanskrit, this is captured by the repetition of the mantra '*I am human*' (*I am a doer, ahamkāra*) and placing the awareness it conjures up at the epicentre of our presence and our experience of life. I realize that I am human, that I am more than what I do or what I particularly identify with.

This knowledge that we are human over and above all our particular identities is a knowledge that we always possess, but which we either (i) pay little attention to, or (ii) we are not absolutely aware of, it being *constantly* present in its full (though silent) sense. Indeed, it is taken for granted in all that 'I' think, all that 'I' know and all that 'I' do. That 'I' am human often becomes explicit only when my human status is challenged in a determinate and fundamental way, as for example, when 'I' am called an animal or treated violently. In the event, my response is usually pinned to this central, often tacit, awareness of being human and 'I' seek refuge in the unmediated dominant conscious experience of that. 'I' react by affirming that 'I' am human, that 'I' do not deserve to be subjected to such treatment. It is in the light of this that *re(an)nunciation* is educationally desirable, providing one with an important creative key, namely *the renaming*, and thus also the re-educating, of one's deepest attitudinal stance. *Advaita* seeks to train us to cultivate keeping this awareness in constant view through philosophy (*lit. darshan*, vision) disciplined (i.e. well-tempered) practices and behaviour and meditation.

Shankara, however, claims that *Advaita* may lead us to a level of awareness that is even deeper and subtler than the realization of our humanity. By shearing off as *not myself*, all that is observable, Shankara claims to be able to help bring our awareness to the point of not merely realizing our humanity, but also something else that is subtler and more refined, something we normally identify by the indexical term 'I' (*aham*). Through this transcendence, the Self will be realized (*mukti* from *moksha*, liberation) while still participating in the events of life. Then, one does not merely embrace the fact of being human, but is liberated and acquires the freedom to bear constant witness to *aham*, the unconditioned 'I', the limitless and simple tranquillity that *is*. In Sanskrit, this is called *Ātman*, the Creative Principle, often identified as the Self. This process ultimately ends in silence, not the silence of the grave, of despondency or a violent silence, but rather a radically different kind of silence called *maunam* in Sanskrit. This is the tranquillity with which Krishna identifies, a virile silence, poised and ready to burst with new experience, a creative urge that redefines presence. It is like light, known only through its effects. Though virile, it is a silence almost indistinguishable from passivity, abetting the solitary self to become independent from and indifferent to what is happening in the field of becoming, the transient yet seemingly real.

Does this however mean that one is not bothered with what happens? Does not this attitudinal shift from the realization of one's humanity to this subtler 'I' suggest an individualism of sorts, some fragmentary and solipsistic celebration of mere personality? Does it not entail that from an epiphany of the *other*, one has shifted to the commonly held egocentric bearing? This is certainly not the case. Indeed, it is the other way round. Non-attachment does not mean a lack of concern about what happens, but a not-being-disconcerted by it. Indeed, the Non-Dualist does not admit to an intrinsically individualist stance even about the intimate features of being, such as beliefs, desires, intentions and performance of actions. Consider intentions. The individualist believes that intentions are internal private states in the minds of singular people. The *advaitin*, however, rejects this view. For him or her the intention of one person *immediately* refers to the intentions of all. Beliefs, desires and actions, then, are by definition, communal and social. Like the air one breathes, they are intimate, though not private in a solipsistic sense. The Self is open to the *other* presupposing it, rather than being radically secluded. In turn, this generates an attitude conducive to genuine peace.

The active discipline of *re(an)nunciation* through participation, then, maps a trajectory that is really a philosophical programme for shifting one's subtlest appreciation of self. *Renunciation* of action then leads to the steadfastness of the attention, which conducts one to realize one's being human. This, in turn, matures into *sankalpa*, a resolution that transforms the (subtlest, uninterrupted) knowledge of the Self, the wisdom that incessantly nourishes the awareness of '*what I am*' and '*what I do*' with creative freedom.

The self-realization through which one may achieve this complete and full awareness is not, ultimately, merely the result of individual effort. *Advaita* claims that the finest human stance consists in grasping that this knowledge is *not* up to the individual to achieve, that it is *not* obtainable through sheer personal effort, but is, rather, received as some kind of donation, a gift (regardless of what one thinks about the nature of the donor). This further affirms that the philosophical trajectory Shankara traces does not end with some individualist, solipsistic self.

Participation

Shankara closes his commentary on Discourse II of *the Bhagavad Gītā* with an exposition of the characteristics of the man *devoted* to wisdom (the *sthitaprajña*, the one who is steadfast in consciousness). To cultivate this steadfastness, this insight, most people simply cannot adapt to the harsh life of a monk. For them, the performance of action (i.e. participation in the events of life) is necessary. So how can they/we live by this Non-Dual wisdom? How ought we to nurture the required *absence of desire for the results of deeds*? What of education if it is from this attitude of complete indifference to success and/or failure that there eventually dawns the knowledge (as also the experience) of the real, call it satisfaction, from the Sanskrit *sat* meaning *truth*? (Sastri 1981, p. 65).

The source of the problem does not lie with objects (*vishayān*) *per se*, which are often the product of some activity or other. The problem is with the *contemplation* (*dhyāyatas*) of them, an architectural term insinuating making these *vishayān* one's *temenos* (in Greek, one's sacred domain) and thus what one deeply and intimately *cares* about.[5] This becomes the source of attachment causing the difficulty as held by the fact that *dhyāyatas* is of the very nature of mental activity. This is why the injunction *not* to entertain the desire for the results of works sounds so alien, so uncanny. Often, we are led to believe the exact opposite (Teschner 1992, p. 6). Work is done for the result and *dhyāyatas*, the steady stream of care, rapidly degenerates to become a source of conflict and violence.[6]

Even though he might not deem the exclusive possession of power and wealth to be the resolution to his state of being, man still acts from egoism, and whereas egoism comes clad in the manic expressions of the euphoria of possessing (and/or being possessed), altruism frequently comes attired in sorrow. Thus the fundamental motive of action is frequently some side or other of a bipolar dichotomy, just as, for example, when one wants to help others in order to be good oneself. In *the Bhagavad Gītā*, this terrifyingly vicious situation is metaphorically represented by having both armies facing each other and making an awful sound, the din of war (Sargeant 2009, pp. 50–7). 'Grief [becomes] the principle manifestation betraying the sufferer' (Kristeva 1987, p. 7).

The sufferer is *the reader* of the epic, humanity at large, and, indeed, you and I. An impasse is reached. In the face of this, Arjuna declares: '*I shall not fight!*' (*na yotsye*)… and having spoken thus, he becomes silent, *tūshnīm*, in a violently despondent sort of silence (Sargeant 2009, p. 94).

Shankara aims to bring some antidote to this impasse. As stated, a predominant human problem lies with our experience of fragmentation in thought and deed. Our submission to the notions that integrity in what we do and think is unsustainable, and that we necessarily develop separate identities, frequently leads to intense solitude, to the fear of being physically alone, socially emarginated, spiritually repressed or speaking without being understood. Not only is an epidemic of loneliness sweeping the world but also to boot, given apparent prosperity, the more successful one is in worldly terms (career, money, etc.), the more likely he or she is to suffer from it. This widespread melancholy is something that we are now quite openly witnessing in the contemporary world. Wealth cannot bail us out. Peace on a personal, social and worldly level fails to ensue.

For Shankara, the attainment of *moksha* (freedom) is a form of immunization against this sweeping malaise. He declares that this achievement would involve *not* moving away from society and its demands, *nor* adopting the lifestyle of a recluse, *nor* assuming an ardent position seeking some divinity, but a different sort of attitudinal refinement that he often calls *turning inwards*. By this he implies remaining active in the world while simultaneously gaining access to the subtler fields of experience, as cited previously. Meditation, reflection and striving to awaken one's finer commands of reason (Sanskrit, *buddhi*) while striving to understand oneself are actions that, while having the aim of reinforcing one's powers of resistance, are also meant to eliminate (*me* as) the *doer* and my claim to the results. This is so even while highlighting one's uniqueness and even if at first, practices such as these might actually seem to *intensify* and *promote* feelings of solitude.

Indeed, why one is not the doer becomes the fundamental philosophical enquiry of the *advaitin*. We tend to see ourselves as the source of our actions. I, for instance, write, eat, sleep etc. Shankara invites us to conceive such events differently. There is eating in the universe. It is adopted variously in many acts and assumed by many creatures, by myself, by other humans and by other animals. My act of eating is regarded as an instantiation of the universal act of eating, something I share with other creatures. This reverses the way of thinking about such acts. The universal becomes the focus of importance, the particular becomes simply an expression of the universal, and in performing my particular and individual act, I partake of the same universal as with countless other beings with whom, given the performance in question, I become akin. In other words any gesture opens me to 'the other'.

Removal of *dhyāyatas* for the results of one's work is sustained by the realization that in the last resort, one is not the real doer of acts. To move from conceiving of oneself as 'I the doer' to recognizing that 'I am not the doer' requires courage. Self-confidence to do this may be obtained from mastering and recognizing, in any given situation, what one's responsibilities *really* are. It requires moving away from an egocentric approach towards the adherence to a tradition: an adherence in the sense of engagement, not blind acceptance. This advocates that while proposing detachment, Shankara is not suggesting that we ignore the world or, indeed, the society we live in. Rather, this attitude occasions engaging with them. It requires a subtle strength (*sattva*) and the cultivation of obedience, a form of hearing (from the Latin *ob audire*) to such a fine pitch as to enable one to hear the voice of one's true self rather than that of one's ego. It necessitates listening to what one really is. A transformation (not necessarily experienced either as sudden or as profound) occurs and one begins to feel dissatisfied with what '*doing*' appears to be in this new light. This is the method that Shankara advocates for coming out of torpor, that so oppressive sort of ignorance and inactivity called *tamas* in Sanskrit.

If the notion that one's self as a particular instantiation of some universal act seems to entail waylaying personhood, and if acts are by definition performed by the said agents and carried out following their individually formed intentions, should agency then be ignored? Obviously, explanations of human phenomena seem deficient when one ignores the beliefs and desires of agents; and it goes without saying that action is distinguished from mere behaviour by virtue of its intentional character. This much is uncontestable, but whereas the individualist position holds that intention exists only as a psychological state in the singular mind of the person, Shankara would add that it also lies deeply as an inbuilt tendency, in processes such as language that belong to the human social dimension. It would therefore be impossible to identify some intent without examining the wider scope and context of human relationships and human gestures within which agents think and act. Unravelling the motives of individuals, therefore, entails that an appeal must be made to the broader beliefs, practices and epistemologies of the human community at large. Ignorance of this larger context would be the cause of a sort of blindness (*avidya, lit.* non-vision) that would necessarily accommodate half-truths, drawing on the sources of human pain, misery and anguish. Moving from the ego to the Self, then, does not occasion closing one's individuality to others … though the reverse does. Thus it does not mean the complete flattening out of one's individuality. Shankara's investigation admits that every individual comes with attributes that are both unique and inimitable. Indeed, karma (action, gesture) captures one's manner (and mannerisms) of life and, as such, is expressive of one's special distinguishing traits.

Shankara's reflections, though, also occasion that anyone who strives to be true to himself or herself would also feel something *subtler* than a mere sympathy for the *other*. He or she *feels* the individuality, the uniqueness of 'the other' and holds *that* as special and, indeed, inviolable, not because of how important or powerful its possessor happens to be, but because from being thus so human, he or she may glimpse and strive to attain to the immediate (non-mediated) stance of that most discrete *Ātman*, which is also the universal (my)Self Shankara terms the *Brahman*.

What the Non-Dual philosophy has to declare is simple. If a limit is placed on how far one can grow in the knowledge of the Self, that is, if one limits one's knowledge of Self to merely one's own self, then one is missing out on something both subtler and truer. Human facts cannot be explained exhaustively in terms of actions, beliefs and the streams of desire of limited and restrained individuals. The duality between thought and action, self and the *other* needs to be deconstructed.

Conclusion

How can this be relevant to peace education? It is necessary when dealing with education, to adopt an approach that enables both educators and learners to realize the insights of Non-Dual philosophy. Along with recognition of the beliefs and intentions of the individual, an in-depth understanding of social practice (call it *tradition* or *language*) is necessary to put *in situ* such beliefs, attitudes, desires and actions. Three conclusions follow from the Non-Dualist's claim.

The first is that a reference to the Universal is inescapable, especially when human affairs are explained in terms of the Non-Dualist theory of action. People need to be educated to adopt this perspective vis-à-vis human action. There seems to be the need for necessarily acknowledging the presence of some Absolute (however this may be construed, and not necessarily in theistic terms).

As even individual affairs come to be explained and understood in terms of the true universal nature of human practices, the *de facto* sustained reference to the merely individually unique actions becomes, in turn, redundant. It is no longer necessary to refer to the individual *per se* except in terms of agency. Educational practice thus needs to forge some means for decomposing this obstinate tendency bent on egocentrism.

Finally, it becomes clear that philosophy is less a function of mental operations in individual heads and hearts, and more of *praxis*. Without such practical live understanding, as anthropologists testify, and as philosophers working on problems of translation and cross-cultural understanding know only too well, mere intellectual effort, no matter how sincere and erudite, turns out to be fatuous. The Non-Dual contribution to this state of affairs promotes the fusion of knowledge and being, providing for a truly enlightened transformation of mankind's awareness of itself. As we strive to cultivate some mastery of the *advaitin* techniques for accessing stillness and heightening our command of presence in all its modifications, we will benefit from the dispelling and undoing of the postmodern fragmentary and jingoistic mentality that has cast its long shadow over these our obsessed and fiercely competitive (i.e. violent) lives encased in a constant stream of deeds. Non-Dual philosophy is less of a function of the mental operations of individual thinkers and more of a way of life, a philosophy in the original sense of the term.

In the light of this, education needs to be primarily philosophical in the sense of drawing out the holistic style of living. The whole of one's being and not merely or exclusively the intellect has to be catered for. Philosophy and education have to respond to the world one lives in. It cannot advocate a mere phenomenological ignorance of war, terrorism, racism and such other forms of violence. *Advaita*, in turn, needs to clearly expose that, indeed, this ignorance *ought not* to be allowed to establish the contemporary fatalistic destiny of humanity, and that by cultivating the skill of *renunciation* in the very act of *participation*, we can free ourselves from this terrible curse. Education, of course, can abet this. In Levinas' words, 'It is not a particular dogma concerning democracy, parliamentary government, dictatorial regime, or religious politics that is in question. It is the very humanity of man' (Levinas 1990, p. 71).

Notes

1 https://www.facinghistory.org/weimar-republic-fragility-democracy/readings/why-study-weimar-germany

2 For Bonhoeffer, a true leader must know not merely the limitations of his authority but must also *'radically refuse to become the appeal, the idol, i.e. the ultimate authority of those whom he leads.'* (Bonhoeffer 1965, p. 195).

3 Sense-mind or *manas* is the faculty of the psyche that reorganizes sense images received. For instance, I have an upside-down image of the computer I am writing upon on my retina, which *manas* then rectifies. The *manas* is different from that other faculty of the mind that discriminates (*buddhi*) and interprets the data gathered.

4 This definitely relates to Levinas' claim that one is responsible even for what occurred before one was born.

5 The contemplation (*dhyāyatas*) in question, then, would be of the very nature of that mental activity that Plato calls *sorge,* the Greek for *exclusive, filial love.*

6 *Dhyāyatas* may engulf even the educational processes. Consider mainstream education in a lot of societies, which has been frequently dominated by the banking concept of education. In the banking concept of education, knowledge is deposited by the teacher in his or her students, akin to someone depositing money in a bank. Now the act of depositing frequently occurs with the intent of receiving a return. Hence, the act in question is instrumental to the return expected. Often, the return aimed for is financial in nature. This becomes then the ultimate object of education: **that** *dhyāyatas* is then contemplated as the end of the educational process.

References

Bonhoeffer, D. (1965). 'No Rusty Swords: Letters, Lectures and Notes 1928-1936, vol. 1'. In E. H. Robertson and J. Bowden (Trans.), Edwin H. Robertson (Ed.), *Collected Works of Dietrich Bonhoeffer*, p. 384. New York: Harper & Row.

Hadot, P. (1995). *Philosophy as a Way of Life: Spiritual Exercises from Socrates to Foucault.* Translated by Michael Chase. Oxford, UK and Cambridge, USA: Blackwell.

Hill, S. R. and Harrison, P. G. (1991). *Dhātupātha: The Roots of Language.* London: Duckworth.

Kristeva, J. (1987). 'On the Melancholic Imaginary'. *New Formations*, No. 3. London: Methuen & Co. (Winter).

Levinas, E. (1990). 'Reflections on the Philosophy of Hitlerism'. In Seán Hand (Trans.), *Critical Inquiry*, vol. 17. Chicago, IL: Chicago University Press.

Levinas, E. (1978). *Existence and Existents.* Translated by A. Lingis. The Hague and Boston: Martinus Nijhoff.

Levinas, E. (1998). *Totality and Infinity.* Translated by A. Lingis. Pittsburgh, PA: Duquesne University Press.

Metaxas, E. (2010). *Bonhoeffer.* Nashville: Thomas Nelson.

Pānini (1980). *The Ashtadhyayi of Pānini.* Translated by Srisa Chandra Vasu. Delhi: Motilal Banarsidass.

Sargeant, W. (2009). *The Bhagavad Gītā.* Translated by W. Sargeant. Albany, NY: State University of New York Press.

Sastri, M. A. (1981). *The Bhagavad Gītā with Shankara's Commentary.* Translated by M. A. Sastri. Madras: Samata Books.

Stutley, M. J. (1997). *A Dictionary of Hinduism.* London and Henley: Routledge and Kegan Paul.

Teschner, G. (1992). 'Anxiety, Anger and the Concept of Agency and Action in the Bhagavad Gītā'. *Asian Philosophy*, 2: 61–77.

12

Schooling for Democracy: Music and Critical Pedagogy in Egypt

Linda Herrera

Introduction

If we take as a given the desirability of an education that promotes principles of universal human dignity, pluralism, rational critical inquiry, compassion, innovation and excellence, then humanistic pedagogies should be paramount to that educational vision. Yet, humanistic education in the Middle East has been on the decline in the past decades because of the intensification of political and economic injustices and the invigoration of nativism, sectarianism and religious fundamentalisms.[1] Also detrimental to the humanistic project are global market-driven education reforms that privilege the human capital or economic imperative of education. With their emphasis on competition, privatization and decentralization of public education, testing, standards and accountability, these global reforms undermine the notion of education for a public good.

In his *Humanism and Democratic Criticism*, the late Edward Said contends that the greatest threats to humanism can be found in the trilogy of 'religious enthusiasm', nationalism and 'exclusivism'. The ultimate mission of the humanist is to 'offer resistance to the great reductive and vulgarizing us-versus-them thought patterns of our time' (Said 2004, p. 50). Humanistic education refers to an approach to learning that is *humane* in that it nurtures respect and compassion, consciously approaching the languages of literature, science and the arts as an inherently collective human endeavour. Humanistic approaches to learning are not the domain of a particular culture or the outcome of a single historical trajectory, but contain universal dimensions.[2]

I pondered questions about humanistic pedagogy from the vantage point of Cairo, Egypt, where I had been living since 1986. At the time of writing in 2003, the region was experiencing a collective dread about the impending US-led war on Iraq. On the very eve of the attack, I had the good fortune to attend a talk by Edward Said at the Ewart Hall of the American University in Cairo. It would be his last trip to Egypt as he tragically died later that year in New York from leukaemia. In a time of so much despair, Said spoke with optimism about the West-Eastern Divan Orchestra, a group he co-founded with the renowned Argentine/Israeli pianist and conductor Daniel Barenboim in 1999. That project, which brought together young musicians from Arab countries, Israel and Iran did not intend to bring 'peace' to the region. Indeed, the intractable military conflicts and occupations in the region need far more than music projects and goodwill to bring about resolutions. Rather, the Orchestra, named after a collection of poems by Goethe, embodies an ethos of humanism, a utopia in the face of so much enmity, suffering and pessimism. The very name of the orchestra, as explained by Barenboim, captures the spirit of the project:

> We took the name of our project, the West Eastern Divan, from a poem by Goethe, who was one of the first Germans to be genuinely interested in other cultures. He originally discovered Islam when a German soldier who had been fighting in one of the Spanish campaigns brought back a page of the Koran to show to him. His enthusiasm was so great that he started to learn Arabic at the age of sixty. Later he discovered the great Persian poet Hafiz, and that was the inspiration for his set of poems that deal with the idea of the other, the West Eastern Divan, which was first published nearly two hundred years ago, in 1819, at the same time, interestingly enough, that Beethoven was working on his ninth symphony, his celebrated testament to fraternity. (Barenboim 2006)

The world view, openness and utopian dream of the humanist, what we can call the democratic ideal, are needed more than ever to confront the polarizing 'us-versus-them' cultural politics evident around the globe. But who are the humanists and what spaces exist for them in contemporary societies? The humanist has historically been associated with the artist and teacher. The teacher should not be reduced to someone who transmits or deposits information in students, what Freire has famously called the 'banking system' of education (1970), but an ethical social actor inextricably involved in the vocation of education for the human good in its broadest sense. It follows, therefore, that education refers not merely to formal schooling – however important schools may be – but also to a range of educational encounters.

During periods of geopolitical conflict, during times of national and regional vulnerability, it seemed especially urgent to venture into arenas of inquiry that address humanism and pedagogies that embody a cosmopolitan ethos. We will explore some of these issues through the life history and pedagogic practices of an Egyptian Muslim music educator, a violin teacher.

Life history and educational practice

The life history of a teacher allows for an investigation of the many influences and conditions that contribute to an educator's formation and pedagogic practices. More than being a mere product of his or her times, a teacher can also motivate change and alternative ways of interacting in the world. In their volume, *Lives in Context: The Art of Life History Research*, Cole and Knowles stress the importance of context and relationality when setting out to conduct a life history. As they reflect: 'Lives are never lived in vacuums. Lives are never lived in complete isolation from social contexts ... To be human is to experience "the relational", no matter how it is defined, and at the same time, to be shaped by "the institutional", the structural expressions of community and society. To be human is to be molded by context' (Cole and Knowles 2001, p. 22).

Profiling an educator working within a humanistic tradition during a period when that very tradition is under threat can provide a way of identifying, with the aim of encouraging and nurturing, these much needed pedagogic spaces.

I became acquainted with the teacher under study in 1997 when my then five-year-old daughter enrolled in his beginners' violin class. As a parent who is also an educational anthropologist, I regularly observed his classes – which included private lessons, multi-age and multi-ability group classes, and rehearsals at the Cairo Opera and elsewhere – with growing professional interest and appreciation.[3] In 2003, I sought the teacher's consent to be the subject of a scholarly study that would entail many hours of personal interviews and a decidedly intrusive shadowing of him throughout his various professional activities for a period of four months. He willingly agreed and generously gave his time without posing any conditions. There was never a serious question of disguising his identity, although I proposed it as an option in the beginning. We always envisioned this as the history of an actual life in the social history tradition. The teacher facilitated the research process by helping me to obtain permission to enter the Cairo Conservatoire to attend his classes twice weekly, and welcomed me into his other lessons at the Cairo Opera House. In addition to observing classes, I interviewed students, their parents, and the teacher's colleagues. He also opened his home for me to conduct a series of tape-recorded personal interviews in five separate sittings that took place in Cairo from January to June 2003. These interviews included reflections on the relationship between music, society, politics and identity. In addition to formal interviews, we also held several impromptu discussions following classes and rehearsals.

The interviews were translated[4] and transcribed, and information derived from them was organized chronologically and topically into categories that included family life, musical life, politics and music, institutions, national identity and the arts, and pedagogy. The teacher read earlier drafts of this chapter and provided additional information, corrections to his life story and suggestions for analysis.

Sceptics of the life-history method often point to the fact that one life is not representative, and, indeed, they are right. But this criticism does not invalidate the method and the riches it can offer for social analysis. In defence of the method, I refer to anthropologist Sydney Mintz who wrote a much heralded life history of a Puerto Rican sugar cane worker in 1960. He posits that life history 'can do no more than offer in broad outline some of the possible meanings of social change against which the personal history of a single individual may be examined. The suggested relationships between social background and life history are intended to serve merely as hypotheses which might be proved or disproved or refined' (Mintz 1960, p. 270).

The hypothesis to be extracted from the life history I consider is that educational spaces rooted in principles of pluralism and humanism are constricting at an alarming pace, and reforms that support humanist education are urgently needed.

Educating beyond nationalism

Since opening its doors in October 1988, The Education and Culture Center, which also goes by the name Cairo Opera House (Dar al-Obra), has served not merely as a professional performance venue, but also as a public, accessible centre for arts education, amateur performance and international exchange. Funded through a grant by the Japanese government, the Opera represents an example of how cultural institutional building can constitute a component of international development aid.

With its mandate for public outreach and international cultural exchange, the present opera house stands in clear distinction to its predecessor, the Khedival Opera House of 1869, which was destroyed by a fire in 1971. Built by order of Khedive Ismael on the occasion of the opening of the Suez Canal, for which Giuseppi Verdi composed his opera *Aida*, that Opera was largely the meeting place of the aristocracy and local and foreign elites. The new opera, in contrast, contains classrooms, art galleries, an outdoor theatre, a small and a large performance hall, museums and public gardens.

It did not take long for the intended cosmopolitan quality of the space to be overshadowed by nationalist tendencies. The Ministry of Culture formally changed its name from The *Education* and Culture Centre, to the *National* Cultural Center (*al-Markaz al-Thaqafy al-Qawmy*). The replacement of 'Education' with 'National' represents more than a semantic change; it reflects an insistence of the primacy of the national over the educational, particularly when the education in question is supposed to advance a form of global, outward-looking exchange that transcends mere national allegiances. While nationalism per se is not necessarily an impediment to cosmopolitanism or humanistic education, the problem arises when nationalism takes a turn into 'nativism', or a defensive posture against 'the other'.

One manifestation of nativism has been the denigration and politicization of aesthetic forms deemed 'outside' the national culture. The so-called Western cultural forms – whether relating to literature, cinema, fashion or music – often get maligned as being inimical to Arab and Islamic culture. These rhetorical and actual responses to non-native arts seem to peak during periods of political repression at home, and vulnerability as a cause of external threats.

Some of the murky questions surrounding nationalism, geopolitics and ways they are connected to the arts came to the fore in a seemingly benign but telling manner in the context of the opera's Talent Development Centre (*Markaz Tanmiyet al-Mowahib*). This public outreach program offers an array of classes in Arabic choir, classical ballet, the Suzuki violin, the oud and the flute.[5] The Suzuki violin classes have been among the Centre's more successful programs. The Suzuki method, a child-centred approach to musical literacy and performance, was developed in Japan by the renowned Dr Shinichi Suzuki (1898–1998) and made its way to Egypt as part of the Japanese cultural exchange.[6] From its inception, the Suzuki violin program in Cairo has constituted a local space for excellence, as evidenced by the prizes awarded its students, critical acclaim of its public performances, rising demand for its classes and kudos for its principal teacher, an Egyptian violinist trained in the method in Japan. Despite its success and high demand, in 2003, within a context of rapidly declining support from the Opera administration for 'non-Arabic' music and a charged anti-Western political environment as the US-led coalition wars waged in Afghanistan and Iraq, the Suzuki violin class began losing institutional support and was in danger of being cancelled. The class, even though based on a Japanese method, was accused by its detractors as representing an expression of Western culture.[7]

Due to efforts by parents, musicians and the principal violin teacher, Osman El Mahdi, the Suzuki class survived and continues to thrive. Yet, educational and artistic spaces that are perceived as being outside national or Islamic culture are under perpetual threat. There is perhaps no better way to illustrate the struggles taking place at the intersection of culture, politics, nationalism and education than through the life history and pedagogy of an educator who straddles multiple and overlapping national and cultural spaces.

'A perfect state of mind': The education of an educator

Born in the cosmopolitan city of Alexandria in 1958, Osman El Mahdi's family life and education reflect larger transformations that occurred in Egypt and the region in the decades of the 1950s to the 1980s.[8]

Osman attended the reputable and architecturally majestic St Mark's, a boys' French Catholic school overlooking the Mediterranean Sea, which was established in 1928. When Osman began his studies at St Mark's, he remembers mixing on a daily basis with Muslim and Christian students of different denominations from Egyptian, Italian, Greek, Lebanese, Armenian and Syrian backgrounds. It was normal for students to be fluent in two to four languages. Yet, with the exodus of large portions of many foreign communities from Egypt throughout the 1950s and 1960s, foreign schools underwent a gradual process of what can be called 'de-cosmopolitanization', accompanied by 'Arabization'.[9] Not only were students proportionately more Egyptian, but new education laws also brought the foreign schools under the regulations of a centralized Ministry of Education to ensure that they did not deviate from the Arab nationalist path.

While a student at St Mark's, Osman recalls comfortably developing his Muslim identity, while also participating in Christian activities and celebrations, the most notable being Easter and Christmas.[10] Among his most cherished activities was participating in the church choir; his family regularly attended the high Christmas mass which, Osman recalls, 'we [Christians and non-Christians] all enjoyed together'.

The religious and cultural mixing that took place in the 1960s and 1970s gave way to divisions by the 1980s that persist in ever-changing manifestations to the present. One such indication of how political-cultural changes have penetrated the school can be found in a school policy dating to the 1980s that forbids non-Christians from joining the choir. The school's outgoing principal and choir director, Father George Absi, explained how the school administration felt compelled to change the choir policy as a result of 'outside pressure'. When today's Egyptian sees a Muslim boy singing in the choir, he explains: 'They misunderstand this and it can cause a lot of problems' (Father George Absi, personal communication, 5 May 2003).[11]

In conjunction with his school-based studies, Osman pursued a parallel music education after school hours at the Alexandria Conservatoire. He began violin lessons in 1964, at a time when classical violin, piano and ballet were flourishing in Egypt as a direct consequence of the country's political, military, economic and cultural exchanges with the former Soviet Union. Given the cultural and linguistic differences between Soviet teachers and Egyptian students, they did not always share a common verbal language, but managed to communicate with a mixture of Arabic, French, sign language and 'anything else that might help'. Osman studied violin with a succession of outstanding Soviet teachers from Armenia, Georgia and Azerbaijan who exerted a lasting influence on musical education and performance in Egypt. They prepared their students to eventually staff and run their own music institutions

By the time Osman reached the critical last year of secondary school in 1974, he had completed eleven years of parallel intensive musical training. He began considering the possibility of pursuing a career in music, a plan entirely vetoed by his family. They put pressure on him to follow in his father's footsteps and study medicine, making the case all the more forcefully since his father had suddenly and tragically died when Osman was twelve years old. His mother dreamed that Osman would continue her husband's work and reopen his medical clinic.

In 1975, Osman entered the Faculty of Medicine at Alexandria University, at a time when the Islamist student movement was starting to organize on campuses.[12] He was unprepared for what he calls 'this terrible change in the logic of things'. He began university along with sixteen boys from St Mark's and eight girls from sister French schools. They naturally provided a support group for each other and the boys felt some sense of responsibility for their female colleagues. The mixed group of friends sat together but noticed hostile looks from other students. It was not long before certain male classmates took it upon themselves to 'advise' Osman and the other Muslim boys from his group that they should not be sitting with Christians, and certainly not with girls. Stunned and offended by their mentality, Osman recalls: 'Of course I never listened to them. We were all friends. We spent twelve years together at school and we have remained friends until today.' By his second year, the university's Student Union, controlled by the fundamentalist Islamist organization, *Jama'at Islamiyya*, instituted sex-segregation in lecture halls, forcibly ending the mixed-sex seating arrangements.

Another medical student at Alexandria University at the time recalls how Islamist students, with the support of the university administration, prohibited a range of student cultural activities from taking place. They stopped, for example, a student-initiated film festival on the grounds that the themes of the art house European films went against the tenets of Islam, using the familiar excuse that they were foreign, or 'not from *our* culture'. They also refused to issue the necessary authorization for an annual student-sponsored Mother's Day celebration because it promoted 'un-Islamic' activities of singing and dancing, albeit between students and their mothers! Islamist student leaders were especially hostile to pop music and Western classical music, claiming that those forms were alien to the Egyptian/Islamic culture, and culturally polluting.[13]

Within this reactionary cultural climate, a group of staff and students from the medical faculty organized regular on-campus classical concerts in which Osman often participated. Although he was not political in the sense of being involved in organized student politics, the very act of participating in classical music concerts at that time assumed a political quality. It represented an insistence on preserving those cultural spaces that were being threatened.

After ten years of intensive medical studies, which included a residency in urology, Osman became a fully certified medical doctor. On the dawn of his new career, he made the unequivocal decision to pursue his preferred vocation: music. When he explains to Egyptians that his honorific 'Doctor' derives from a medical degree, not a doctorate in music, they usually express a sense of disbelief.

They are astonished that someone could abandon medicine, the most prestigious of professions, for music and teaching – two vocations of considerably less social value and economic reward. On numerous occasions, he has been asked: 'How? Why? Surely what you mean to say is you're doing music for fun, as a hobby?' He adds, only half joking: 'I think many people think I'm not in a perfect state of mind!' Yet, he believes in the value of music to change the individual and society for the better. Like science, music in all its complexity and beauty provides the potential to develop one's perception and understanding of the world.[14] He explains:

> Music and the arts in general do change a lot in the personality. If we speak of music, the mere fact of knowing not only the music of your own country but of having some idea about the music of other countries or other cultures, allows you to have a broader understanding [of the world]. Music makes you a different person. Even listening carefully to a piece of music can enhance your perception. It is a very important part of the educational process and I do believe it is an important thing to teach.

In 1985, Osman enrolled at the Geneva Conservatoire in Switzerland where he majored in chamber music and supported his studies by playing in different chamber orchestras and taking on private students. The differential treatment the Swiss exhibited towards Osman the musician, versus Osman the Arab foreigner, pressed upon him the role of the musician as a cultural bridge. He recalls:

> I will tell you something that used to happen to me in Switzerland that I will never forget. I look very Middle Eastern, no doubt about that, and the Swiss tend to be reserved *[with foreigners]*. I used to take public transport regularly in Geneva and when I was without my violin nobody ever sat next to me. When I had my violin, people had a completely different attitude. Someone would invariably sit next to me and start up a conversation by asking, 'Is this a violin? Are you a musician?' This would almost always lead to, 'Where are you from? Ah Egypt! It is my dream to visit it one day!' So they dream of visiting Egypt but wouldn't sit next to me, because of the fear of *[Arab/Muslim]* strangers! The only thing in common was music as represented by the violin I was holding! This is to tell you that there the musician is seen as someone who is doing something special and is considered someone worth knowing and talking to.

On completing his master's degree in 1989 with a specialization in string quartets, Osman returned to Egypt to pursue the career of a professional musician. Like many musicians, Osman divided his time between teaching and performing. He joined the Cairo Symphony Orchestra as a first violinist in 1989 and in

1993 moved to the Cairo Opera Orchestra as first violinist and concertmaster. Since 1989, he has been teaching at The Cairo Conservatoire. In 1993, he was selected to attend a workshop on the Suzuki method, and subsequently attended a training session in Japan and became principal teacher of the Suzuki violin class at the Cairo Opera House.

Towards a humanistic and critical pedagogy

Osman's experience with institutions and educators from Egypt, the Arab world, the former Soviet Union, Japan and Europe has culminated in his forming an eclectic pedagogic style and philosophy about teaching. Taken as a whole, his style can be characterized as humanistic, but what does this mean and how can a humanistic pedagogy be practised?

Osman tries to instil in his younger students a sense of pleasure, discernment and discovery in music through a combination of questions, stories and humour relating to each new piece. He is careful not to differentiate in his treatment of students based on their aptitude, a quality that especially endears him to the parents of slower learners. A technique he uses with students of all levels, but more so with younger students, is a strategy of positive reinforcement and humour. He usually comments on an individual performance with a positive comment followed by a more critical one. To the student who produces a screeching sound and plays out of tune but is clearly making a good effort, he comments: 'I can see you've worked very hard on memorizing the piece which is good, but you need to concentrate more on the tone.' For the more gifted student who is producing a superior sound, he will recognize his or her efforts by saying, 'The sound you're producing is definitely becoming more beautiful. It would be even better if . . .', at which point he will show him or her how to get a better sound and work with him or her through a passage of the music until he hears a discernible improvement. Every student, even the most gifted, is encouraged to attain greater levels of excellence.

Osman acknowledges that he learnt the technique of positive reinforcement later in life, while studying the Suzuki method. He had previously been more influenced by his Soviet teachers who, in the method of the 'old school,' exhibited more severity and criticism towards their pupils in an attempt to discourage any complacency and propel them to excel. He recalls that after a violin exam where he performed especially well, his teacher commented: 'It wasn't bad, but you did so and so wrong' and proceeded to produce a long list of his deficiencies.

Another salient characteristic of Osman's pedagogy is patience. Being the teacher of an especially difficult instrument, Osman makes every effort to cultivate in the learner a love of the instrument and of music, which means, especially in the earlier stages, making allowances for slower learners. In one of his group classes, two students aged nine and ten years consistently came to class ill-prepared and produced an especially squeaky sound. They remained on the same piece several weeks after others in their class had moved ahead. Over the course of some months, they did not appear to be making any noticeable progress. Nevertheless, Osman attended to them with his characteristic diligence, scrupulous attention to detail and encouragement as they struggled and fumbled through their lessons. Recalling these two students, I later asked Osman if he had ever had a student who he simply did not think had what it took to continue with the violin. He responded:

> It's very easy to say don't come back if the student isn't practicing, if the parents aren't following up at home, and if you don't feel that he is giving his best effort. The easiest thing to say is 'Thank you, bye-bye, see you, or try another instrument.' But it's not always the best choice because I have seen children that have had a very slow start and then after a while, without knowing why or when, something clicks; something happens and they start improving so fast, you can't imagine how fast. So you have to be patient. You have to hope for this to happen during some step of their studies.

Because of his perseverance and results with students of varying abilities, Osman has gained a reputation for working with students who have been labelled 'problem cases'.

At the Cairo Conservatoire, a free vocational institution to train future professional musicians, students are under a lot of pressure. The Conservatoire's rigorous system of formal assessment means that teachers cannot allow students the luxury of developing at their own paces. In fact, if a student fails to pass his music exam at the critical stage of third-year preparatory (Grade 8), he is expelled from the Conservatoire without the option of repeating the year.

Dr Osman has taken students from the brink of expulsion to the path to a promising career. One of his current Conservatoire students, eighteen-year-old 'Ahmed' is one such example. In the three years since Osman has been his teacher, Ahmed has gone from being perpetually on the verge of getting expelled to becoming a fine musician with an advanced musical repertoire. A major source of Ahmed's troubles in the past was his 'difficult' confrontational character. He regularly questioned his teachers' judgement, was often defensive, and gained a reputation for being not only a poor musician, but also an especially wearisome student. Osman allowed Ahmed the space to question and discuss the music. During lessons, they often took time to analyse a passage of music and decide how best to interpret it. Rather than imposing his will, Osman allowed Ahmed scope to experiment with an alternative interpretation. Osman also paid meticulous attention to every detail of Ahmed's playing.

During their twice-weekly hour-long lessons, Osman used the most exacting standards in assessing his student. In his tidy practice room in the Conservatoire, furnished with music stands, a desk, extra violins and hanging plants, they worked through some of the most difficult music written for violin. Osman alternated between standing and sitting by his student's side and listened to him with great intensity. He drew Ahmed's attention to even the slightest error in an effort to heighten his awareness of the importance of every detail, all the while remaining faithful to the spirit of the piece. He physically inserted himself into the piece by snapping his fingers, clapping his hands or stamping his feet to the tempo, humming to correct the tone and constantly reacting to his student's performance through facial expressions and gestures. He was also quick to tackle and solve problems. When Ahmed's playing became strained and his shoulders tense, Osman instructed him to slouch down in his chair with his legs sprawled out, and to play the piece from that position. He then asked him to stand up and walk around the room, while still playing: 'Relax, enjoy yourself as if you're strolling along the Nile.' Osman guided Ahmed into becoming a better musician, and, no doubt, a better person.

Osman stresses the importance of remaining open to alternative interpretations: 'You cannot be narrow-minded with music,' he insists. 'You have to be open to other ideas or you will never be a good musician.' He encourages his students to constantly seek out other sources of knowledge and instructs them to knock on the doors of other teachers and play for them, get their feedback, criticism and ideas. He also encourages them to learn from everyone and from everywhere. He continuously reminds student-musicians that the more sources they consult, the greater will be their experience and exposure to different styles, cultures and perspectives, and the closer they will arrive at being great musicians and also finding their own voices.

Pluralism does not deny politics

As a performing musician, Osman adds to the local music scene in whatever way he can. He often plays the works of lesser-known contemporary composers and premieres the works of Egyptian and other Arab composers in the repertoire of his quartet. His choices, however, are not always appreciated. Osman recalls that after the performance of *Nigun* by Swiss composer Ernest Bloch (1880–1959), an Egyptian colleague questioned why he played a piece by a Jewish composer, especially given the injustices inflicted on the Palestinians by the Jewish state of Israel. Osman explained that he chose it because of its merit as a piece of music, and added that not playing the piece on the basis of the composer's ethnic or religion identity would constitute an act of bigotry, not a stand of solidarity with the Palestinian people.

Yet, his position on the universalism of music does not deny his strong identification as an Egyptian and an Arab, and his firm political convictions. As he explains: 'As an Egyptian I do have some political ideas and sometimes I like to take a position. I believe, as most Egyptians do, that the American policy in the Middle East is very biased. As Arabs we have to convey the message that we are not happy with what's going on.' In 2002, during the second Palestinian *intifada*, Osman answered a pan-Arab call to boycott American and Israeli institutions. At the time he was heading an after-school Suzuki strings program and community orchestra at the American school in Cairo. He made the decision to resign his job in protest against US foreign policy: 'Some people take to the streets and demonstrate, and some others take a different approach. I chose not to cooperate directly with an official American institution.' Although he severed institutional ties, he maintained individual relations with American students and also continued his volunteer position as director of the community orchestra, which moved from the school to the living room of an orchestra member.

A school for life

Part of becoming a fine musician is learning to work within a group in that quintessential musical institution, the orchestra. The orchestra, made up of members of different backgrounds, specializations, temperaments, abilities, ages and experiences, can be conceptualized as a microcosm of a pluralistic society. On the parallels between playing in an orchestra and living in a democratic community, Daniel Barenboim has cogently said: 'If you wish to learn how to live in a democratic society, then you would do well to play in an orchestra. For when you do so, you know when to lead and when to follow. You leave space for others and at the same time you have no inhibitions about claiming a place for yourself' (Barenboim and Said 2002, p. 173).

The metaphor of music, with its potential to forge democratic learning communities, serves as a powerful affirmation of Daniel Barenboin's dictum that 'music can be the best school for life', that is, if it does not become 'the most effective way to escape from it' (Barenboim and Said 2002, p. 174). This story of a music educator serves as a reminder of the urgency for pedagogies, for educational spaces and learning communities that promote principles of respect, pluralism, rational critical inquiry, fairness and rigour. As communities in the Middle East and beyond grapple with political and economic injustices, growing sectarianism and struggles for democratic change, it becomes ever more urgent to support and nurture those inclusive educational spaces that are constricting at an alarming pace. An education grounded in principles of openness and humanism may be among the best possible means for confronting and overcoming the despair, inequities and injustices of our times.[15]

Notes

1 Some of the injustices referred to here are linked to the politics of empire. It is beyond the scope of this chapter to deal in any depth with questions of empire in the Middle East; however, for an outstanding overview of the issue, see Rashid Khalidi's *Resurrecting Empire: Western Footprints and America's Perilous Path in the Middle East* (2004).

2 In his tremendously erudite volume, *The Rise of Humanism in Classical Islam and the Christian West*, George Makdisi demonstrates the influence of Arabo-Islamic culture, especially with regard to humanism and scholasticism, in intellectual cultures of the West.

3 Osman al-Mahdi's reputation as an outstanding violin teacher is well established by the fact that his classes have been consistently in high demand. Similarly, he is highly regarded by his peers as evidenced by the fact that Egyptian composers Mona Ghoneim, Awatef Abdel Karim and Khaled Shukry have all dedicated compositions to him.

4 All of the interviews with Osman were conducted in English. Interviews with some of his students and their parents took place in Arabic. All translations were done by the author.

5 At the time, the fee per month, which covered four weekly classes, was LE 100, or roughly $20.

6 Dr Suzuki developed what he called the 'mother tongue' method in musical instruction. Following the logic of children's language acquisition, he advocated that

children first learn to listen, absorb and imitate music before learning its formal rules. According to the Talent Association of Australia, Suzuki's goal was to 'embrace the whole child, nurturing a love of music and the development of a fine character rather than just the mastering of a musical instrument'. Suzuki called his idea 'Talent Education' and soon established a school in Matsumoto. Talent Education refers to the development of skill, knowledge and character. Suzuki took a great deal of time and care developing the repertoire, which presents technical and musical concepts in a logical sequence. The Suzuki method, which began in Japan, in 2003 included over 8000 Suzuki teachers and more than 250,000 children learning it worldwide (Talent Association of Australia 2003).

7   It is worth noting that Western classical music is an eclectic form that draws on a vast resource of secular and spiritual musical traditions from the East and the West, which includes, as musicologist Estelle Jorgensen points out, 'the musics of Eastern Orthodoxy and Judaism, and … the secular musics of Middle Eastern and Northern African countries in which Islam took hold' (Jorgensen 2003, pp. 134–5).

8   The cosmopolitanism of Alexandria was legendary and immortalized in works of art and fiction such as Lawrence Durrell's *Alexandria Quartet*. But the city's cosmopolitanism, as Sami Zubaida reminds us, flourished in an imperial context and was steeped in layers of exclusions and segregation. As Zubaida relates: 'Cosmopolitan Alexandria … included a rigorous system of exclusions for native Egyptians, including segregation or exclusion on buses and trams, and certainly from clubs, some bars and cafés and many social milieux. Native Egyptian society provided servants, functionaries and prostitutes for the cosmopolitan milieu' (2002, pp. 37–8). André Aciman's autobiographical history of the de-cosmopolitanization of Alexandria, *Out of Egypt* (1994), with its absence of native Egyptians except in the roles of servants and odd characters, confirms Zubaida's observation.

9   Not unlike what occurred in Alexandria, Istanbul experienced its own de-cosmopolitanization and Turkification, as portrayed in Orhan Pamuk's *Istanbul, Memories of a City* (2005, p. 215).

10 In its earlier years, the policy at St Mark's was to allow Muslim boys to attend what at that time was a boarding school, but to keep practices and signs of Islam at bay. A student boarder from the 1940s recalled that Muslim students were not allowed to fast during the holy month of Ramadan. By the 1960s, the school administration embraced a principle of religious pluralism, not merely because of legal obligations to do so, but also because of a seeming change of attitude regarding religious education.

11 The author interviewed Father George Absi on 5 May 2003 at St Mark's School, Alexandria.

12 According to French sociologist Giles Kepel, 'the *jama'at islamiyya* were the Islamist student associations that became the dominant force on Egyptian university campuses during Sadat's presidency. Although they were at first a

minority within the Egyptian student movement (then dominated by the Nasserist and Marxist currents) that arose just after the country's defeat in the 1967 war, the Islamist students made their breakthrough during the relative calm that prevailed in the campuses after the October war of 1973' (1985, p. 129).

13   Interview with Dr Ibrahim Karbouch in Alexandria, May 2003.

14   Indeed, throughout history music has been an integral part of scientific study. The ancient Greeks studied harmonics, a subject that combined music, arithmetic, astronomy and geometry (Postman 1996, p. 103). Similarly, in the time of medieval Islam, music was 'studied by the scholars and favored by the Sufis' although it did not make up a formal, independent subject of school curricula (Dodge 1962, p. 87).

15   The author would like to thank the students and parents who participated in this study, with special mention of Tara Bayat. The members of the Culture and Education in Egypt working group in Cairo, the education reading group of the Institute of Social Studies, the anonymous reviewers from Teachers College Record, Susan Hack, Lila Abu-Lughod and Osman El Mahdi provided insightful critical comments on earlier drafts of this chapter. A different version of this chapter was published in Arabic, titled: 'Al-Amkanat al-Tarbawiyya: al-Musiqa wa Hudud al-Thaqafa fi Misr' [Pedagogical Possibilities: Music and the Borders of Educational Culture in Egypt] (Herrera 2003, pp. 23–46).

References

Aciman, A. (1994). *Out of Egypt*. New York: Farrar Straus Giroux.

Amin, G. (2000). *Whatever Happened to the Egyptians?* Cairo: AUC Press.

Barenboim, D. (2006). *In the Beginning was Sound*. Jerusalem: Reith Lectures.

Barenboim, D. and Said, E. (2002). *Parallels and Paradoxes: Explorations in Music and Society*. In A. Guzelimiam (Ed.). New York: Pantheon Books.

Cole, A. L. and Knowles, J. G. (Eds) (2001). *Lives in Context: The Art of Life History Research*. Walnut Creek, CA: AltaMira Press.

Dodge, B. (1962). *Muslim Education in Medieval Times*. Washington, DC: The Middle East Institute.

Freire, P. (1970). *Pedagogy of the Oppressed*. New York: Continuum.

Gardner, H. (1993). *Frames of Mind: The Theory of Multiple Intelligences*. New York: Basic Books.

Greene, M. (1995). *Releasing the Imagination: Essays on Education, the Arts, and Social Change*. San Francisco: Jossey-Bass.

Herrera, L. (1999). 'Song Without Music: Islamism and Education, a Case from Egypt'. *Revue des Mondes Musulmans et de la Méditerranée*, 85–6: 149–59.

Herrera, L. (Ed.) (2003). *Qiyam! Julus! Thaqafat al-Ta'alim fi Misr [Stand up! Sit Down! Cultures of Schooling in Egypt]*. Cairo: The Population Council.

Herrera, L. and Torres, C. A. (Eds) (2006). *Cultures of Arab Schooling: Critical Ethnographies from Egypt.* New York: State University of New York Press.

Jorgensen, E. R. (2003). 'Western Classical Music and General Education'. *Philosophy of Music Education Review*, 11 (2): 130–40 (Fall).

Kepel, G. (1985). *The Prophet and Pharaoh: Muslim extremism in Egypt.* Translated by J. Rothschild. London: Saqi Books.

Khalidi, R. (2004). *Resurrecting Empire: Western Footprints and America's Perilous Path in the Middle East.* Boston: Beacon Press.

Makdisi, G. (1990). *The Rise of Humanism in Classical Islam and the Christian West.* Edinburgh: Edinburgh University Press.

Mintz, S. (1960). *Worker in the Cane: A Puerto Rican Life History.* New Haven: Yale University Press.

Iran's President Bans All Western Music (2005). *New York Times.* Retrieved 19 December 2005, from http://www.nytimes.com/aponline/international/AP-Iran-Music-Ban.html.

Pamuk, O. (2005). *Istanbul: Memories of a City.* Translated by M. Freely. London: Faber and Faber.

Sonbol, Amira el-Azhary (Ed.) (1996). *Mémoires d'un souverain: Par Abbas Hilmi II, Khédive d'Egypte [Memoires of a Monarch: Abbas Hilmi II, Khedive of Egypt] (1892–1914).* Cairo: Centre d'Études et de Documentation Economique, Juridique et Sociale (CEDEJ).

Said, E. (2004). *Humanism and Democratic Criticism.* New York: Columbia University Press.

Talent Association of Australia (2003). Accessed 20 October 2003, http://www.suzukimu-sic.org.au/homepage.html

Zubaida, S. (2002). 'Middle Eastern Experiences of Cosmopolitanism'. In S. Vertovec and R. Cohen (Eds), *Conceiving Cosmopolitanism: Theory, Context, and Practice*, pp. 32–41. Oxford: Oxford University Press.

Epilogue

Carmel Borg and Michael Grech

Introduction

The main thread linking these writings is a critical challenge to some ideas concerning peace that have entered the common sense (in the Gramscian understanding of common sense) that is influenced by Western thought, academia and media. The chapters examine items concerning peace that pertain to this common sense, hoping to contribute towards promoting Critical Education regarding peace. Critical Education refers to those educational engagements – formal and informal – that encourage the examination of the limits and possibilities[1] of the myths, impressions, pictures of the world or of some aspects of it, clichés, opinions, received wisdom, institutions and relations between human beings (on a micro and macro level) that are predominant in a society and in the world in general, and to consider these in relation to structures of domination and empowerment of different classes and groups. It is a kind of education that pays particular attention to how education itself occurs, the limits and possibilities of different pedagogical encounters. The aim of these exercises is not a sterile intellectual venture, but an undertaking that involves cognitive, practical and affective aspects, seeking to nurture in those involved in the educational sites in question the awareness, sensitivity and motivation to bring about justice and equity.

In the 'common sense' being considered, 'peace' is normally understood as the mere absence of violence in relation to some groups, especially nations. This 'common sense' seems to enshrine the following assumptions:

1. War is evil; peace is preferable to war.
2. Peace, understood narrowly as the absence of war, is generally preferable to violence and conflict.
3. Humanity as a whole would benefit without war.

4. War is, however, an inevitable feature of human existence; there will be moments when a situation cannot be resolved if not through war.
5. War may be morally legitimate and justified; it may involve a 'good side' fighting a morally legitimate war against an 'evil side'. A consequence of this is that the 'good side' ought always to be ready to fight for the rightful cause.

This book adopts a broad and flexible understanding of the term 'peace' – a concept that is taken to involve not merely a definite set of entities (e.g. nation states and armies) or situations (e.g. war in the conventional sense of the term), but involving various dimensions, including an international sphere (involving global, regional and transnational dimensions) implicating nations and sets of people; a national dimension, involving different groups and classes within a social formation; and an intimate/personal sphere comprising family and intimate relations.[2] Even regarding the very meaning and extension of the term, we adopt a broad understanding of 'peace'.

Many philosophers of language distinguish between a common core content of a linguistic expression (what the linguistic expression says in any context of use), involving 'features of the meaning of a linguistic expression that stay invariable in whatever context the expression may be used' (Kratzer 1977, pp. 3–6) and the enriched content that tokens of the linguistic expression may have in determinate contexts. The former would be 'the meaning proper of [the] expression' (Kratzer 1977, p. 3). In this epilogue, we adopt a similar strategy in relation to the term 'peace'. 'Peace' has a common core content, which is its proper meaning. Yet, in specific and different contexts of use, the term may mean and entail different things. Indeed, a common mistake regarding 'peace' is supposing that the term will evoke the same things, have the same attributes and entail the same characteristics in any context of use. The contexts to which we refer would involve not simply speakers, times and locations where the term is used, but will involve features like history, gender, ethnic groups, class, culture, subcultures within the same social formation and political set-up, and international and regional junctions of these features.

Peace, pacification and passive resistance

Peace is frequently characterized as the absence of war and violence, involving primarily (if not exclusively) armies and nations. This is the first thing the book seeks to problematize. There cannot be peace if unjust and inequitable relations between nations, peoples, classes and other groups of peoples, and between different individuals, exist. If such unjust relations exist, 'peace' understood as the mere absence of conflict would abet an unjust *status quo*. Moreover, peace understood in this way would not be a state of affairs that could subsist forever; the *status quo* it abets will, realistically, occasion violence of different sorts. Some of these aspects are highlighted by Marianna Papastephanou in *Where Does True Peace Dwell?* Papastephanou begins by distinguishing peace from pacification. Peace entails justice and equity; pacification may conceal and abet unequal and unjust relations.

Papastephanou also examines the above-mentioned idea that war is an inevitable feature of human existence, noting that this has been consistently hammered into the minds of many, even by eminent intellectuals and philosophers. At the dawn of modern philosophy, one finds thinkers like Hobbes who buttress the idea that humans are by nature aggressive and warlike by what he takes to be an empirical characterization of human nature (this characterization of humanity includes predominantly male attributes, war being frequently a patriarchal construct). Even many postmodern philosophers who would shy away from the idea of there being a human nature, however, tend to implicitly accept that war is the obvious condition of human beings, since the tendency among them is to consider peace as a meta-narrative that is now passé. The obvious consequence of this is to accept war as inevitable, what remains when the meta-narrative of peace is debunked. Papastephanou, on the other hand, claims that what is artificial – what is imposed by culturally hegemonic means – is the idea that humans are destined to an existence of war, a belief that is made an item of common sense for reasons that are not innocent. War (and peace understood as mere absence of physical violence) is necessary for the powers that be to have those who are hegemonically subordinated to them accepting their lot, and to justify their policing and aggression in the name of peace. It is vital for Critical Education to be aware of these hegemonic manoeuvres, particularly when they are couched in humanitarian and progressive guises. A trivial reading of Papastephanou's argument might suggest a rejection of most of modern and contemporary thought. Such a reading, though, would be superficial. The author rightly warns about those lines of thoughts that have served to cement the hegemony of some groups and the exclusion and suffering of others. Yet, it definitely does not exclude the fact that people involved in Critical Education may help themselves to the intellectual, cognitive and philosophical resources that these traditions offer and put these to emancipatory purposes.

'Peace', then, cannot be understood as the mere absence of conflict, the coming into being of which may justify aggression and war. A different common core content of the term 'peace' is henceforth required. A contribution in this regard is made in Joseph Gravina's piece *A Gramscian Analysis of Passive Revolution and Its Contribution to the Study of Peace:* which starts with a definition of 'peace' as 'the absence of violence together with the existence/coming into being of relations of justice and equity'.

This can be taken as the proper meaning of 'peace', the common content of the term. It is deeper than the characterization of 'peace' as the mere absence of violent conflict, because it refers to justice and equity, and hence entails dignity, respect for rights, well-being and welfare. It is also quite general and vague, and may be enriched in various contexts.

The distinction that needs to be made between peace and its travesty is a running theme in Gravina's chapter. By referring to four historical examples, the author presents situations deemed to be peaceful but which do not, in fact, entail peace as understood here. Specifically, he considers Italian Unification, Fascism, post-World War II Italy (from the boom to the 1970s) and the process of European Integration, claiming that what occurred in these different contexts was a 'passive revolution', the immediate aftermath of which was 'pacification' (meaning an end to widespread social and political violence), but not peace. 'Passive revolution' refers to processes that are measured and piecemeal, and frequently entail the adjustment of existing social, political and economic structures, instead of their elimination. These processes were accompanied by educational reforms that sustain the 'change' in question. If the social, political and economic structures in question are unjust and inequitable, unjust and inequitable relations would have been perpetuated, albeit under a different guise and in a relatively 'peaceful' manner.

Gravina's piece is important for the relationship between peace and Critical Education in a number of respects. It cautions those who are involved in Critical Education not to be deceived by processes and phenomena that appear to be progressive, but, in fact, are not. Critical educators need to go beyond such rhetoric and judge initiatives, including educational initiatives, as truly progressive if and only if they help in achieving justice and equity.

More importantly, the chapter raises important questions that go beyond the remit of the chapter and the book. Can peace, defined as the absence of violence together with the existence/coming into being of relations of justice and equity, ever occur? Can peace occur in class-based societies (as hitherto most/all societies) and in a global scenario involving unequal exchanges, however mild these may be? Can peace, understood as 'the absence of violence, together with the existence/coming into being of relations of justice and equity', ever be achieved by non-violent means, since the powers that would presumably be unwilling to change unequal relations that are favourable to them? Did the world ever experience peace? Or is it the case that peace can only occur in small spatio-temporal pockets? Is the achievement of peace so understood too onerous, and maybe we should settle for something else; accept some state of affairs involving some unequal exchanges, but where the basic needs of the majority are satisfied? Could one envisage what Giovanni Franzoni calls a truce rather than peace, a 'temporary respite from a reality marked by suffering, massacres and destruction?' (Franzoni 2015, p. 151).

These grave questions hover over the entire work, and it would be preposterous for us to claim that the book is able to answer them. Problematizing 'peace' in relation to these aspects may count as some form of humble contribution that the book may make, which will hopefully stimulate further thinking. Critical Education that aims to achieve 'peace' as understood in this book cannot avoid tackling such questions, both theoretically and in the distinctive concrete contexts in which education initiatives occur. The relation of 'peace' to unequal and unjust economic situations is not, however, the only aspect of peace (as the term is normally understood) that is problematized in the book.

Women – inclusion and a new paradigm

Peace is frequently discussed in vague and theoretical terms, often in relation to abstract and totalizing categories like 'humanity'. Even the early Paulo Freire, with his emphasis on 'becoming fully human', was prone to this. In mainstream peace discourses, including in a lot of formal and informal education related to the topic, a common assumption is that war and peace are aspects of human existence that affect everyone more or less in the same way. This assumption belongs to the common sense of many. A positive aspect of this is recognizing and postulating peace as a universal ideal, a goal that all human beings ought to aspire to achieve. Yet, this approach has an important limit; that humans belong to different social classes, nations, cultures, ethnic groups and sexes is ignored or not considered as relevant to the achieving of peace. This is a limit that Critical Education ought to highlight. Since humans fall in different categories, their experience of, thoughts about and, indeed, the very understanding of, the term 'peace' may differ fundamentally, and be enriched in various contexts and in relation to several variants.

Simone Galea's chapter '*Breathing Peace*' criticizes mainstream peace discourses from a feminist perspective. Galea focuses on how women experience war, violence and peace, claiming that these experiences are usually not taken into consideration in mainstream peace discourses and initiatives. These frequently imbue a patriarchal and phallocentric ethos that limits and hampers their effectiveness. This ethos implicitly marginalizes women, reproducing relations of domination to which many women are subjected. Such peace initiatives cannot be successful and comprehensive. An education that is not critical in this respect will reproduce this exclusion and strengthen it. Critical Education that seeks to promote peace ought to encourage educational encounters where such logic is challenged.

Galea proposes a new paradigm for peace building, one that draws inspiration from Luce Irigaray's thoughts about the maternal aspect of women and its liberatory potential. Certain feminists have traditionally considered the maternal aspect and the roles that are associated to it as limiting and debilitating. Irigaray, on the other hand, highlights their possibilities and liberatory potential, even in relation to peace. Pregnancy, birth and the mother's breath may symbolize relations that respect differences are genuinely peaceful. Motherhood for instance, involves three poles: the mother, the offspring and a third space where the two come together and relate to each other, enacting their different roles and subjectivities. Regarding breath, the mother breathes for herself but also sustains the breath of a different, autonomous, creature, who in due course will breathe on his or her own. In both cases each subject approaches the other, respects his or her subjectivity and undergoes a reworking and rethinking of his or her personality and character. Education that relates to peace might attempt to re-create such multipolar approaches, bringing participants together and creating a distinct space, rather than a one-to-one relation that may end up in an uneven rapport between parties. (Initiatives that somehow embody such ethos may already exist as in Neve Shalom/Wahat as-Salam in Israel.) Very pertinently, Galea highlights that in such educational encounters, even the characterization of peace, what characteristics are concretely included in the understanding of this term, cannot be determined a priori.[3]

Though drawing important insights from Irigaray, Galea also discusses limits in her work, like her fatalistic and negative understanding of terms like 'conflict'.

Irigaray fails to notice the potential that phenomena grouped under the term 'conflict' may have in relation to peace. Peace is implicitly conceived by Irigaray as the state where different persons have reached a consensual agreement on some issue. This overlooks the possibility of developing relations where conflicts and disagreements arise, but where peace exists despite them. Galea rightfully suggests that one should deconstruct the dichotomy of peace–conflict, rather than simply seeking to eliminate always and everywhere one of these termini. Teaching peace, therefore, entails creating a hospitable space where differences and healthy conflicts (ones that do not involve violence, inequity and injustice) exist, rather than ignoring, playing down or dismissing them. Another limit of Irigaray is arguably her failure to consider identities that cannot be identified as strictly male or female (See Poe 2011; Gerada, Mercieca and Xuereb 2014).

'Liberal peace' from above

It is not only gender that is caricatured in a generalized characterization of peace. 'Peace' ought also to be enriched in relation to other variants, relating to history, cultures, economic development, religious identities and regional situations.

The benefits of a Critical Education that takes this into consideration emerge if one considers how the ideals of 'democracy' and 'peace' were (mis) implemented in Iraq after the US Invasion, something discussed in Arsalan Alshinawi's *The Limits of Exogenous Initiatives in Peacemaking, Focusing on Iraq after the US Invasion*. Alshinawi discusses endogenous and exogenous change aimed at bringing about peace and democracy, focusing on the shortcomings that the latter type of change generally entails. He focuses on the ill effects of the American exogenous initiative; an initiative that was meant to enhance democracy and peace in the country and region.

One limit of the initiative is already evident in its characterization of 'peace' as the mere absence of conflict. Indeed, Iraq was supposed to be restructured along neo-liberal lines, something that would have unlikely achieved justice and equity, even if the post-Saddam transition had been free from violence. The chapter clearly illustrates the dangers involved in imposing peace from above, especially when those imposing it have only superficial and biased knowledge of the terrain on which the ideals are being imposed, superficial knowledge that does not reflect the perspectives, world views and aspirations of those on whom the ideal is being forced. The contents that the terms 'democracy' and 'peace' will have for those implementing the ideals will inevitably differ from those for the people that are supposed to benefit from their implementation. Awareness of the impact that the religious and/or ethnic identities of different groups would have had on how Iraqis would understand 'peace' in the post-Saddam era, for instance,[4] was apparently missing from the thinking of those who imposed 'peace' and 'democracy'. Historical features like the fact that Sunnis had ruled the land for a thousand years and would not easily accept being sidelined, that the Shias were seeking a share of power in a country where they are a majority, the aspirations of the Kurds, the fears and prospects of other minorities and other specific features ought to have constituted the backdrop in relation to which the content of 'peace' could have been fleshed out. Instead, these considerations were by and large missing. The results have been disastrous.

Nicos Trimikliniotis and Dimitris Trimithiotis (*Critical Peace in the Digital Era of Austerity and Crisis*) move along similar lines with Alshinawi, broadening their concern regarding (and diminishing the focus of) peacemaking in general. Adopting a postcolonial reading of peace initiatives, they note that the dominant approach in peacemaking has, for the past forty years, been largely dictated by the West. While confirming Al Shinawi's claim that many exogenous peacemaking initiatives are insensitive to the particularities of individual realities, the two throw doubts on the motives behind such initiatives, holding that most of these missions have economic purposes as their ultimate end. A thorough analysis of these initiatives reveals not merely structural defects like unidirectionality and failure to take into consideration particular contexts, but also features like high-level prescriptions involving invasive 'peace dividends' and other aspects that reflect an imperialistic framework that ultimately benefits the economic, legal and geopolitical interests of former colonial masters and of current hegemonic powers.

Trimikliniotis and Trimithiotis focus on 'Liberal Peace Processes', which, behind the liberal rhetoric, involve a largely economistic, Western-centric model of peacemaking and peace agenda. Elements of this model have entered the common sense of many in various parts of the world. One element that has become predominant in thought and talk about peace in recent years is 'security', leading to a territorial and an extra-territorial paranoia that has led to the building of all types of walling, surveillance technology, border brutality and militarization, as well as to overt and covert mass repression. Apart from the moral, economic and political contradictions such initiatives entail, wall-building and other means of keeping people apart from each other are pedagogically debilitating in relation to peace education since they discourage dialogue and the transcending of limits, borders and boxes.

Trimikliniotis and Trimithiotis seek to theoretically dismantle the Liberal peace model and promote 'Critical Peace' in contrast. Critical peace processes are historicized and sociology-driven models involving an in-depth and multidimensional understanding of the structural issues that perpetuate hostilities, contestations and divisions. They exhibit a heightened awareness of the geographical intersectionality of phenomena and the dialectics that emerge from the tension between de- and re-territorialization. What ought to follow from such analysis, though, are not merely models through which to understand particular situations, but a critical-social-scientific engagement with the wounded world, rooted in transformational struggles, seeking social and economic justice. Indeed, Trimikliniotis and Trimithiotis set as the ultimate benchmark of peace education the building of socialities (i.e. people and groups converging, developing social relations and building communities) that imbue values that are antithetical to those of contemporary hegemonic order. Anything else is tantamount to pacification rather than genuine peace.

Interestingly, Trimikliniotis and Trimithiotis discuss digital technology and relate this to the new possibilities it might entail in relation to peace and justice. This is a very important aspect, which is not highlighted by other contributors to the book. Quite frequently, when pedagogical issues are discussed in relation to ideals like peace and to political factors, the means that are used in our pedagogy are dismissed or simply related to economic features, as Trimikliniotis and Trimithiotis note when they refer to the digital divide. Indeed, digital technology is often presented as an obstacle to justice and genuine peace, given the divide that persists in relation to access to it between people belonging to different groups and societies. Yet, the authors hold that this field is, in fact, opening new terrains of struggles. Studies show that disadvantaged groups, such as migrants and refugees, often use digital media and social networks in their border crossings, contributing considerably to a 'mobile commons'. Critical Education committed to peace, then, cannot ignore digital technologies and should harness the potential of politically productive digital spaces that are constitutive of new social dynamics, and connect such spaces to contexts where different humans exist and operate, especially those who belong to marginalized groups and realities. On the other hand, it should not exaggerate the role digital technology may play, or consider these technologies as socially and politically neutral (something that may be suggested by some parts of Trimikliniotis and Trimithiotis' chapter), coming into being, existing and operating in some politico-economic-cultural vacuum. Digitality also involves forms of power-laden processes such as coding and decoding. The ability to perform these is a form of powerful knowledge (Williamson 2015).

Cementing common sense

Common sense does not come into being spontaneously. There are various sources from which it is built. One of them is formal education. In her chapter *Dreaming of Peace in a Culture of War: Revolutionary Considerations*, Antonia Darder discusses how common sense in relation to war is built in the United States in various educational set-ups: creating cognitive and emotional consent around the idea that ongoing, unprovoked aggressive and violent behaviour is morally justifiable if it pre-empts perceived aggression by 'the other' is inflicted in the name of national and international security. At school, many Americans covertly experience a curriculum of war, which is, however, frequently hidden behind benign language – a curriculum that provides ideological priming and legitimation for a 'violent' state. In this regard, Henry Giroux writes extensively and prolifically on the culture of militarization to which US youths are exposed through all sorts of discourses in which they are immersed, such as computer games simulating war combat. (Apart from citing books and other available material, Darder recounts her personal experience as a woman, wife and scholar, belonging to an ethnic minority, growing up in the United States.[5]) The mantra sustaining this exercise in hegemony is that citizens cannot experience freedom unless the state exercises permanent aggression, that for the state to guarantee freedom and democracy, its citizens have to accept constant surveillance,[6] the presence of militarized police (including armed security guards in high schools), as part of the communal landscape, civilian casualties resulting from military initiatives, and walls and fences that keep out undesirable aliens. They also need to be made to approve overt and abrasive militarism as permanent features of US foreign policy, and to condone selective and covert military initiatives aimed at destabilizing other countries and regions. Patriotism and nationalism are reified through daily rituals, textbooks and symbols that promote allegiance to an aggressive state. The end result is that war comes to be perceived as an act of allegiance to one's country and of love of one's nation, something that is indispensable to the communities (local and national) one inhabits. Opt-out options as conscientious objection are vilified and portrayed as acts of desertion and betrayal.

In contrast to the universal condemnation of the indoctrination processes that lead jihadists to explode themselves in the name of God, the normalized massive indoctrination to war occurring within the institutions of learning is rarely censored. (Indeed, the existence of such a curriculum of war is ignored by many, including most of its victims). The fact that the curricular experience children undergo in US schools is devoid of the language of critique in relation to acts of state aggression ensures such failure, and provides the ideal habitat for curricular initiatives that reinforce aggression and violence in the name of lofty ideals like democracy, human rights and peace.

Schools however, are not the only institutions that cement common sense in relation to war. The media, in its multiple forms, is another terrain where the violent state has successfully (albeit not without resistance) achieved legitimation for violent acts in exchange for perceived safety, security and freedom. The scripts prescribed by the dominant media, portrayed as neutral entertainment, present violent heroes as decisive characters and carriers of moral authority.

Very pertinently, Darder relates the implementation of this curriculum of war to the social set-up in the United States, noting how the primary victims at home are people from the lowest echelons of society. Schools, home or cinema screens, to mention three examples, serve as public pedagogy that delinks war from the war industry, from the accumulation of wealth and from the pain inflicted by the perceived necessity of war. They also promote a false sense of self-worth derived from acts of 'hypermasculinity'. For people serving in the army, the war-spectacle they view on TV, is transformed into a theatre of real war where predominantly working-class youth end their lives on behalf of their beloved *mother/fatherland*. For young people from deprived backgrounds, the army might constitute the only means of getting a decent education and employment. Those who reap the benefits of war generally, shirk from participating directly in such ventures and hence must convince others to fight these wars for them.

Darder's agenda is clearly for a pedagogy that deals with complex moral questions in an equally complex way, distant from dualisms and essentialisms – an educational agenda that promotes collective dialogical experiences that critically reflect on the historical and structural roots of violence with the purpose of structurally breaking the cycles of violence within our homes, communities and beyond. What perhaps should be emphasized is that, as the common sense for war is cemented in concrete sites, at what a Gramscian might call national-popular level, attempts to amend common sense should also operate at this level, seeking elements of good sense to use for critical and peaceful purposes. Just as the military and economically hegemonic establishment can use a whole array of figures to glorify wars and aggression in the name of peace and democracy, Critical Education that is committed to 'peace' should hook to its own pantheon of the American great and good who challenged imperialist wars; people like Dorothy Day, Martin Luther King and Mark Twain.

The myths of peace and war

Critical Education has traditionally attempted to apply to education insights that draw their origin from critical thought in philosophy and elsewhere. Critical thought, bent on the examination of the limits and possibilities of human phenomena, cannot exempt from its scrutiny the human faculty from which it issues: rationality. Indeed the masterpiece of the harbinger of critical thought, Immanuel Kant's *Critique of Pure Reason*, is an analysis of the limits and possibilities of reason, focusing primarily on the types of judgements this faculty emits. Kant, however, stood at the height of a movement, the Enlightenment, the affirmation of which saw the celebration of the possibilities rather than the limits of rationality. Many Enlightenment thinkers sought to curtail the wings of Revelation, to banish what they considered superstition and to eliminate myth. Reason was used not merely to trace boundaries and limits, but also to suppress and banish. In their enthusiasm, many Enlightenment thinkers thought that, in both the theoretical and the practical domains, humans could and ought to be guided, moved and motivated by reason alone. Education had to reflect this banishing of thoughts and ideas deemed to be mythological. Critical Education seems to have imbued this ethos. Freire, for instance, uses 'myth' pejoratively, considering myths as narratives that somehow distort reality (see *Pedagogy of the Oppressed*, Chapter 4)

This picture of reason reigning supreme drew criticism from various sources even in its heyday, (e.g. Rousseau's *First Discourse on the Arts and Science*, where it is claimed that the elevation of reason over feeling had led to a degeneration in behaviour and morals, and Hume's *Treatise of Human Nature* where reason is declared the 'slave to the passions'). Freud later demonstrated that the idea of rationality having total control over human action is fabulous; in steering and controlling human action, reason has to compete with the equally strong 'impulse of the unconscious' (Solomon 1988, p. 143), which includes 'urges and impulses [that are] indifferent to [reason's] demands' (Solomon 1988, p. 143). Regarding myths, Nietzsche positively reconsidered the role of myths, and claimed that the enlightenment itself contained its own set of mythological narratives (See Mangion 2003, p. 2). Recently, Karen Armstrong has argued that mythological and rational discourses serve different purposes, involve different types of meanings and approach reality in different ways. These two types of discourse concern different faculties and aspects of the mind, and should not be seen as mutually exclusive (2004, pp. ix–xvi).

Rather than banishing myth, critical thought and education might attempt to engage with its limits and possibilities. This is what Clive Zammit does in *The Myth of the Inevitability of War: A Mythico-Historic Hybrid Discourse*, regarding myths that concern peace. The author refers to two uses of the term 'myth': the first refers to traditional mythological narratives, the second to a different use of 'myth' by Ronald Barthes.

Clive Zammit first discusses myth understood in the first sense of the term: a narrative drawn from familiar tales, which focuses on some theme (e.g. abduction, gift giving, the fall). He contrasts myth with history understood as the rigorous investigation of the past. The two types of discourse have distinctive characteristics. Historical discourse is characterized by its factual character, and the use of evidence and sources to sustain conclusions. The events it concerns are contingent. A historian may discuss the Battle of Waterloo and adduce evidence to buttress his conclusion. Yet, the battle is a contingent event; it could not have occurred. Mythological discourse, on the other hand, is characterized by 'thematic necessity'; it concerns things that occur necessarily and go beyond contingent events and happenings. 'The myth of the "fall"' for instance, refers to intrinsic characteristics of the human species, frailty and the propensity to do what one ought to avoid. Though myths may refer to real events and concrete individuals, they need not be buttressed by factual evidence. Also, while the themes of myths are constant across different times and narrations, their content (what the stories say) and the morals drawn from them are reworked, reinterpreted and reconsidered in different contexts.

Zammit, however, refers to another kind of 'myth', one used by Barthes. This is a hybrid between historical discourse and myth in the traditional sense of the term. This kind of discourse, however, (a second-order discourse, one that produces second-order signifiers) does not normally present itself as 'myth' or expose its 'mythical' facets.

Myth in this second sense is concerned with things that are normally the subject-matter of historical narratives. Yet, within this kind of 'myth', the events, characteristics and features narrated lack the contingent character they normally have in historical writings. Instead, they evidence the necessity typical of traditional mythology, without, however, admitting the possibility of different interpretations. This discourse would, then, both concern history, in the sense of dealing with concrete events that occur in the material world, and transcend it, possessing characteristics that historical events normally lack, such as inevitability and necessity. Indeed, unlike historical discourses, mythological discourse in the Barthian sense would not require factual corroboration to justify it. Rather, the tendency for people who accept such discourse is to dismiss a priori conflicting evidence. Barthian 'myths' seem to be a fundamental feature of any common sense.

Critical Education that promotes peace as an ideal ought obviously to deal with this second type of 'myth'. Some such myths, for instance, are used to sustain the so-called war on terror, and to justify militarization and rearmament. Zammit considers the myth of the inevitability of war. One may, however, also consider other myths, like the myth that Islam is a violent religion and fundamentally antithetical to Western values.[7] This myth influences a lot of ideas found in Western common sense about war, peace and how to achieve the latter.

The discourse in which such myths are imbued seems to refer to something that is very concrete: Muslim people interacting with others. It tries to appear as a discourse that is corroborated by evidence, if not as being actually positivistic. It attempts to explain certain concrete phenomena and happenings like the 9-11 attacks, the failure of the Arab Spring, IS and Al-Qaeda, and to unearth the links between them. Yet, it is a discourse that exudes the necessity typical of traditional myths, rather than the contingency that characterizes historical narratives. Thus, though the events in question refer to historical phenomena, the underlying causes seem to be supra-historical: Islam and Western values are considered as having some existence of their own (one that transcends historical events and epochs) and to be necessarily and fundamentally antithetical. Historical events would merely enact in time and space the supra-historical battle between the two; they would be a mere manifestation of a deeper necessity; they could not be otherwise or occur differently from how they occur. If these narratives enter common sense, people will accept this necessity and reject possible alternative interpretations of the events: Muslim radicalism as a result of concrete political and economic phenomena, geopolitics related to different power struggles in the Middle East and the Gulf, etc. Common sense would close itself to any contrary evidence. Narratives of Muslims who work hand in hand with others, who participate in democratic activities, who uphold Western values (whatever these may be) and lifestyles, would be denied or sidelined as marginal. Peace between these two monoliths would be dismissed a priori. Educational sites and initiatives might end up fostering, reproducing and propagating such myths.

Given that myths play such an important role in the common sense of different sets of people, Critical Education cannot ignore or dismiss them. It must separate clearly historical and mythological discourses, being aware of the different types of narratives these involve. It ought to expose myths, in the Barthian sense, for what they are: narratives that conceal their non-concrete nature, and present as necessary features that are contingent and limited. Zammit does an excellent job in exposing these myths, how they function and what effects they have. Yet, he does not spell clearly and completely (after all, he is not a professional pedagogue) what people engaged in Critical Education ought to do in concrete circumstances. This is for pedagogues in different sites to establish.

Reading the world in the word

As emerges from Clive Zammit's piece, an education that is committed to peace cannot limit itself to the cognitive dimension: to examining the thoughts, notions, ideas and beliefs people harbour. One area where education ought to operate is the sensibility of different parties and groups. This emerges clearly from Carmen Sammut's *The Face of Evil in the Era of Liberal Peace: Media Debates around the Cases of Jyllands-Posten and Charlie Hebdo*. While not directly addressing the issue regarding whether the publication of religious caricatures ought to be allowed or not (Sammut, though, seems to have no objection to laws that allow such publication), she does favour an approach to media management that promotes responsibility in relation to the possible effects that the publication of similar pictures may have on the relations between different communities, particularly between Muslim communities in different parts of the world including the West, on the one hand, and mainstream Western society (whatever this means), on the other. What may appear to be innocuous publication of cartoons or other material may end up fomenting real or apparent clashes between different groups, sustaining myths in the 'Barthian' sense regarding some eternal war between different civilizations whose sensibilities, beliefs and values are (obviously) incompatible. Such publication may end up targeting communities that are weaker and cannot reply in kind to what they see as an unjust attack on what they hold to be sacred and dear.[8]

This latter aspect points to a limit of traditional liberal and libertarian discourses, even in relation to peace within a society. These tend to conceive of issues concerning the media and freedom of speech in abstract and legalistic terms; laws ought to be enacted regarding whether or not there should be censorship of any kind, what rights (frequently conceived in abstract terms) writers, illustrators, publishers and audiences have, etc. Many liberal and libertarian discourses tend to view satire as some kind of sacred cow, not to be trampled on for any reason. This in many cases reflects a bourgeois and Western (or Westernized) ethos, frequently ignoring or dismissing the fact that most of the so-called free media is an uneven playing field. Different individuals, social classes and groups that rally around some particular identity and/or concern may have different access to the media, and different and unequal possibilities of pushing their views, concerns and agendas (even in relation to peace, including peace in a particular society), as well as of making fun of each other. These inequalities both reflect and reinforce uneven relations of power. Considering the issues excessively in terms of what rights there ought or ought not to obtain misses out this dimension. Very sensibly, Sammut suggests that publishers, academics and, one might add, educators be thoughtful regarding the sensibilities of different groups, especially if they cherish the ideal of peace.

Critical Education ought to teach and learn to read the world behind the word or picture, to make people aware of power relationships and of uneven distribution of power, whenever issues concerning freedom of expression and the media are raised. A very concrete exercise Lorenzo Milani used to carry out with his students at Barbiana when they would engage in collective reading of Italian newspapers was asking questions like: 'What is being said and what is being left out in the report/article in question?'; 'Who is represented and who is not?'; and 'Who owns the newspaper and what may be her/his interests?', Critical Education cannot exempt satire from an analysis of its limits and possibilities, or fail to see connections between this and concrete power relationships. 'Who is being satirized and who is not?'; 'From which point of view is satire being carried out?'; 'What Barthian myths are possibly being sustained or punctured by the satire in question?' are fundamental questions.

Being open to the sensibilities of different groups and communities does not entail ignoring that these sensibilities may change, a feature that Sammut does not explore. Change need not entail one community completely abandoning its outlook and sensibilities, and becoming assimilated entirely into another. Members of a community may, however, attempt to understand how what from their own perspective appears to be abhorrent is perfectly acceptable (if not reflective of some positive value) from another. This entails dialogue at a level that involves more than token encounters. Once again we take cue from the school in Barbiana, wherein an exercise the school suggested in order to enhance peace is reading the histories of countries with which one's own is/had been at war, countries that are normally demonized in one's historical narrative. Similar initiatives involving culture, religion and civilizations ought to be encouraged. Such educational encounters, though, were largely missing in the Danish and French sagas, especially where the media was involved. The media ought to have been one of the major spaces for such dialogue, a third space as described by Galea in her chapter. Instead, it generally failed to provide this space, focusing instead on the clash of words (and not just) between different sides to the debate. It ended up sustaining existing myths. This was perhaps the greatest failing of mainstream media in the whole saga. Critical Education ought not to merely highlight such failures, but should also provide sites and spaces where such dialogue may occur. Yet, it is not obvious that most peace education is providing such a space, as Michalinos Zembylas and Zvi Beckerman indicate.

Critical education for peace – the basics

Zembylas and Beckerman lament the lack of critical engagement that characterizes peace education as this is frequently implemented, a vacuum that is frequently filled by positivist views of peace and peace education. These positivist characterizations tend to essentialize peace, to frequently endorse the definition of peace repeatedly censured throughout this book, and to fail to problematize pseudo-peaceful situations where stability is bartered for an oppressive, social, economic and political *status quo*. They are inclined to trivialize or ignore the diverse and multiple possibilities of conceiving of peace that, as the chapters by Alshinawi, and Trimikliniotis and Trimithiotis indicate, are necessary to achieve this ideal. Apart from the epistemological and academic shortcomings of such an approach, positivist characterizations of 'peace' often ignore asymmetrical power relations, reducing conflict to individual misunderstanding, prejudice, ignorance, tribalism, radicalization and other simplistic explanations. The programmes such type of peace education often offer involve universal, dehistoricized, undertheorized and conceptually superficial curricular experiences, frequently avoiding interrogating power relations, 'technologies' of surveillance, the practice of 'othering' and manipulation by state aimed at achieving collective consent. They also tend to prescribe harmonized, skills-based programmes involving routines that train rather than educate, promoting efficiency and proficiency (buzzwords of the dominant neo-liberal economic model) rather than the depth and growth that emerges from meaningful encounters with various contexts and their constituents. While leaving very little room for critical engagement, such programmes have served to alienate educators from their ethical role of intellectuals and cultural workers, and to cement the aforementioned common sense in relation to peace and war, including the contradictions relating to these. They are thus part of the problem that they are trying to address. Zembylas and Beckerman point to the need of reclaiming critical peace education through dialogical encounters aimed at having educatees challenging widespread and fallacious notions of peace, tolerance, justice and equality.

Zembylas and Beckerman do not limit themselves to exposing the shortcomings of mainstream peace education, but make important suggestions regarding how peace education ought to be structured. While recognizing that a one-size-fits-all educational programme to abet peace that fits all contexts is a chimera, they do not exclude general guidelines for a pedagogy of peace, which could then be fleshed out in particular circumstances according to particular features. These general guidelines should rest on four philosophical principles: reinstating the materiality of 'things' and practices, reontologizing research and practice in peace education, becoming 'critical experts of design' and engaging in critical cultural analysis. A limit of their writing is that they do not provide examples of how this may be done (or, rather, the examples are vague). But this perhaps is understandable given that what they are proposing are general principles, all of which recognize human beings as historical subjects, subjects whose thinking and actions are socially mediated.

Quite sensibly, Zembylas and Becker do not shirk from highlighting the limits that educational initiatives alone, however critical these might be, could have. Since this epilogue has focused on common sense in relation to peace and war, one might be tempted to think that to achieve peace in the proper sense of the term in one's context, all one needs to do is to alter this common sense through some educational exercise(s). While educational initiatives aimed at nurturing critical thoughts and aptitudes are important to achieve peace, Becker and Zembylas are rightly aware of the limits of education as a transformative tool. Education and educational programmes cannot be the panacea to all problems; they have to be wedded to political and social initiatives, lest they turn into intellectual jugglery.

From myths to music

Deconstructing Barthian myths concerning war and changing common sense in relation to peace is not a mere intellectual activity. Change also requires operating in concrete sites and not just at the level of notions and arguments. Linda Herrera's *A Song for Humanistic Education: Pedagogy and Politics in the Middle East* considers a concrete arena where stereotypes are challenged and myths are debunked, a site 'on the other side of the border': the teaching of classical music in Egypt, focusing on the life and pedagogy of Osman El Mahdi, a music teacher in Cairo. The 'other side' also has its myths and common sense that need to be tackled critically.

In Egypt, classical music is frequently shunned as elitist, and as fundamentally non-Arabic, non-Muslim and Western, and hence associated to colonialism and imperialism. Moreover, as in other parts of the globe, in Egypt and parts of the Arab world, the teaching of humanities and arts is being increasingly considered a field that is not worth investing in, in contrast to other areas of education that are seen to be more economically rewarding. El Mahdi's choice to teach classical music, then, is not devoid of political connotations.

In relation to peace, Herrera claims that the teaching of classical music may abet a humanistic education that involves 'an approach to learning that is human [and] nurtures respect and compassion, ... [by] consciously approach[ing] the language of literature, science and the arts as an inherently collective human endeavour' rather than as pertaining to this or that culture. It is an education that promotes human and academic encounters, valuing humanity and its endeavours regardless of their origin, and promoting values such as respect, pluralism, rational critical inquiry, compassion, innovation and excellence. It is fundamentally inimical to irrationality, inequity and injustice.

The promotion of such values, though, is not something that is intrinsic to the teaching of music and art. Art in general and music in particular have frequently served to promote divisions and ideologically consolidate arrangements of power that may be deemed anything but pluralist, compassionate and just, promoting feelings, attitudes and moods that are antithetical to peace and justice. Hence, it is not by their very nature that the humanities, arts and music are conducive to such values as 'peace', 'justice' and 'compassion', something that Herrera herself concedes at various points throughout her article.[9]

Music and art may enhance humanistic goals and values provided that those engaged in them adopt these values themselves and incarnate them in their performance and pedagogy. El Mahdi consciously does so, promoting values like egalitarianism, cosmopolitanism and inclusion in his teaching. He adopts a pedagogy where he consciously puts students at ease (starting lessons with storytelling about composers and their times), avoids any exclusion of sorts (taking troublesome students and getting the best out of them) and considers diversity an asset. A musician has to learn to work within a group, with others who are of different ages, and come from different social groups, and who have different specializations and experiences. In line with what Critical Education ought to be, learning becomes an engagement that involves 'integral human beings … in an educational process that has love as its core' (English and Mayo 2012, p. 18).

Apart from its educational and pedagogical value, Herrera's piece is also important in another respect. Alshinawi's piece about exogenous 'peace' and its emphasis on the need to enrich the common core content of 'peace' in relation to particular features belonging to specific realities might tempt some to think that what is being suggested in this book is that particular realities are somehow sealed from each other, that we are promoting some form of nativism. This is not the case. While attention to particular regional, national, religious and social features is fundamental for 'peace' to be achieved in particular realities, these features cannot be considered as existing in a vacuum or in isolation from each other, and one should not ignore the specific limits and possibilities particular realities involve. El Mahdi's educational engagement and Herrera's piece, though, require that this critical gaze involve a human and humanizing encounter, not one that involves one culture looking down from some pulpit on another that is viewed as intrinsically inferior.

Portraying and creating realities

Another critical exercise on the 'other side of the fence' is André Mazawi's '*School Textbooks and Entanglements of the "Colonial Present" In Israel and Palestine*'.

The chapter specifically concerns textbooks, including textbooks produced by the Palestinian Authority and the thinking that went behind their production.

Textbooks are sites where the identities of groups are constructed and moulded. They influence the values that members of a group will likely nurture, the outlook on the world they will have and the skills they will acquire in relation to them. Citing Rancière, Mazawi claims that textbooks construct a 'political aesthetics of the sensible', a system of a priori categories that determine how one experiences reality. They serve to 'normalize' and to 'otherise'; to suggest what is acceptable and what is not; to indicate what belongs to 'us' and to 'them'. Textbooks make visible some groups, phenomena and characteristics, and fail to accord visibility to others. Even when visible, different groups, phenomena and characteristics will be accorded different prominence. Such differences may reflect and/or abet hierarchical and uneven relations between different sets of people, interests and perspectives. As it is obvious when one considers all this, textbooks are sites of contestation.

Historically, Palestinians followed foreign curricula in their schools. In 1993, following the Oslo peace accords, Palestinians were for the first time in history accorded responsibility for their educational set-up, including writing their own curricula. (This does not mean, a fact which Mazawi repeatedly highlights, that colonialism and colonial legacies could be erased at one go.) The curricula were written in light of what was then considered to be a long-term peace process between Israel and the Palestinians, a process, though, that never came to fruition. They were therefore an important aspect of the peace that was supposedly being enacted.

Mazawi considers the writing of this curriculum in relation to three factors: the Israeli–Palestinian issue involving a colonizer – colonized relation; different groups, formations and interests within Palestinian society itself; and the Israeli political Left and Right. In what follows, we refer to the second.[10] The major question that cropped up in the production of the texts in relation to this issue was: 'What "image reality" of Palestine ought the curricula to present/construct?' The writing of the curriculum involved tensions between the Palestinian Authority and various groups and organizations belonging to civil society (both in the actual Palestinian territories and in the Palestinian diaspora), as well as between different individuals who took part in its formulation. It involved divergences between different conceptions of Palestine that different groups and individuals had/have, especially in relation to the role to be accorded to Islam (Should Palestine be characterized in secular-national terms or in primarily Islamic ones?), to representations of women and to the visibility (or lack of it) of different groups that make up the Palestinian people (city dwellers, refugees in the West Bank and Gaza, Bedouins, Diaspora Palestinians). The overall result is one that, according to Mazawi, generally reflects 'world views of able-bodied men and women from urbanised classes, of particular ideological backgrounds'. For instance, the author notes that with regard to certain representations of Bedouins, their 'lifestyle … is emptied of creativity, depicted as incompatible with modernisation and progress. Bedouins are cast as pathologised outliers within a semiotic hierarchical rendition of Palestinian society.' This aspect points to an important feature. Palestinians as a group are generally the victims of colonialism and brutal policies. Yet, even at a time when peace with Israel seemed to be a feasible possibility, mechanisms of marginalizations, inequities and exclusion between Palestinians themselves were in existence, something that would not have enabled the achievement of peace in the substantial sense characterized in this book at an intra-social level. This fact demonstrates the importance of constant critical vigilance at all levels within a particular context, even in relation to things so intimate and so important in the context of colonial oppression as one's identity. Peace education should play an important role in this regard.

Re(an)nouncing and participating

As already stated, Critical Education for achieving peace ought not simply to involve notions, ideas, pictures of the world or points of view. Education to peace has to educate holistically. This requires educating one's attitudes and approach to others and to reality, something that is frequently ignored in a lot of educational set-ups and critical engagements. One needs to learn the practical (not merely academic) means of seeing the limits and possibilities of concepts, categories and characterizations of reality that may abet war and violence. Michael Zammit's *The Long Shadow Thrown over the Actions of Men* is a contribution in this regard.

Zammit starts by noting that peace, education and academia are intimately related to one another. Referring to pre-World War II Germany, Zammit argues that an academic and educational environment may abet, even if indirectly (through failing to oppose), war, and violent and unjust political set-ups. In this regard, he refers to totalizer and infinitizer philosophers (the two are defined at length in his chapter), charging the former of posting unbridgeable chasms in reality, chasms that prevent one from being struck by the face of 'the other' and feeling responsible for him or her. Zammit does not actually state this, but one may add that critical thought and Critical Education themselves may turn into a sterile totalizing exercise.

Critical Education suggests that we go beyond phenomena, by engaging with their possibilities and limits. Michael Zammit presents a philosophy that may help one to (1) get beyond fixed and rigid identities, and 'given' chasm lines that are thought to exist between groups and sets of human beings; and (2) become involved in activities and exercises that are not merely academic but which also concern one's attitude and affections. The philosophy in question is Shankara's non-dual *Advaita* philosophy. This philosophy teaches techniques that enable one to re(an)nounce one's identity/ies, and the dichotomies and systems of characterizing the world these entail. This enables one to view what one is critically and not be pinned down by one's identity. It also enables one to open oneself to the 'other', since one cannot characterize what one is without implicitly referring to some 'other'. Such openness, then, is not a mere concession to the 'other', but something entailed by one's very being.

Zammit does not refer extensively to phenomena like exploitation and uneven economic relations with particular societies and globally, and to hegemonic relations between different groups and classes. Yet, the attitude *Advaita* fosters may play an emancipatory role even in this regard. It may help in attempts at challenging sociopolitical–socio-economic mantras, common sense and myths that abet the dominant economic and political *status quo*, which *status quo* prevents the world from achieving true peace. For instance, whereas the dominant common sense in a lot of societies considers acquisition and accumulation of wealth as obvious motives that are natural to human beings (they would complement the other characteristic presumed to be intrinsic to human beings that Papastephanou mentions in her chapter, aggression, which would make war natural), *Advaita* would teach people to renounce the desire for the results of their work and re(an)nounce their relationship with them (an example Zammit himself discusses). They would do this while still being involved in their daily practices. This re(an)nouncing might facilitate concrete attempts at changing the *status quo* in question, to achieve a more just and egalitarian social and world set-up. It might get people one step closer to peace as characterized in this book. To do this, though, one should always, in our opinion, keep in mind that humans do their history, including re(an)nouncing their identities and striving for peace, in set contexts; in circumstances that they do not create. This avoids the Scylla of naïve voluntarism and the Charybdis of defeatist fatalism.

Notes

1 A characterization of 'critique' dating back to Kant.

2 See *Lorenzo Milani's Culture of Peace: Essays on Religion, Education, and Democratic Life*, 2014

3 See Mayo, P and Al-Siwadi, N., 2014.

4 In Iraq, contrary to what may be the case in Western Europe and the United States, it is not possible to characterize peace without considering religious and/or ethnic variables.

5 Parts of her work are almost autobiographical. Some of the stories of aggression are shared through the experienced eyes of Antonia the child, the mother and the citizen.

6 Darder notes that when the ideological means of control of the state over its citizens fail, the state will not refrain from using violent means to restrain resistance and restore 'legitimacy'. The story of the Occupy Movement, particularly in New York and San Francisco, is a case in point. Pepper spray, rubber bullets, detention, incarceration, summons in front of water cannons, life bullets – all were used by the state.

7 Obviously, one could have mentioned contrary myths that exist in certain Muslim circles concerning Western values, Jews, Americans and the like.

8 The two incidents were, however, also used by powerful elites in the Muslim world to tighten their repressive grip, a fact that Sammut generally overlooks.

9 Indeed, thinkers like Adorno hold that contemporary music is beyond redemptive purposes in current capitalist society, and can only serve to alienate people from themselves and from each other.

10 Regarding the characterization of Israel in Palestinian textbooks, the tensions are numerous. Following the Oslo accords, the tone of the curriculum was conciliatory, even if reality on the ground was still one of colonization and Israeli annexation of Palestinian land. Hence, a tension developed between what Palestinian textbooks taught and concrete reality. Another source of tension between Israeli and Palestinian authorities, though, concerned history. The land of Israel exists on land that was previously Arab. This was recognized in Palestinian texts, a feature that was contested by Israelis.

   Mazawi also refers to tensions between those who conceive of Israel as a fundamentally democratic and Jewish (hence ethnically monolithic) state and those who conceive of Israel as a pluralistic society in terms of ethnicity and culture, something that in the Israeli context raises the question as to which characterization of Israel ought to be promoted by Israeli curricula.

References

Armstrong, K. (2004). *The Battle for God*. London: Harper Collins.

Borg, C. and Grech, M. (2014). *Lorenzo Milani's Culture of Peace: Essays on Religion, Education, and Democratic Life*. New York: Palgrave MacMillan.

English, L. and Mayo, P. (2012). *Learning with Adults*. United Kingdom: Sense Publishers.

Franzoni, G. (2015). 'The Truce'. In M. Grech (Ed.), *Jottings and Reflections*. Malta: Faraxa Publications.

Freire, P. (1996). *Pedagogy of the Oppressed*. London: Penguin.

Gerada, M., Mercieca, C. and Xuereb, D. (2014). 'Peace and Sexuality – Two Reflections'. In C. Borg and M. Grech (Eds), *Lorenzo Milani's Culture of Peace: Essays on Religion, Education, and Democratic Life*. New York: Palgrave MacMillan.

Hume, D. (2015). *A Treatise of Human Nature*. United Kingdom: CreateSpace Independent Publishing Platform.

Kratzer, A. (January 1977). 'What "Must" and "Can" Must and Can Mean'. *Linguistics and Philosophy*, 1 (3). The Netherlands: Springer Science and Business Media.

Mangion, C. (2003). 'Nietzsche's Philosophy of Myth'. *Humanitas, Journal of the Faculty of Arts*, 2. Malta: University of Malta Press.

Poe, D. (2011). 'Can Luce Irigaray's Notion of Sexual Difference be Applied to Transsexual and Transgender Narratives?' *Ecommons*. Dayton: University of Dayton.

Rousseau, J. J. (1992). 'First Discourse on the Arts and Science'. *Collected Writings of Rousseau: Discourse on the Sciences and Arts (First Discourse) and Polemics v. 2*. Dartmouth: Dartmouth College Press.

Salomon, R. (1988). *Continental Philosophy Since 1750 – The Rise and Fall of the Self*. Oxford: Oxford University Press.

Swanson, D. (2011). *War is a Lie*. London: Biteback.

Index

abstraction(s)   101, 154
Adenauer, Konrad   41
Advaita (Non-Dual)   181, 187, 188, 191, 193, 197, 239
Afghanistan   83, 98, 131, 139, 205
Al-Dawa Islamic Party   69, 70
Alexandria   205, 206, 214, 215
Al Jazeera   129, 130
Al-Maliki, Nur   63, 68, 69, 70
Al Qaeda   71, 78, 87, 98, 131, 132, 133, 230
anti-terror ideology/anti-terrorism   40, 127, 131
apartheid   20
Apel, Karl-Otto   16
Arabian Gulf   62, 70, 231
Arab League   73
Arab Spring   70, 132, 230
Aristophanes   7, 12, 14, 15, 18, 26
Armenia   205, 206
Ātman (creative principle)   189, 192, 196
Australia   87, 214
Austria   34, 35, 44
autonomy (metaphysical)   185
autonomy (political)   57, 71, 74
Azerbajan   77, 206

Ba'ath Party (Iraq)   67
banking concept of education   198, 201
Barthes, Roland   111, 114, 119, 120, 121, 122, 124, 125, 126, 229
Bhagavad-Gita   181, 187, 188, 193, 194
Bologna Accords   43
Bosnia War   98
bourgeoisie/bourgeois   33, 35, 36, 40, 232
breath/breathing   3, 47, 49, 55–9, 222
Britain   22, 27, 42
British Empire   20, 82, 165

Cabral, Amilcal   106, 107
Cairo   xvi, 201, 203. 204, 201, 215, 235
Cairo Conservatoire   202, 209, 210

Cairo Opera House (Da-al-Obra)   202, 203, 209
Calasso, Roberto   114, 116, 117, 126
Calgacus   7, 8,9, 10, 26, 27
caliphate   63, 132
Cambodia   97
capitalist/capitalism   18, 32, 33, 35, 36, 41, 44, 86, 103, 204
Casati Law (Italy)   34, 35
Catholic Church   32, 38, 39
censorship   129, 135, 137, 140 232
Charlie-Hebdo   3, 127, 133, 135–40, 231
chess-board model   52, 53
Chicana-Chicano activists   97
Christian Democratic Party (Italy)   32, 40
Christianity/Christian   69, 162, 185, 186, 190, 191, 205, 206, 207
clash of civilisations   127, 132, 135, 136
class (social)   19, 34–37, 39–44, 53, 88, 98, 99, 100, 103, 105, 131, 168, 170, 171, 183, 184, 191, 217–21, 227, 232, 238, 239
Cold War   41, 44, 82, 97, 127, 128, 129, 133, 136
colonialism/colonisation   11, 12, 16, 18, 19, 20, 27, 28, 42, 82, 127, 131, 150, 161, 164, 171, 176, 224, 235, 236–8
competition/competitiveness   17, 42, 43, 84, 116, 197, 200
conceptually mediated   152, 157
conflict   xvii, 3, 7, 17, 19, 21–6, 29, 30, 33, 36, 40, 41, 48, 49, 58, 59, 62, 66, 67, 70, 81–90, 97, 106, 127, 129, 130, 132, 133, 139, 147–9, 154, 155, 157, 161, 163, 164, 165, 169, 174, 176, 188, 190, 193, 201, 202, 217, 219, 220, 222, 223, 224
conflict resolution   19, 29, 81, 82, 84, 139, 148, 149
consensus   22, 24, 33, 59, 72, 84, 130
construct/ed   22, 24–9, 49, 50, 56
consumerism   150, 168
contingent   118–24, 187, 229–31
Contras   98

Cook, S. A.   21, 29, 30
Cornelius Tacitus   7, 9, 26
cosmopolitan/cosmopolitanism   10, 18, 19, 20, 30, 202, 204, 205, 214, 236
crimes against humanity   26, 103
critical/criticality   1–4, 8, 9, 16, 22, 27, 29, 41, 44, 55, 57, 63, 65, 67, 75, 81–5, 87, 88, 90, 99, 100–7, 114, 125, 139, 140, 147–58, 168, 173, 184, 200, 205, 209, 210, 213, 215, 217, 219–25, 227–36, 238, 239
critical education   2, 55, 114, 125, 139, 217, 219–23, 225, 228, 230–3, 236, 238, 239
critical experts of design   3, 152, 153, 155, 157, 158, 234
critical peace   2, 81, 82, 84, 85, 87, 88, 90, 101, 103, 104, 106, 148, 152, 153, 154, 158, 225, 234
critique   3, 7, 8, 21, 24, 25, 28, 29, 77, 81, 85, 104, 149, 158, 171, 172, 227, 228, 240
Cuoco, Vincenzo   30, 34
Curriculum Development Centre (CDC) Palestine   166, 167, 168
Cyprus, Republic of   86, 151

Declaration of Principles on Interim Self-Government Arrangements (Oslo Accords)   166
deconstruction   19, 23, 24, 155, 196, 223, 235
dehumaniz/ed   2, 22, 99, 102, 132
democracy/democratisation   2, 12, 32, 34, 41, 43, 58, 62–7, 73–5, 86, 87, 98, 100, 106, 107, 124, 128–30, 132, 134. 135. 137–9, 173, 174, 184, 197, 200, 201, 212, 213, 223, 224, 226–8, 231, 240
Denmark   134, 141
desire   188, 192, 193, 195, 196, 239
dharma   187, 188
dhyāyatas   193, 195, 198
dialectic   35, 88, 101, 102, 105, 120, 225
dialogue   2, 3, 16, 105, 106, 127, 128, 131, 138, 139, 140, 155, 186, 191, 225, 227, 233, 234
dichotomy/dichotomies   147, 149, 188, 193, 223, 239
digitality   xiii, 81, 84, 88, 89, 90, 225, 226

discourse   2, 3, 7, 17, 20, 22, 24, 32, 33, 58, 90, 98, 99, 100, 106, 111–19, 121–6, 134, 138, 156, 171, 186, 221, 222, 224, 226, 229, 230, 231, 232
diversity   21, 29, 113, 115, 130, 170, 176, 236
divinity/divine   13, 14, 15, 28, 112, 182, 183, 187, 194
domestic violence   48
Dominican Republic   97
dualism   101, 152, 153, 227
Dussel, Enrique   16, 30

economic apartheid   100
egalitarian femminism   48, 60
Egypt   69, 139, 165, 201, 202, 204–9, 211, 212, 214, 215, 235
Egyptian text-books Palestine   166
Einstein, Albert   98
El Madhi, Osman   205, 206, 207, 208, 209, 211, 212, 213, 215, 235
emancipation   35, 38, 167
empire   7, 11, 78, 86, 123, 213
Enlightenment, the   50, 228. 229
epiphany   187, 189, 192
epistemic signatures   165, 168, 171, 173
epistemology   104, 125, 149
equality   8, 10, 60, 150, 151, 234
equity   3, 33, 35, 37, 217, 219, 200, 221, 223
Eretz Yisrael (Land of Israel)   172
essence/essentialist/essentialism   26, 34, 50, 51, 54, 120, 149, 154–6, 183, 185, 227, 233
ethics   1, 16, 21–3, 25, 29, 47, 49, 58, 59, 85, 101, 103, 106, 107, 124, 137, 163, 186, 187, 201, 234
European Economic Community (EEC)   41, 42
European Monteray Union (EMU)   43
European Union (EU)   32, 41, 43, 44
exile   12, 20, 24, 25, 50, 141
exogenous   62–5, 67, 71, 73–5, 223

Face of Evil   127, 129, 133, 136, 140
fascism/fascist   34, 36, 40, 44, 57, 220
FIAT (Fabbrica Italiana Automobili Torino)   39, 40, 44
First World War   128, 131, 184

Fordism/Fordist 36, 41, 42
fragmentary/fragmentation 66, 84, 98, 165, 174, 182, 192, 194, 197
France 35, 133, 134, 136, 161, 162, 176
freedom of speech 136, 232
freedom of the press 133, 134, 140
Freire, Paulo x, xvi, 102, 105, 108, 109, 201, 215, 221, 228, 241
French empire 123, 176
French revolution 34, 162
Führer, Der 184, 185
Fukuyama, Francis 76, 77, 86
functionalism/functionalistic 148, 167, 169, 214
fundamentalist/fundamentalism 3, 17, 82, 132, 200, 207

Gaza Strip 135, 166–8, 177
gender 48, 54, 103, 169, 176, 218, 223
Geneva 68, 208
genocide 21, 22, 26, 103
Gentile, Giovanni 38
Georgia, Republic of 206
Georgia Tech University 105
Germany 21, 35, 39, 67, 75, 184, 185, 238
Giroux, Henry 104, 108, 226
good, Plato's characterisation of 186
Gorbachev, Mikhail 128
Gramsci, Antonio 32, 33, 34, 35, 41, 45, 46, 92
Greece 86, 88, 151
Greene, Maxine 215
Grenada 97
Gulf War (First) 98, 131, 169

Haiti 98
Hall, Stuart 136
Hamas 132, 135, 140
hegemony/hegemonic 2, 3, 21, 24, 34, 39, 41, 44, 70, 82, 84–6, 89, 100, 103, 104, 106, 150, 164, 173, 219, 224–6, 228, 239
Heidegger, Martin 181, 182, 185, 186
Hendrix, Jimi 103, 108
hermeneutics 176
Herodotus 114, 117, 118, 126
Hesiod 110, 117, 118, 125, 126
hidden curriculum 4, 98–100, 102
historical discourse 112, 118, 119, 122, 123, 229, 230

history textbooks (Israel) 173
Hobbes, Thomas 9, 10, 17, 31, 219
homeland protection 99
hope 2, 3, 8, 15, 19, 20, 24, 83, 106, 117, 124, 125, 139, 210
humanistic education 200, 204, 235, 236
humanistic pedagogy 3, 200, 201, 204, 209
humanizing/humanistic 3, 38, 200–4, 209, 213, 235, 236
human rights 2, 29, 51, 60, 103, 106, 107, 129, 131, 148, 227
human spirit 185
Hussein, Saddam 62, 63, 64, 65, 67, 69, 70, 72, 131
hybrid discourse 111, 114, 119, 121–4, 229
hyper-masculinity 99, 227

identity 34, 50, 55, 74, 97, 132, 134, 137, 138, 152, 155, 156, 155, 166, 168, 173–6, 186, 187, 190, 202, 203, 206, 212, 232, 238, 239
incarceration 26, 102, 103, 104, 240
indigenous 2, 11, 84
inequality 1, 7, 29, 41, 44, 51, 84, 88, 100–2, 136, 139, 147, 154, 232
infinitizer/s 181–4, 187, 238
injustice 3, 11, 13, 17, 22, 23, 25, 40, 41, 51, 60, 149, 154, 163, 176, 200, 212, 213, 223, 235
International Monetary Fund (IMF) 43, 88
interpretative possibility 116, 117, 119, 122, 123, 125
intifada 167, 177, 212
inviolability 186, 187, 196
Iran 62, 69, 70, 74, 77, 86, 87–98, 135, 141, 201
Iraq 12, 15, 16, 49, 67–75, 83, 87, 98, 129, 131, 132, 139, 201, 205, 223, 224, 240
Iraqi Constitution 67–69, 71–5
Iraqi Constitution Drafting Committee 68, 72, 73, 77
Ireland 86, 135
Irigaray, Luce 47, 49, 50, 51, 52, 53, 54, 55, 55, 56, 57, 58, 59, 60, 61
Islam 63, 70, 74, 127, 131–6, 138–41, 168, 169, 201, 204, 205, 207, 213–15, 230, 237

Islamic State (IS)   63, 132, 133, 140
Islamism   132, 206, 207
Islamist Student Movement (Egypt)   206, 207, 215
Islamophobia   127, 131, 133
Israeli Colonialism/Military Occupation   161, 163–6, 171–3, 176, 237, 238, 240
Israeli Military   166, 171
Israeli textbooks   172, 173, 176
Istanbul   214
Italy   32, 34–44, 86, 88, 135, 220

Jama'at Islamiya   207, 214
Japan   39, 67, 75, 203–5, 209, 214
Jewish Identity   175, 176
Jewish State   172, 212
jihad   171
John Hopkins University   105
Jordan   66, 165, 166
Jordanian text-books Palestine   165, 166
justice   1–3, 8, 10, 13, 22, 23, 29, 33, 35, 85, 101, 106, 107, 110, 135, 147, 149, 150, 151, 176, 217, 219–21, 223, 226, 235, 236
Jyllands-Posten   3, 123–5, 127, 137, 139, 140, 231

Kant, Immanuel   10, 27, 228, 240
karma   187, 188, 196
Korean War   97
Kosovo   98
Krishna   187, 189, 192
Kurdistan   63
Kurds   70–2, 74, 224
Kurukshetra, battlefield   187, 188

language-game   111, 112, 119
Lateran Pacts   37, 38
Lebanon   70, 83, 97
Levinas, Emmanuel   110, 181, 182, 184, 185, 186, 187, 197, 198, 199
liberal democracy   128, 132, 139
liberal peace   81, 83, 84 86, 87, 90, 102, 127, 129, 130, 139, 224, 225, 231
liberal triumph   86
Liberia   98
Libya   83, 98, 139
linguistic sign   119, 120, 121, 125

Mahabharata   187
manas (sense-mind)   188, 198
Mandanean   69
market economy   60
Marshall Plan   30
martyrdom   171
materialities/materiality   3, 82, 152–4, 157, 234
maternal, the   47–9, 53–6, 59, 60, 222
maternalist femminism   48, 49, 60
media   3, 19, 33, 64, 65, 70, 84, 88, 98, 99, 102, 105, 111, 125, 127–41, 157, 165, 171, 174, 217, 225, 227, 231–3
meditation   191, 194
Mexico   87
Middle East   62–4, 82, 86, 87, 103, 131, 132, 200, 208, 212–14, 231
militarization   1, 87, 100, 103, 105, 224, 226, 230
mobile commons   89, 225
mode of signification   119
modernization/Modernity   10, 18, 19, 149, 162, 164, 170, 181, 185
moksha   192, 194
morality   100, 101, 181, 182
Mosul   63, 132
motherhood   53, 222
Muhammad   133, 134, 137
Muhammad cartoons   133–5, 137
Muslim brotherhood   132, 140
myth   1, 18, 99, 110, 111, 113–25, 217, 228–33, 235, 239, 240
mytho-historic discourse   111, 121, 122, 124, 229

nakba   174
Napoleonic Wars   161, 162, 176
narrative   3, 20, 24, 25, 34, 35, 99, 105, 115–19, 123, 125, 130, 132, 133, 139, 163, 164, 172–6, 187, 219, 228–31, 233
National Culture Centre, the (Egypt)   204
national identity   34, 132, 168, 187
nationalism   42, 85, 132, 155, 200, 203–2, 226
nation state   11, 32, 44, 83, 149–51, 173
nativism   3, 200, 204, 236
naturalizing   7–10, 13, 14, 17, 24–6, 99, 121, 170

Nazism, (National Socialim) 30, 182, 185, 186
neo-liberalism 19, 42, 66, 83, 86, 89, 101, 104, 130, 223, 234
neo-Platonism 90
neo-Schmidtean 90
Nicaragua 98
Nigeria 198
non-dualist 3, 187, 189, 192, 196, 197
normalized/normalization 1, 99, 148, 157, 227, 237
North Africa 87, 132
Norway 135

objectification 99, 164
objective /objectivity 18, 98, 110, 112, 118, 152, 156, 182, 186, 189
occupation (military) 66, 67, 104, 161, 162, 166, 171, 173, 201
Occupy Movement 19, 100, 240
ontologizing 3, 25, 152, 153–5, 157, 234
Operation Desert Storm 129
Operation Enduring Freedom 98
Operation Uphold Democracy 98
oppression 2, 21, 22, 51, 69, 103, 238
orientalist 171
Orwell, George 128, 142
Oslo Accords 166, 169, 237, 240
other, the/otherness 13, 16, 23, 54, 55, 58, 59, 151, 176, 186, 187, 189–92, 195, 196, 201, 204, 222, 226, 238
Ottoman Empire 82, 161, 165

Pakistan 98
Palestine 83, 163–6, 168, 171, 175, 176, 236, 237
Palestine Liberation Organisaation (PLO) 166, 167
Palestinian Authority (PA) 166–9, 171, 172, 175, 237
Palestinian Ministry of Education 167
Palestinian National Council 167
Panama 98
Pan-Arabism 131
paradox 24, 25, 164, 187
Paris 135, 137, 161, 176
participation (Advaitin) 181, 188, 189, 192, 193, 197

passive revolution 4, 32, 33, 36–9, 41, 43, 44, 220
patriarchy/patriarchal 3, 16, 48–53, 56, 99, 101, 219, 222
patriotic/patriotism 8, 99, 101, 155, 226
peace building 4, 84, 85, 89, 139, 222
peacekeeping 4, 29, 48, 84, 85
peace maker/peace making 1, 13, 23, 29, 50, 62, 63, 65, 67, 75, 81, 83, 84, 87, 90, 129, 163, 223, 224
peace movement 100
pedagogy of peace 103, 106, 234
Penn State University 105
periphery/peripheral 43, 86
permanent possibility of war 110
Persian Gulf 87
phallocentric/phallocentricism 47, 50, 52, 53
Philippines 98
pluralism 3, 130
Popular Front Party (France) 136
Portugal 86, 88
positivism/positivist 35, 38, 102, 148, 157, 158, 230, 233
post-Cold War Era 129, 133
post-foundational ideas 158
postmodern/ity 7, 9, 24, 25, 197, 219
post-positivist realism 157
post-World War II 32, 220
power-games 86
power relations 103, 105, 149
pragmatic/pragmatism 22, 148, 152, 158
pravritti (participation) 188, 189
praxis 81, 150, 197
privatization 131, 200
progress 20, 35, 36, 41, 42, 44, 60, 63, 65, 74, 104, 151, 164, 170, 171, 219, 220, 238
proletariat (Working Class) 36, 37
pseudo-peace 8–10, 12, 22, 233
psychologized/psychologistic 3, 15, 22, 23, 149, 150, 154, 155, 157
Puerto Rico 97, 203

Qattan Centre for Educational Research and Development 167
Qu'ran 201

racial   16, 58, 102, 104, 138, 174
racializing economy   102
racist/racism   20, 21, 85, 103, 151, 154, 176, 197
Radical Islam   131
Ram, Uri   175
Ramallah   167
rationalize/ation   27, 98
Reaganism   130
realism/realist tradition of international relations   128
reason   148, 182, 185, 194, 228, 229
recognition   17, 49, 53 107, 116, 150, 151, 196
reconciliation   63, 81, 82, 84, 85, 89, 90, 163
refugee camps (Palestinians)   169, 171
refugee/s   24, 25, 66, 87, 88, 169, 170, 225, 238
religion   17, 38, 58, 69, 115, 134, 140, 168, 170, 212, 230, 233
renounciation/re(an-)nounciation   186, 189–92, 238, 239
respect   3, 21, 29, 53, 54, 59, 103, 123, 140, 151, 200, 213, 222, 235, 236
revelation   27–8, 112
revolutionary   4, 24, 33–5, 38, 101, 103, 106, 107, 162
right to offend   133, 137, 139, 140
Risorgimento   32, 34–6, 40, 44
Rousseau, Jean-Jacques   10, 228, 241
Russia   86, 130

Said, Edward   92, 131, 142, 167, 200, 201, 212, 213, 215, 216
San Francisco   240
sanitization   xvii, 98
satire   131, 133, 232
Saudi Arabia   62, 70, 77, 86, 87 130, 135
school textbooks   161–6, 168, 171, 172, 174–6
science   35, 105, 115, 117, 182, 200, 208, 235
scripture   101, 112
sectarianism   3, 200, 213
secular/secularism   64, 86, 131, 132, 13, 135, 139, 162, 175, 214, 237
securitization   84, 87
security   xv, 9, 15, 48, 63, 65, 69, 70, 86–8, 98, 102, 105, 130, 139, 140, 224, 226, 227

self-determination   11, 207, 102, 161, 163
semiotic/s   162, 164, 170, 173, 238
settlers (Israel)   171, 174, 175
sexual/sexuality   15, 47–9, 51, 53, 57, 58, 99, 103
shadow   181, 197
Shankara   181, 187, 188, 189, 191, 193, 194, 195, 196, 199, 239
Shia Islam   64, 68–74, 77, 224
signatures   164, 165, 173
signification   111, 119–22, 125
signified   120–2, 124
signifier   50, 120–2, 124, 125, 229
silence   22, 103, 162, 176, 192
Single European Act   43
slavery   48, 103
Social Europe   42, 43
social group/s   136, 164
social interaction   127, 156
sociality/socialities   84, 88, 89–90, 225
social justice   2, 29, 106, 107, 147
social media   105, 132, 133, 138, 140, 174
social responsibility model of the freedom of the press   127, 135
solipsism/solipsistic   192, 193
Somalia   98
sorge   198
Southeast Asia   100
South Sudan   98
Soviet Union   128, 129, 141, 206, 209
Spain   86, 88, 135
Spanish-American War   97
Spanish Civil War   128
Spinelli, Alterio   41
spirit   16, 28, 185, 188
Sri Lanka   83
State, the   37, 38, 40, 49, 52, 66, 67, 102, 128, 137, 150, 175, 226, 240
St Mark Catholic School (Alexandria)   205, 214
Structural Adjustment Program (SAP)   88
subaltern   90
subjective/subjectivity   50, 53, 88, 182, 222
Sudan   98
Suez Canal   204
Sunni Islam   64, 68–74, 77, 224
surveillance   84, 87, 90, 149, 150, 224, 226, 234

Switzerland   208
Sykes-Picot Agreement   131
Syria   63, 66, 70, 87, 98, 132, 205
Syria, Operations in   87, 98

Taliban   132
Tamas (oppresive ignorance and
   inactivity)   195
Tel-Aviv   172
terrorist/terrorism   xv, 16, 127, 131, 133,
   134, 140, 197
thematic necessity   116, 177, 122–5, 229
third world   32, 88, 128
third space   3, 54–6, 59, 222, 233
tolerance   16, 21, 29, 138, 150, 151, 234
totalitarian   184
totality   86, 153, 182–4
totalizer/s   23, 107, 181–4, 221, 238, 239
tragedy of the commons   89
transformative agency   150
transformative peace approaches   103
transnational   4, 42, 43, 83, 87, 90,
   104, 218
Tunisia   139
Turkey   62, 86
Twin Towers   131, 133

Uganda   90
ultra nationalism   184
Ultra-Orthodox Jewish schools   175
UNESCO   149 166
UN High Commission for Refugees   66
United Iraqi Alliance   70
United Kingdom   8, 20, 69, 132
United Nations General Assembly,
   Resolution   110–11, 1941
United Nations (UN)   xvi, 21, 73, 128,
   166, 172
United States of America (US)   27, 39, 41,
   42, 49, 62, 63, 65–75, 86, 97–105, 107,
   128, 131, 167, 171, 201, 205, 223, 226,
   228, 240

UN Report on Women, Peace and
   Security   48
US Foreign Policy   62, 75, 212, 226
Utopia/Utopian   7, 10, 13, 19, 28, 106,
   147, 201

Ventennio (20 year Fascist Rule in
   Italy)   32
Vietnam   97, 99, 128
Vietnam War   97, 99, 128
violence   1, 4, 8, 9, 16, 17, 22, 24, 25, 29,
   33, 36, 48, 53, 57, 60, 81–4, 88, 130, 136,
   163, 171, 193, 197, 217–25, 227, 238
visual order(s)   165, 168, 171

war industry   22, 99, 227
war in North/West Pakistan   98
war journalism   124, 125
war of manoeuvre   33
war of position   33
war on terror   xv, 49, 98, 127, 131, 239
Watts Riots   97
Weimar Republic   184
welcoming   54, 59
welfare state   83, 88
welfarism   88
West Bank   166–8, 174, 175, 177, 238
Western media   130–2, 137, 139
Western philosophy   181, 185
wilderness   2, 7–13, 16–18, 21, 22, 24–8
Wittgenstein, Ludwig   111, 112, 113,
   119, 126
Workers Charter (Italy)   40
working class   40, 43, 44, 104
World Bank   166
World Trade Centre   131
World War II   27, 32, 220, 238

Yazidi   69
Young, Iris   19, 31

Zionist   165, 173, 174